WAyne +

MW00680805

MANAGEMENT
And
DISEASES
OF DAIRY GOATS

MANAGEMENT and DISEASES OF DAIRY GOATS

by
Samuel B. Guss, V.M.D.
Professor Emeritus, Veterinary Science Extension
The Pennsylvania State University

DAIRY GOAT JOURNAL PUBLISHING CORPORATION
Scottsdale, Arizona 85252

Library of Congress
Catalog Card Number: 77-84438

ISBN-0-930848-01-2

PRINTED IN THE UNITED STATES OF AMERICA

FOREWORD

This book was written to serve both practitioners of veterinary medicine and owners of dairy goats. The author does not claim to be a dairy goat specialist nor one who has had a lifetime of experience with these animals. During my early twelve years of experience in general veterinary practice in Pennsylvania and Virginia, I treated many dairy goats because my associates disliked working with them.

I found the same frustration many younger practitioners find today — very little textbook reference material available for assistance on medical and surgical problems for goats. I realized over a period of time that the veterinary education I received pertaining to other ruminants, the cow and sheep, could very well be applied to dairy goats. In fact, the day-to-day education the bovine practitioner receives in his work with high-producing dairy cows can very well be applied to the problems of dairy goats. In the past twenty-five years, enormous progress has been made in the nutrition and other aspects of management of dairy cows. Much, if not all of it, can be directly applied to the dairy goat.

It may be fortunate and it may be unfortunate that the dairy goat is such a highly intelligent, affectionate animal. Its endearing qualities often overshadow its utilitarian purpose as a food-producing animal. The average owner of a small herd of dairy goats becomes so fond of them that he finds it very difficult to do some of the things necessary to really improve a herd. For example — a particularly lovable animal may not be culled after it becomes infertile or hopelessly mastitic.

The animal-owner interrelationships in dairy goat practice, in at least the smaller herds, are very much the same as they are in (pet) animal practice. These owners demand for their animals the very best medical attention, and they often disregard completely the economics involved in treating a particular animal or a particular herd problem. Owners of the great majority of dairy goat herds do not depend for their livelihood upon income derived from the animals. Persons engaged in business and the professions, full-time and part-time workers in government, business, and industry own small herds of dairy goats. These people gain great satisfaction in producing milk for family use, perhaps having some surplus to sell to people who have children who cannot digest cow's milk, or others for whom goats' milk has superior nutritional value. The upper middle class owner of dairy goats gets the same satisfaction and rewards, regardless of cost, which he gets from producing vegetables and fruits from his own garden, and eggs and meat from his own poultry, rabbits, etc. Few have agricultural backgrounds but most of them are eager to learn about all aspects of their chosen hobby or part-time business. Most farm animal practitioners are involved in the economics of farm animal treatment. This is, of course, the only way to keep down production costs and keep the producer in busines. For example — in sheep practice, necropsy is an important and valuable assistance in establishing diagnoses and developing a flock health program, and the sheep owner is not reluctant to sacrifice a few animals to do this, if necessary. To even suggest sacrificing a chronically ill goat for the sake of the herd may be shocking to owners of small goat herds. In this respect, dairy goat practice resembles that related to amateur breeders of dogs and cats.

The shepherd of today routinely castrates lambs, docks their tails and administers biologics. Hopefully, he does this job better and more productively when he depends upon his veterinarian for counsel. For the owner of a small herd of dairy goats, dehorning, castrating, and removing supernumerary teats, even administering biologics, may be expecting too much. Many dairy goat owners today have no farm background and no inclination to do such things. They expect somebody else to do them. When they find veterinarians unavailable for assistance, they often turn to others who willingly provide far less competent assistance.

Many veterinarians are unaware of the value of dairy goats today. Purebred kids with fashionable prefix names, but without any production records behind them, readily bring hundreds of dollars in sales. Many breeders today who own larger herds are well aware of the progress which can be made by production testing, rigid culling and attention to type, and giant strides forward are being made. The modern dairy goat today is truly an animal which can hold its own against any other in production of food.

Progress in the dairy goat industry has been held down by a number of things which are gradually passing from the picture. For many years, type standards laid more emphasis on appearance than on improving the utility of the animal. This is rapidly disappearing from the show ring. The length of a Nubian doe's ears is today much less important than the conformation of her udder. This change of emphasis from companion animal status to utility animal status has come about as a result of the efforts of a few leading breeders and a few courageous judges. The progress they have sponsored has been increasingly evident in the show ring over the past few years. Animals which have the ability and capacity to produce milk are gradually getting the recognition which the petite "pretty" animals have gotten in the past.

The greatest frontier for progress in the dairy goat industry is in nutrition. Authors and owners, in the past, have insisted that among ruminant animals, dairy goats are unique. Many have emphasized that "dairy goats cannot be fed like cows," when there is little or no evidence to support that. Many strongly insist that feeding animals capable of superior milk production according to their needs will "burn them out." These expressions were equally prevalent among the uninformed and intransigent cow dairymen thirty years ago. Fortunately, the dairy goat industry today can ride along on the bandwagon of nutrition progress made in feeding dairy cows. In the goat industry, there are many vendors of "organic" and other "pseudo-medicinal" products for which undocumented extravagant health claims are made. Happily, these are gradually passing from the scene.

Veterinary medicine has a very important role to play in the future of the dairy goat industry. Animals and herds capable of high production demand good veterinary care. Treatment of sick animals is not enough. Veterinary medicine must provide preventive medicine, surgical assistance, and management counsel on the same level it now so competently supplies the dairy (cow) industry. Fortunately, modern veterinarians have basic education which renders them highly competent to provide the necessary service to support the current progress in the dairy goat industry. The author, in writing this book, has attempted to fortify the basic education all veterinarians have, with emphasis on problems peculiar to dairy goats. My own experience, correspondence, and discussions with veterinarians and dairy goat owners have provided most of the information in this book. The literature is not overburdened with reference material on dairy goats. Much of the literature available applies to goats, diseases, and management conditions far removed from the American or European situations.

It is the author's fervent hope that this book will stimulate clinical investigations and generate more scholarly textbook and reference approaches to veterinary medicine for the dairy goat industry. I am indebted to a host of people for information and assistance which has made this book possible. Dozens of dairy goat breeders have been most helpful to me, voluntarily providing information and criticism involving my efforts to write a veterinary column for the American *Dairy Goat Journal* over the past several years. Kent Leach, publisher of the *Dairy Goat Journal*, and Dr. A.J. Durant, the dean of American dairy goat veterinarians, have been most helpful. My colleague in Dairy Science Extension at the Pennsylvania State University, Professor Donald Ace, has been of valuable assistance. Together, we wrote the Penn State Dairy Goat Correspondence Course which has been a stimulus for continuing education for both of us. To Dr. Richard S. Adams of the Pennsylvania State University, I owe a special measure of gratitude for his untiring and candid efforts to teach an almost unteachable veterinarian something about modern concepts of dairy nutrition.

The number of veterinarians who have influenced the writing of this book is legion. I am greatly indebted to those who have goaded and encouraged me via pen and telephone to "stick my neck out" and make this effort. To Dr. Clifford Beck of the Parke Davis Company and to Dr. Donald Bailey, practitioner, of Roseburg, Oregon, I am especially grateful for counsel and education. I am indebted to Dr. James Wadsworth, Extension Animal Pathologist at the University of Vermont for the chapter on Neoplasia in Goats. Dr. Wadsworth has been interested in neoplasia of domestic animals for many years. I was very happy when he agreed to furnish that chapter of this book.

Dr. Lester Griel, clinician for the Pennsylvania State University Veterinary Science Department reviewed what I had written regarding anesthesia, and we concluded that there are many things in that area which were worth using. He, therefore, kindly consented to write what is in that chapter. I am grateful for his contribution.

Finally, to my wife, Jean, who spent many mornings during our freighter trip enroute to Africa, and many more days after our return home, deciphering manuscript and typing it for publication, I express my appreciation. Without her assistance, this effort would never have been attempted.

Dr. Sam B. Guss

x

Table of Contents

Chapter   **Page**

Foreword v

I   The United States Dairy Goat Industry 1
     A.   Distribution, Numbers, Growth, Herd Size 2
     B.   Economics of the Dairy Goat Enterprise 10

II   Environment and Physiological Data 13
     A.   The Goat In Its Natural Environment 14
     B.   Physiological Data 15

III Management 19
     A.   Housing 21
          1.   Environmental Requirements 21
          2.   Tie Stall Housing 23
          3.   Free Stall Housing 27
          4.   Loose Housing 28
               Water Facilities 28
               The Milking Parlor 28
               The Milking System 29
               The Milk House 30
          5.   Keyhole Feeders 30
          6.   Baby Kid Housing 30
          7.   Herd Sire Housing 32
          8.   Pastures, Dry Lots 32
          9.   Fencing 34
          10. Available Building Resources 35
     B.   The Herd 35
          1.   Managing Milking Animals 35
          2.   Care of the Dry and Kidding Doe 36
          3.   Starting Healthy Kids 44
          4.   Care of Herd Sires 50
     C.   Nutrition 50
          1.   Special Feeding Requirements 50
          2.   Exercise and Appetite 52
          3.   Feed According to Needs 53
          4.   Feeding Forage 55
               a.   Forage Quality 56
               b.   Factors Which Influence Palatability
                    of Forage 57
               c.   Hay Equivalent Intake 58
          5.   Feed Additives 59

6.   Nutrition Resources for Dairy Goat Owners . . . 59
7.   The Eye of the Master 61

IV   **Quality Milk Production** **63**
A.   Introduction 64
B.   Factors Which Influence Keeping Quality of Milk. 64
        1.   Sanitation 64
                a.   Milking Area 64
                b.   Milking Animals 64
                c.   Hand Milking 64
                d.   Milking Equipment 65
        2.   Off-Flavors in Milk 65
        3.   Milk Holding Temperatures 67
        4.   Somatic Cells in Milk 67
C.   Resources Available 67

V   **Nutritional Deficiency Diseases** **69**
A.   Specific Deficiencies 70
        1.   Calcium 70
        2.   Cobalt 70
        3.   Copper-Molybdenum 71
        4.   Energy 71
        5.   Iodine 72
        6.   Iron 72
        7.   Magnesium (Hypomagnesemia in
                Grass Tetany) 73
        8.   Phosphorus 74
        9.   Protein 75
        10.   Salt — Sodium Chloride 75
        11.   Selenium (White Muscle Disease) 75
        12.   Sulfur 77
        13.   Vitamin Deficiencies 77
                a.   Avitaminosis A 77
                b.   Avitaminosis B 78
                c.   Avitaminosis C 78
                d.   Avitaminosis D (Rickets) 78
                e.   Avitaminosis E (White Muscle Disease) . . 79
        14.   Zinc 79

VI   **Metabolic Diseases** **81**
A.   Indigestion 82
        1.   Acute — Bloat 82
        2.   Chronic — Rumen Impaction 83
        3.   Abomasal Ulceration 83
B.   Ketosis — Pregnancy Disease 83
C.   Laminitis (Founder) 85
D.   Milk Fever (Hypocalcemia) 86
E.   Osteopetrosis (Nutritional Arthritis) 88

F. Polioencephalomalacia
    (Cerebrocortical Necrosis) 89

VII Contagious and Infectious Diseases 91
A. Abscesses...................................92
B. Anaplasmosis................................97
C. Anthrax.....................................98
D. Arthritis....................................99
    1. Non-suppurative Arthritis..................99
    2. Suppurative Arthritis.....................100
        a. Navel Ill............................101
E. Bluetongue.................................101
F. Brucellosis 101
G. Coccidiosis 102
H. Contagious Ecthyma 104
I. Dermatomycosis (Ringworm).................106
J. Enterotoxemia 106
K. Foot Rot and Foot Abscesses................109
L. Infectious Bovine Rhinotracheitis............110
M. Infectious Keratoconjunctivitis..............111
N. Johnes' Disease............................112
O. Leukoencephalomyelitis (Progressive
    Paralysis of Kids) 113
P. Listeriosis..................................114
Q. Malignant Edema — Blackleg 116
R. Mastitis....................................116
S. Pneumonia 127
T. Pox..128
U. Toxoplasmosis..............................129
V. Traumatic Testiculitis......................129
W. Neoplasias 131

VIII Diseases of Kids 137
A. Colibacillosis, E. coli Septicemia,
    Diarrhea, Scours............................138
B. Hypoglycemia — Birth Chilling...............139
C. Navel Ill — Omphalitis, Arthritis of Kids 140
D. Salmonellosis — Bloody Scours, Black Scours ...141
E. Stressors Which Lower Disease
    Resistance of Baby Kids 141
    1. Environmental 141
    2. Erratic Feeding.........................142
    3. Lack of Space...........................142
    4. Lack of Attention.......................142

IX   **Internal Parasite Control**. **143**
    A.   Herd Worm Problems 147
        1.   Blood Sucking Worms 147
        2.   Tapeworms 147
        3.   Lungworms 148
    B.   Symptoms of Excessive Worm Burdens 149
    C.   Diagnosis of Worm Infections 149
    D.   Management and Facilities to
        Prevent Ingestion of Worms 150
    E.   Management During Tapeworm Treatment. 152
    F.   Management to Control Lungworms 152
    G.   Medication 153
    H.   Drugs Available for Treatment 154
    I.   Liver Fluke Disease 156
    J.   Cysticercosis (Bladderworm Disease) 157
    K.   Nose Bots, Head Grubs, Oestrus-ovis Infection . . 158
    L.   Herd Parasite Control —
        A Challenge to Veterinarians. 158

X   **External Parasites and Their Control** **161**
    A.   Lice Infestation — Pediculosis 162
    B.   Goat Scabies. 163
    C.   Demodectic Mange — Demodicosis 163

XI   **Reproduction** **165**
    A.   Physiology 166
        1.   Genital Tract in Pregnancy 166
    B.   Artificial Insemination 166
    C.   Improving Herd Fertility 168
        1.   Factors Which Affect Heats and
            Fertility in the Doe. 168
            a.   Environmental 168
            b.   Nutritional 168
            c.   Social 168
            d.   Hermaphrodism 169
            e.   Congenital Reproductive Hypoplasia . . . 169
        2.   Pregnancy Diagnosis 170
        3.   Preparing Bucks for Breeding 171
        4.   Using Bucks to Best Advantage
            in Large Herds 171
        5.   Heat Synchronization 171
    D.   Problems of Reproduction 173
        1.   Abnormal Cycles 173
            a.   Weak or Silent Heats 173
            b.   Cystic Ovaries 173
            c.   Heat During Pregnancy 173

           d.   Abnormally Long
                Periods Between Heats 174
      2.   False Pregnancy 174
      3.   Metritis................................. 174
      4.   Infertility Hazard in Polled Goats........... 175
      5.   Problems in Bucks 176
           a.   Cryptorchidism (Undescended
                Testis, Retained Testis) 176
           b.   Varicocele 176
      6.   Causes of Abortion........................ 176
           a.   Vibrionic Abortion.................... 176
           b.   Chlamydial Abortion.................. 176
           c.   Q Fever 177

XII   **Anesthesia And Surgery** **179**
     A.   Anesthesia For Dairy Goats.................. 180
     B.   Surgical Procedures......................... 183
       1.   Dehorning Adults........................ 183
       2.   Disbudding Kids — Descenting,
            Wattle Removal 183
       3.   Castration of Buck Kids 186
       4.   Foot Trimming 186
       5.   Caesarian Section........................ 187

XIII **Poisonous Plants.**.......................... **189**
     A.   Factors Involved in Plant Poisoning........... 190
       1.   Starvation 190
       2.   Accidental Plant Poisoning 191
       3.   Amount of Plants Eaten 191
       4.   Desire for Browse........................ 191
       5.   Fertilization Practices and Weather 191
     B.   Locoweeds 192
     C.   The Nightshades............................ 192
     D.   Nitrate-Accumulating Plants.................. 192
     E.   Ornamental Plants 193
     F.   The Prunus Family......................... 193
     G.   Plants Which Contain Oxalic Acid 193
     H.   Plants Which Cause Photosensitivity 194

XIV **Chemical Poisoning** **195**
     A.   Ammonium Sulfamate (Ammate) 196
     B.   Arsenic 196
     C.   Borax..................................... 196
     D.   Dinitro Compounds.......................... 196
     E.   Fluoride 197
     F.   Lead...................................... 197

G.   Pentachlorophenol 198
H.   Salt 198
I.   Sodium Chlorate 199
J.   Trizine Compounds 199

XV   **Routine Herd Health Program for Dairy Goat
Herds in Mid-Atlantic States of the U.S.** 201
A.   Seasonal Health Considerations 202
B.   Health Recommendations for
Classes of Animals 203
1.   Dry Does 203
2.   Kidding Does 203
3.   Baby Kids 204
4.   Weaned Kids 204
5.   Milking Herd 204
6.   Bucks 205

XVI   **Dairy Goat Resources** 207

INDEX 213

CHAPTER I

THE UNITED STATES DAIRY GOAT INDUSTRY

A. Distribution, Numbers, Growth, Herd Size 2
B. Economics of the Dairy Goat Enterprise.............. 10

A.   Distribution, Numbers, Growth, Herd Size

G oats have been domesticated at least as long as any other domestic animals. There is good evidence that nomadic people of the Middle East tended goat herds as early as ten thousand years before Christ. Domestic or semi-feral goats are found throughout the world excepting arctic regions. Nearly three hundred recognizable breeds occur. Most are found in dry climates where temperature extremes are great. In Africa, goats thrive in areas where cattle barely exist. Few goats are given preventive vaccination in countries where foot and mouth disease, rinderpest and other dread animal diseases occur. There are some losses during periodic epizootics of disease, but the goat has developed remarkable resistance to diseases capable of wiping out populations of animals in those countries. In Africa, the Middle East, Asia, South America, and the Caribbean Islands, goats are favored meat animals and their hides are valuable export items.

In the United States, the dairy goat industry was slow developing. Most of the purebred animals arrived in the United States in very small importations early in the twentieth century. Today, there are five major purebred breeds and there is a registration system used whereby bucks which are 15/16 purebred and does which are 7/8 purebred can be registered as "Americans."

Nubians are the most numerous breed. They were developed in England by crossing British dairy stock with Indian Jumnapuri and Egyptian Zariby types. Outside the United States, they are known as Anglo Nubians. Because they are short-haired, heat-tolerant and have meatier carcasses than the Swiss breeds, they have been used extensively to upgrade native goats in tropical countries. Nubians are distinguished by their long wide pendulant ears and Roman noses. They produce milk of good quality with relatively high butterfat content. They are found in many colors and color patterns and they have a shorter hair coat than the Swiss breeds.

Toggenburgs originated in the Toggenburg Valley of Switzerland where they have been bred for hundreds of years. They occur in shades of brown with characteristic erect white ears, white facial markings and white lower legs. They are remarkably uniform animals and the highest milk production records have been recorded from Toggenburgs. The high record, made in 1960 by "Puritan Jon's Jennifer" (owned by the late Mrs. Carl Sandburg, Flat Rock, N.C.), of 5750 lbs. milk in 305 days still stands.

The French Alpine breed originated, too, in the Swiss Alps. All of the animals in the United States trace their ancestry back to an importation of 21 animals in 1922. Alpines are relatively large animals with erect ears and they come in many combinations of white, black, and brown in characteristically named color patterns. They are excellent producers of good quality milk.

The Saanen breed originated in Switzerland. They are the largest dairy goat breed. They are by far the most popular breed in Israel, many European countries, Australia, and New Zealand. They are docile, white or cream-colored, erect-eared animals. They are called the Holsteins of dairy goat breeds by many because of their relatively large size and the slightly lower butterfat content of their milk.

American LaManchas are a relatively new breed of dairy goats in the United States. The first animals were registered in 1958. Breeders in California crossed goats of Spanish origin with purebreds of the Swiss breeds. The distinguishing characteristic of LaManchas is their small rudimentary ears which are genetically dominant. Because good animals were used in the development of this breed, there are some excellent milking herds and milk records. They come in all colors and color patterns, and they have no really distinguishing characteristic other than their tiny ears.

Dairy Goat Numbers — Who Owns Them

Figure I-1 reveals a dramatic and continuous increase in the number of purebred animals registered annually by breed by the American Dairy Goat Association in the United States.

Figure I-2 shows, perhaps, even more dramatically, the current trend when registration of all breeds are plotted together. Not only are numbers of purebred animals increasing dramatically, but production records shown in Figure I-3 indicate that there is continuous steady progress in that respect. Recently, Dairy Herd Improvement Recording Associations in most dairy states of the United States have moved to accommodate production testing of dairy goat herds into their centralized computerized testing systems. This is resulting in production testing of many more animals.

Progress in the show ring has been even more dramatic (Figure I-4) than in production. Show-winning dairy goats of the 1970's in the United States are clearly dairy animals. Dairy temperament, body capacity, and udders have improved rapidly. The author can remember a show only twenty years ago when a superlative milking Nubian with dairy

Dairy Goat Registrations
According To Breeds
(Data compiled from Dairy Goat Journal, Vols. 48 — 54)

* ( ) times as many registered in 1969

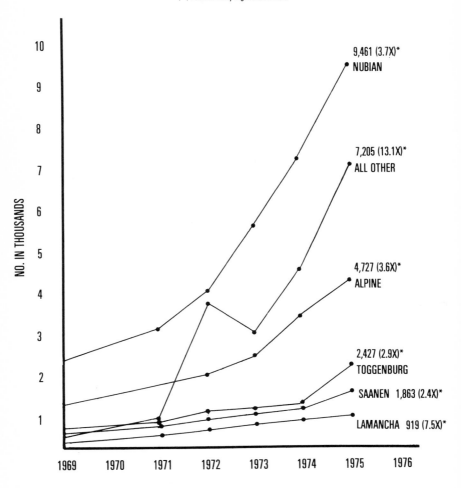

Figure I—1

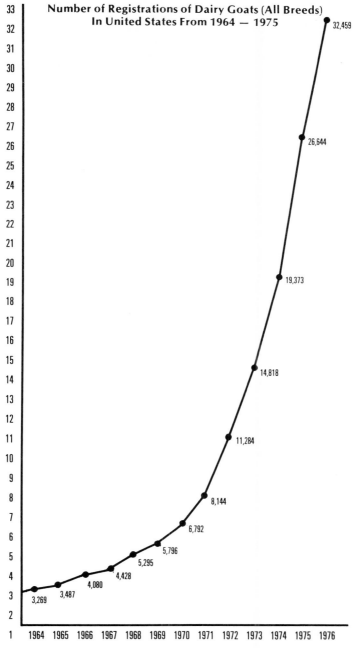

Number of Registrations of Dairy Goats (All Breeds) In United States From 1964 — 1975

33
32 — 32,459
31
30
29
28
27
26 — 26,644
25
24
23
22
21
20
19 — 19,373
18
17
16
15
14 — 14,818
13
12
11 — 11,284
10
9
8 — 8,144
7
6 — 6,792
5 — 5,796
4 — 5,295
 — 4,428
3 — 4,080
2 — 3,487
1 — 3,269

1964 1965 1966 1967 1968 1969 1970 1971 1972 1973 1974 1975 1976

Figure I—2

6

attributes far ahead of any other animals in the ring was put at the bottom of her class because her ears were about three-quarters of an inch shorter than the others in the class. Judging has been slower to improve than the goats themselves. In the past several years, ADGA has made progressive moves to improve the number of competent judges and the standards by which all breeds are judged.

Value of Purebred Dairy Goats in the United States

At the National Spotlight Sale, a consignment sale of purebred dairy goats of all breeds, records of prices paid for dairy goats over the past nine years reveal that people are willing to pay high prices for dairy goats. As production records are submitted along with show winnings of the consignments and their progenitors, prices paid are rising higher with each successive sale. (Figure I-5).

Dairy Goat Breed Leaders in Milk
Production and Butterfat (DHIR Records)

Breed	1972	1973	1974	1975	1976	All-Time Record
Toggenburg						5,750 (1960)
lbs. Milk	4,072	4,250	4,690	5,416	4,223	Puritan Jon's
lbs. B.F.	153	173	139	193	160	Jennifer
Saanen						* 5,496 (1972)
lbs. milk	*5,496	4,160	3,550	4,140	4,610	Morka Acres
lbs. B.F.	186	145	133	147	179	Sally
Nubian						* 4,420 (1973)
lbs. milk	3,200	*4,420	3,845	3,552	4,130	Albuquerque
lbs. B.F.	139	224	189	159	211	Estrallita's Myra
Alpine						*4,880 (1975)
lbs. milk	4,194	4,120	4,268	*4,880	4,508	Rofred's
lbs. B.F.	152	139	196	165	174	Sydelle
LaMancha					Marita	*4,510 (1975)
lbs. Milk	2,603	3,260	3,408	*4,510	4,130	Goat City
lbs. B.F.	133	114	137	156	141	Marzipan
No. of A.R. Lactations	805	1312	659	1547	1802	

Data compiled from ADGA Handbook (yearbook) Vols. 18-22, 1972-1976.

Figure I—3

Size of Purebred Dairy Goat Herds in the United States

Examination of the data available on the number of purebred dairy goats and the number of ADGA members (Figure I-6) shows that numbers of owners are increasing even more rapidly than the numbers of registered animals.

Some Serious Concerns About the Current Popularity of Dairy Goats in the United States

Following are the author's observations based on efforts to learn about the current American dairy goat situation at many educational meetings and via communications of all types. It is the author's opinion, based on these observations over the past twenty years, that the current situation can be interpreted as extremely good for the industry. However, unless owners and the industry in general make concrete efforts to develop a dairy goat milk production industry from its present state, the long range results may be bad.

At many meetings where the author has addressed avid goat owners

OFFICIAL ADGA SANCTIONED SHOWS

	1970	1971	1972	1973	1974	1975	1976
No. of Shows	154	168	210	248	277	353	417
No. of Entries	15,936	19,403	24,476	28,175	30,942	43,632	52,672
No. of Perm. Cham-'pions	61	71	90	100	122	161	234
Largest Show & No. of Entries	CA. St. Fair 240	Ohio St. Fair 444	L.A. Co. Fair 639	Natl. S.CA. 836	So. CA. Expo. 631	Natl. Ohio 638	Natl. CA. 1,005
No. of ADGA Licensed Judges	41	39	34	47	47	40	44

Information compiled from ADGA Handbook (Yearbook) Vols. 17—22

Figure I—4

NATIONAL SPOTLIGHT SALE
A Consignment Sale of Dairy Goats of Five Breeds

Year	No. Of Goats	Top Price Doe	Top Price Buck	Av. Price Doe	Av. Price Buck *	Total Income
1968	22	$ 445 N	$ 400 A	$ 305	$ 306	$ 6,715
1969	22	$ 410 N	$ 390 N	$ 280	$ 294	$ 6,230
1970	23	$ 375 L	$ 400 N	$ 214	$ 264	$ 5,262
1971	19	$ 1,000 S	$ 560 N	$ 510	$ 367	$ 8,975
1972	26	$ 1,300 N	$ 1,300 T	$ 524	$ 549	$ 13,745
1973	23	$ 1,725 T	$ 1,725 T	$ 792	$ 1,100	$ 19,755
1974	22	$ 2,250 N	$ 750 L	$ 772	$ 519	$ 15,975
1975	19	$ 2,700 N	$ 2,550 A	$ 828	$ 1,112	$ 16,875
1976	24 †	$ 5,600 T	$ 3,900 S	$ 1,393	$ 1,810	$ 35,525

Data compiled from ADGA Handbook (Yearbook) Vols. 15—22, 1969—1976.

* *Only one buck per breed is accepted:*
N = Nubian; S = Saanen; A = Alpine; T = Toggenburg; L = LaMancha.

† *Data obtained from ADGA office, not yet published, sale held Oct. 23, 1976.*

Figure I—5

American Dairy Goat Association Memberships

YEAR	MEMBERSHIP	RATIO MEMBERS	REGISTERED GOATS
1966	1,062	1:	3.8
1967	1,089	1:	4.0
1968	1,224	1:	4.3
1969	1,305	1:	4.4
1970	1,594	1:	4.3
1971	2,114	1:	3.9
1972	2,698	1:	4.2
1973	3,722	1:	4.0
1974	5,228	1:	3.7
1975	6,844	1:	3.9
1976	8,645	1:	3.8

Figure I—6

in groups often exceeding one hundred, he has tried to find out the nature of the audience. It would be a great surprise if one percent of those present are engaged in dairy goat production as a full-time enterprise. The average goat owner is a middle class or upper middle class skilled worker or professional person. Audiences at goat meetings in eastern United States typically contain skilled workers, business people, clergy, lawyers, architects, and doctors — those who live in suburbia with small acreages of land.

The dairy goat industry, in the author's humble opinion, has profited by Americans' increased desire to produce at least some of their own food without chemical additives and pesticides. The current class of goat people is easily "hooked" by the intelligence and tractability of the animals. They look forward to a continuous succession of goat meetings and shows held during every week-end during the warm weather months. Here they enjoy the competition and camaraderie of others like themselves. They think nothing of taking their camper or mobile home and a trailer or station wagon full of goats for distances of several hundred miles each successive week-end throughout the late spring, summer and autumn seasons.

In spite of the fact that many of the typical dairy goat owners find a ready market for all of the milk they can produce at prices up to $1.00 per quart, there is, in the East at least, little real interest in producing milk. The author knows many owners who may have three or four animals of all five breeds, who keep bucks and milking animals under the same roof, who produce milk which must often be discarded or used for swine or poultry feed because it is really unfit to drink.

On the other hand, there are a minority of individuals throughout the country who are in the primary business of producing milk. There are also a number of good, though small, goat milk processing plants around the country, producing excellent goat milk products, and they currently pay (at least in Pennsylvania) 20 cents per pound for milk delivered to them. The author is aware of many "natural food" stores which are literally begging for goat milk products of all kinds. Numerous conversations with these tradesmen indicate that a great untapped market is available. Perhaps, the development of profit-making opportunities during the current periods of relative affluence will soon influence the dairy goat industry to move toward the challenge offered it at the present time.

Once the American dairy goat is recognized and exploited for what she already is — a useful domestic animal which will profitably produce excellent quality food — then there will be real long-term progress and opportunities for profitable full-time enterprises for thousands of goat milk producers in the United States. The trend toward development of a goat products industry is there, but the author, for one, believes that its expansion is very slow in the light of the current economic factors which favor expansion.

B. Economics of the Dairy Goat Enterprise

Efficient production of goats' milk is very similar to the same enterprise with dairy cows. One can start with excellent animals, good housing and excellent equipment. However, these do not insure success. The key ingredient is **management**. One must like the animals and enjoy working with them, and one must be business-person enough to make the hard decisions. (Culling is one of the most important and difficult of these.)

The foundation of any profitable dairy enterprise is keeping good records and using those records to make management decisions. Many good dairy herd record systems are available through Dairy Herd Improvement Associations, from the very simplest to very detailed systems. These are essential. Production testing of all milking animals, use of sires known to be superior for production, and sound economical scientific feeding programs are basic tools for dairy profits and for improvement of the value of the herd over a period of years. The field in the United States is wide open, and the potential is great for those in the goat dairy enterprise to use the basic production tools which, for 30 years, have been available to dairy cattle enterprises.

For a number of reasons, it is very difficult to obtain cost figures for the operation of dairy goat herds. In the United States there are relatively few dairy goat herds managed as a full-time farm enterprise. Most herds are small, have several breeds, and maintain excessive numbers of bucks. The great majority of United States goat dairy herds are hobby enterprises where costs are often not important. Markets for the product of small herds vary tremendously. Goat milk may be sold on the farm to retail customers, or in some areas it may be sold to local processing-distributing enterprises. Some producers sell their product as cheese or yogurt, or they market it as goat milk fudge. Whether or not a good market is available for the milk to be produced is the first and most important consideration in the development of a goat dairy herd large enough to furnish income for part-time or full-time work of the operator and/or his family.

Some few dairy goat owners feed much of the herd product to veal calves or pigs, but these operations are not usually profitable.

The costs for necessary elements (land, housing, equipment, labor) vary so much for small part-time enterprises that this writer's efforts to try to list them have been fruitless. However, the basic costs for a 100-milking-doe herd which will produce enough net income to support a farm family can be considered realistically. Donald Ace, Dairy Extension Specialist at the Pennsylvania State University, has used some basic considerations for a 100-milking-doe herd which appear to furnish realistic guide lines.

Don Ace's basic assumptions used for cost projections for the dairy goat enterprise:

1. Good purebred mature milking animals may cost an average of $600/head.
2. One may expect to get five lactations from does in a well-managed healthy herd.
3. Milk production from reasonably good does can be calculated at 6 lbs./day over 365 days.
4. To maintain an average of 100 milking does, it is necessary to keep an additional twenty dry does, and start 50 new kids each year.
5. All young does should kid by the time they reach eighteen months of age. Well grown doelings can be bred to kid at twelve to fourteen months of age.
6. Housing for animals and feed storage should be depreciated over a twenty-year period with no salvage value.
7. Equipment should be depreciated over a ten-year period with 10% final salvage value.
8. Barn space can be calculated at $4/sq. ft.
9. Land area space can be calculated at $1/sq. ft.
10. Hay values (1976) at $90/ton.
11. Grain value (1976) at $140/ton.
12. Salvage value — culled does — $25/head.
13. Male kids sale value — $25/head.

**Considerations Which May be Helpful When Planning
For a 100-Doe Production Unit**

Milk production — 219,000 lbs./year

Buildings and paving — $29,100

Equipment — $7,700

Milking facilities and equipment — $13,780

Operating expenses — $18,480/year

Replacement costs — $6,555/year

Depreciation — $.0187/lb. milk

Interest — $.0207/lb. milk

Animal depreciation — $.0806/lb. milk

Operating expenses — $.0844/lb. milk

Replacement costs — $.0299/lb. milk

Total production costs: $.2343/lb. milk

Income from sale of young — 1.8 kids/milking doe

Male kids 117 @ $25. —	$2,925.00	
Female kids 67 @ $100. —	$6,700.00	
Total	$9,625.00 or .044/lb. milk	
Total production costs —	.2343/lb. milk	
Income from sale of young stock —	.044/lb. milk	
Net Production costs —	.1903/lb. milk	

Generally speaking, at current 1976 costs, the selling price for goats' milk must be approximately twice that of cows' milk for profitable production. Thus, when cow's milk sells retail at 35¢/qt., goats' milk sold at retail should sell at 70¢/qt.

When cows' milk cheddar cheese sells for $1.50/lb., goats' milk cheddar cheese should sell for $3.00/lb.

Acknowledgment: The author is indebted to Ms. Cynthia Knudson for statistics regarding the U.S. Dairy Goat Industry, which she presented at a Pennsylvania State University Animal Science seminar in October 1976.

Economics figures for the dairy goat enterprise were furnished by Professor Donald Ace, Pennsylvania State University Dairy Science Extension Specialist.

CHAPTER II

ENVIRONMENT AND PHYSIOLOGICAL DATA

A.   The Goat In Its Natural Environment 14
B.   Physiological Data 15

A.   The Goat in its Natural Environment

The exact ancestral lines for the modern dairy goats bred today in North America are not known. It is believed, however, that wild goats of the mountains of Asia Minor may be at least the major source. The goat is probably second only to the dog in early domestication, and like the dog and sheep, its origin in domestication is obscure.

In order to understand the adaptation and capabilities of the modern milk-producing goat, it should be helpful to examine both the habitat and the goats of the regions of the world where goats have been known to exist in domestication for thousands of years. The Middle East is such a region of the world where goats have been important domestic animals for all of recorded history.

The wild goats of the Middle East and Asia Minor are wary, highly intelligent animals which live in the most rugged rocky mountain climates of the world. The weather at its very best is harsh. Strong winds, bitter cold winter weather, and very hot summer weather are the rule. Rainfall, for most of the region, is less than fifteen inches per year. Under such severe arid conditions, vegetation is scanty and growth of plants occurs spasmodically when scanty rains fall. Populations of wild goats are small. They usually exist in small family parties living in the highest mountains in summer and descending to lower altitudes in winter. The hair coat of the wild goat is marvelously adapted to its environment. Hollow erectile hairs furnish excellent insulation from the cold in winter, and the hair is shed and replaced by a short coat of hair for the hot summer weather. The feet of wild goats enable them to move through precipitous rocky areas with ease. In the high mountain areas where rock formations are formidable, wild goats are safest from predators because they can easily escape from them over the terrain. Only eagles which attack the young from the air are significant predators during the time when baby animals are present.

In the Middle East, scanty vegetation forces those who herd domestic goats to lead a nomadic existence to find enough forage to sustain their animals. The Bedouin of the mountains of Jordan must continually move his flocks of sheep and goats to new pasture. Both animals live together in harmony, the goats browsing perennial shrubs and the sheep grazing the short grasses. The author, on a visit to the area, was impressed by the good condition, the vigor, and the productivity of goats living under conditions where it is difficult to see how they find enough food for survival. In the mountains of Jordan, for example, kids are born in late winter when vegetation, such as it is, is greenest.

Does rarely have more than one kid, but they are as strong, vigorous, and growthy as the best kids grown in relative luxury in the United States. Size and weaning weight of kids at the age of six to eight weeks under desert conditions in the Middle East compares favorably with those of the larger milk producing breeds in the United States. There is abundant evidence that the wild goat and the domestic goat are remarkably adapted for living a nomadic existence under conditions of weather and forage which would not sustain other animals. Only the camel and the wild ass can tolerate similar conditions at lower altitudes, and they cannot survive the high-altitude rocky summer home of the goat.

Good evidence of the adaptability of goats to harsh alpine or desert conditions has been shown by research experiments conducted on dehydration of goats and their subsequent response when given access to water. Non-lactating goats were completely deprived of water for a period of twelve days during which time they remained alert and active although they refused to eat the last several days. When given free access to water, all responded and blood studies showed complete recovery in a short time.[1]

It is remarkable, indeed, that the goat has been transported to all sections of the world inhabited by man. This unique animal is a profitable producer of food, hides, and fiber under a wide variety of climatic conditions which have only two common features: scarcity of forage and outdoor existence.

Dairy goat herd owners should recognize the fact that the animals they are attempting to manage are, at best, far removed from conditions to which they were well adapted before their recent domestication. However, the modern dairy goat must be managed for optimum milk production. This can be done best without detriment to health when the environmental requirements and adaptations are understood.

B. Physiological Data

Parameter

Temperature (rectal)........ 101.5 ° — 104.0° F.

Pulse........ 70 — 80/min.

Respiration........ 12 — 20/min.

Rumination........ 1. — 1.5/min.

Puberty........ 4 — 12 mos.

Estrum (Length of Heat)........ 12 — 36 hrs. (Avg. about 18 hrs.)

Estrus Cycle........ 18 — 23 days

Gestation. . . . . 148 — 153 days (Avg. 150)

Birth Weight. . . . . Dependent upon breed and number (from 4.5 to 9.0 lbs., or 2.2 to 4.1 kgms.)

Urine Specific Gravity. . . . . 1.015 — 1.035

Hematology

Blood Volume. . . . . 7.0% body weight

Hemoglobin. . . . . 8 — 14

Packed Cell Volume (PCV). . . . . 30 — 40%
Hematocrit

Red Blood Cells (RBC). . . . . 8 — 17.5 millions/ml.

White Blood Cells (WBC). . . . . 6 — 16.0 millions/ml.

Clotting Time. . . . . 2.5 minutes

Differential

Neutrophils. . . . . 30 — 48%

Lymphocytes. . . . . 50 — 70%

Basophils. . . . . 0 — 2%

Monocytes. . . . . 1 — 4%

Eosinophils. . . . . 3 — 8%

Clinical Chemistry

Blood Glucose. . . . . 40 — 60 mg%

Blood Urea Nitrogen. . . . . 13 — 28 mg%

Creatinine. . . . . 0.9 — 1.8 mg%

S.G.O.T.. . . . . 50 — 100 S.F. Units

S.G.P.T.. . . . . 12.17 S.F. Units

Calcium. . . . . 9.5 — 10.5 mg%

Magnesium. . . . . 2.5 — 3.5 mg%

Phosphorus. . . . . 3.8 — 7.6 mg%

Sodium. . . . . 135 — 154 mg%

Potassium. . . . . 3.9 — 6.3 mg%

Chloride. . . . . 105 — 120 mg%

Ca: P Ratio. . . . . 1.7:1 in milking does
2.0:1 in others

Temperature

Rectal temperature of goats varies tremendously with the length of hair coat, ambient temperature and excitement. Before deciding whether or not a particular animal has a fever temperature or a subnormal temperature, it is best to take rectal temperatures of at least two other animals in the herd. On a hot summer day, a doe with acute mastitis may have a rectal temperature of 106.5°F. when "normal" animals housed with her may have 104.0°F. rectal temperature. In cold winter weather, a doe with acute mastitis may have a rectal temperature of 105.5°F., when "normal" animals housed with her have rectal temperatures of 102.0°F. It is not uncommon to find rectal temperatures of 106.5°F. in apparently normal animals which have been chased to catch them in hot weather. The only way to be reasonably sure whether or not a particular animal's temperature is abnormal is to compare it with others at the same time.

Hemoglobin

Goats in heavy lactation show lower normal hemoglobin values (8-9) than others. This is also true of dairy cows in the peak of lactation.

Packed Cell Volume (PCV) Hematocrit — Dairy goats milking over 8 pounds daily usually have PCV of 30-32. The higher values listed (up to 40%) are normal for dry does, bucks and young animals.

Calcium — Blood calcium levels exceeding 10.0 mg% (up to 11.5 mg%) are commonly found in herds with milk fever problems where late pregnancy does receive excessive calcium in their diet. Where blood calcium levels of 9.0 to 10.0 mg% are found in animals in late pregnancy, milk fever is rare.

Magnesium — Blood magnesium levels under 2.0 mg% indicate grave danger of hypomagnesemia outbreak in milking does.

---

[1] *M. Szabuniewiez and D. Clark, Am. J. Vet. Res. 26 (114) 1079-1085, 1965.*

CHAPTER III

MANAGEMENT

A.   Housing. 21
     1.   Environmental Requirements 21
     2   Tie Stall Housing 23
     3.   Free Stall Housing. 27
     4.   Loose Housing 28
        Water Facilities 28
        The Milking Parlor 28
        The Milking System 29
        The Milk House 30
     5.   Keyhole Feeders 30
     6.   Baby Kid Housing 30
     7.   Herd Sire Housing. 32
     8.   Pastures, Dry Lots 32
     9.   Fencing 34
     10.   Available Building Resources. 35
B.   The Herd 35
     1.   Managing Milking Animals 35
     2.   Care of the Dry and Kidding Doe 36
     3.   Starting Healthy Kids 44
     4.   Care of Herd Sires. 50
C.   Nutrition. 50
     1.   Special Feeding Requirements. 50
     2.   Exercise and Appetite 52
     3.   Feed According to Needs. 53
     4.   Feeding Forage 55
       a.   Forage Quality 56
       b.   Factors Which Influence Palatability of Forage . . . 57
       c.   Hay Equivalent Intake 58
     5.   Feed Additives. 59
     6.   Nutrition Resources for Dairy Goat Owners 59
     7.   The Eye of the Master 61

A. Housing

T he purpose for the following discussion of housing of dairy goats is primarily directed toward those aspects of housing which are related to health.

1. Environmental Requirements

Temperature — There is no necessity for attempts to provide warm housing for goats in winter. They are comfortable in the coldest weather if they are provided draft-free quarters and dry bedding. Any attempt to close doors and windows in wintertime to increase the temperature in the barn is accompanied by respiratory problems resulting from excess moisture, noxious odors, and increased carbon dioxide in the air. Any condensation of moisture on windows, walls, or bedding is evidence that wintertime environmental conditions are undesirable.

Air Requirements — The air requirements for mature milking does in tie stall housing in winter are at least 200 cubic feet per minute per thousand pounds of goat. Attempts to provide mechanical ventilation in closed housing reveal inadequate control of moisture when a 50°F. temperature is maintained even in housing where the animals are kept in tie stalls with minimal bedding and daily manure clean-out. When goats are kept in loose housing on a deep bedded manure pack, any attempt to raise the inside temperature with or without mechanical ventilation and insulation is impossible without excessive moisture build-up. For summertime conditions, most milking does perform best under the same temperature limits as do dairy cows, with the exception of Nubians which are slightly more heat tolerant than the Swiss breeds.

Light — Provision for plenty of light from the southern or south, south-eastern aspect is highly desirable in the northern hemisphere for any type of goat barn. This provides maximum sunlight (with its warming and drying properties) in the winter months and a minimum of inside sunlight during the summer months.

All of the barn, milking parlor and milk house plans were drawn with the assistance of Roger Grout, Penn State Agricultural Extension Engineer.

22

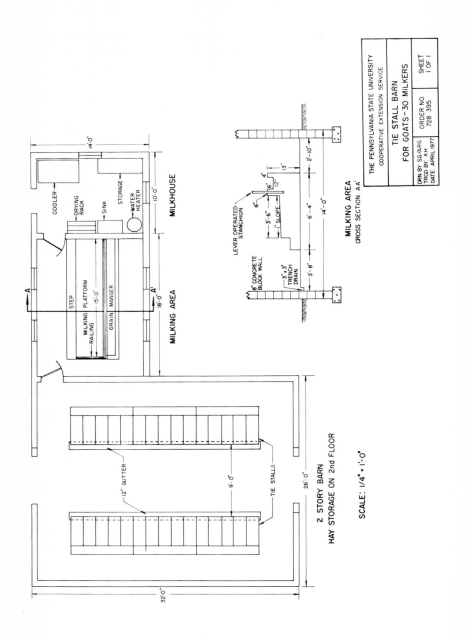

Figure III—1

2. Tie Stall Housing

There are many advantages in closed stall housing for milking animals. Where animals are tied or otherwise restrained in individual stalls, they can be individually fed and cared for. Dominant animals in the herd are prevented from bullying more timid individuals. Labor requirements, however, are much greater and housing costs can be at least double that of loose housing. In addition to the facilities and equipment necessary to restrain the animals (collars, chains, stall partitions), concrete flooring, manure removal equipment, mangers, water buckets, mechanical ventilation, and supplementary heat are necessary. Stall housing requirements for goats are similar to the best of conditions for rearing calves separate from cows in calf barns.

Although they are rather expensive on the basis of cost per cubic foot of housing space, new prefabricated calf houses are ideal for a herd of up to forty milking does kept in stalls. They are temperature controlled with electric heat for winter, air conditioning for summer, and automatic fans. Liquid manure systems available for prefabricated calf housing are not necessary for goats. The tie stall area in this barn may be of pole-type construction. If the building has a solid ceiling and windows, it is absolutely necessary to provide mechanical exhaust ventilation.

In cold climates, any effort to provide an inside temperature higher than the outside temperature in winter time will require ceiling and sidewall insulation and some supplementary heat. It is not possible to provide conditions in a closed insulated stable similar to those found in dairy cow barns without providing supplementary heat. The suspended plastic air duct system used for housing veal calves is ideal for dairy goat barns but it is expensive. If a warm barn is required by the owner (it is not required by the goats), an agricultural engineer who specializes in veal calf housing should be consulted.

Raised slatted floor stalls will provide comfortable confinement with minimal fighting and easy cleaning. The solid fronted, partitioned manger allows individual feeding and minimal feed waste. When animals are restrained in tie stall or stanchion-type stalls, they should be allowed outside for exercise for at least a half hour daily during winter weather. Owners of breeding herds where emphasis is directed toward the best individual production records and individual attention given to each animal will find that individual tie stall housing most nearly fills their needs. (Figure III-1).

24

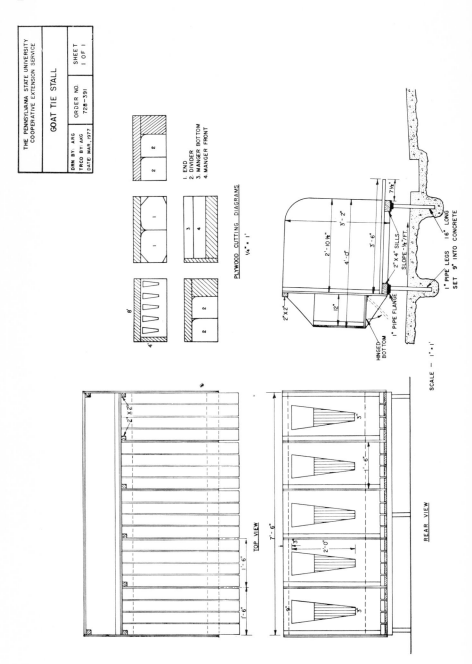

Figure III—2

Restraint in Tie Stall Housing — Use of heavy leather collars (hame straps for horse harness are good), short smooth chains with a swivel and snap next to the collars are the best means of restraint. Chains are fastened to one side of the head opening. Any device which restrains movement of the head and prevents normal rising and lying down makes it difficult to keep bedding under the animals and increases teat and udder injuries. Keyhole stalls and lever operated stanchion stalls are examples of this. Animals should be released for milking and water twice daily. (Figure III-2).

Stall Width and Length — Stalls should be 18 to 20 inches wide and 40 inches in length. The height of mangers determines to a great extent whether or not goats will stay clean in stalls. When the floor of feed mangers is at least eight inches above the stall floor and the depth and forward length of the mangers prevent the animals from pushing forward against the manger to reach food, both feces and urine are dropped well back in the rear of the stall. Wooden stall floors raised above a concrete floor at least eight inches are drier and cleaner than concrete stalls. They permit the floor to be washed down periodically in winter and daily in summer. Individual water pails in a boxed-in corner of the manger (so goats will not upset them) are especially desirable during days when the goats are housed most of the time.

A holding area should be provided at the end of the stable next to the milking parlor and the animals can be returned to their stalls after they have been milked and have drunk water.

26

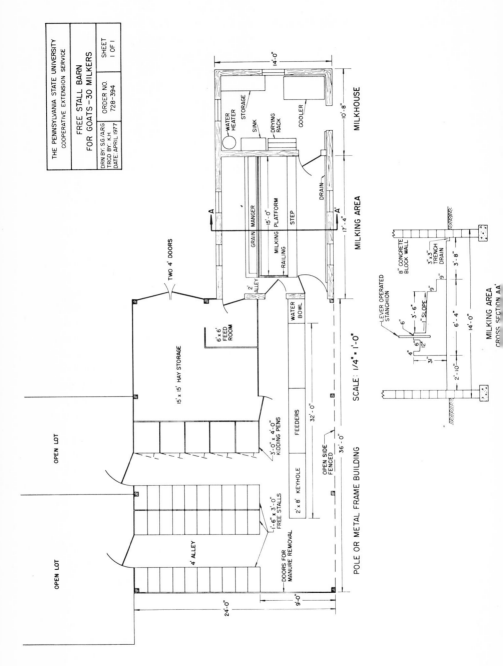

Figure III—3

3. Free Stall Housing (Figure III-3)

This relatively new method of housing large dairy cow herds economically is adaptable for dairy goats. Free stalls provide does with privacy and security lacking in open loose housing. Free stalls save bedding, and sanitation is enhanced by concrete alleyways which can be scraped or washed down regularly. It is imperative in free stall or other loose housing that body heat from the animals be quickly removed from the building. Free stall barns and loose housing barns should be made with ridged roofs which are open the entire length of the ridge to permit free movement of air upward from beneath open eaves and outward through the open ridge. Unless an open ridge at least 6 inches wide or some other means of providing for rapid elimination of heat is provided, condensation occurs in winter weather. When this occurs, conditions are most unfavorable for health of the animals.

Free stalls effectively help the animals stay dry and clean and they eliminate much of the fighting which is continuous in loose housing.

The aisles should be concrete in free stall goat barns. A snow scraper can be used to clean the manure out every few days and aisles can be washed down occasionally. Free stall barns provide an excellent environment for dairy goats at low cost. Fiberglass roofing panels greatly improve the amount of light and if placed where sunlight comes through them, they help to keep the building drier in cold weather. Drop panels at the top of the side walls are useful for better ventilation in hot weather. Stalls should be filled with packed clay, sand or crushed rock to within an inch of the top of the rear curb.

The free stalls themselves should be 18 - 22 inches wide and about 36 inches long. The rear curbs of the stalls should be at least eight inches above the floor. The front wall stalls should be made of plywood. Expanded metal, plywood or non-climbable wire can be used for partitions. The bottom of the free stall should be built up level to about one inch from the top of the rear curb. Tamped clay is the best stall flooring. Inedible bedding material such as sawdust, shavings, shredded corn fodder, sugar cane bagasse, or old hay can be used for bedding. Combinations of these are usually better than use of a single type. Bedding should be placed in stalls at least six inches higher in the stall front than in the rear because goats prefer to lie uphill. Horizontal bars placed across the front of the stalls one foot toward the rear end about 30 inches from the stall floor help to prevent does from standing too far forward in the free stalls. Facilities for feeding and watering should be the same as those recommended for open loose housing.

4. Loose Housing

The most economical way to house mature goats is in a simple open shed in which a deep (at least 15-18 inches) bedded manure pack is provided. The same basic stable plan is satisfactory for goats kept in loose housing on a deep bedded manure pack. Deep bedding produces some heat and a tremendous amount of moisture. At least 20 square feet per animal is necessary. A concrete walk-way across the open end, which can be scraped regularly, will help to keep the bedding cleaner and drier. Goats should never be fed or watered on a bedded manure pack. Part of the same space can be used for feeding forage and water, but it should be physically separated and have a concrete floor which can be scraped clean regularly. Open shed-type barns should have some provision for additional ventilation during summer weather. Drop-down panels at the top of the back wall, or mechanical ventilation with exhaust fans, are necessary. It is imperative in loose housing that no effort be made to keep temperatures inside the stable above those outside it. Condensation of moisture under the roof, on the walls or on the surface of bedding reveals an environment intolerable for dairy goats. Bedding should be kept at least 15 to 18 inches deep at all times. The kidding pens provided alongside the hay storage area may have solid plywood sides but at least one side should be open to the floor.

Feeding Goats in Loose Housing — Keyhole feeders with large mangers elevated at least eight inches from the floor level are excellent for feeding hay, green food or ensilage. Goats can be held in them until the feed is eaten. This prevents much fighting and it gives the more timid animals an opportunity to eat. The arrangement illustrated (see Figure III-3) provides opportunity for individual grain feeding beyond the amount which can be fed in the milking parlor. All loose housing systems for dairy goats require some means of supplementary grain feeding for the highest producing goats beyond that which is fed in the milking parlor. Heated floor-type water troughs provided with keyhole access openings prevent water contamination and provide warm water in wintertime.

Water Facilities — This author favors the float-type cattle waterer which can be fitted with an electric heater to prevent freezing in cold weather. This should be surrounded by key-hole openings to prevent water contamination. Lick type waterers are satisfactory in the shade outdoors, but they usually have a muddy mess around them, and they may not foster sufficient water consumption where there is opportunity for fighting.

The Milking Parlor — This milking parlor is similar to that used by Harvey Considine of Portage, Wisconsin. As many as ten or twelve does stand side-by-side on a raised concrete platform on which the operator can sit down and operate the milking machine. A lever-operated arrangement of stanchions similar to that available for calf housing is ideal in this milking parlor. They should close to a four inch space. Openings should be 15 inches to 18 inches O.C. apart.

The feed trough floor should be at least 6 inches above the platform. Partitions may help to prevent fighting and individual feed pans would provide for individual feeding.

The Milking System — A small size suspended-type milker pail with an attached pulsator is ideal. The 35 lb. milker pail with the vacuum operated Surge pulsator sold by Babson Brothers Co. can be slid under the animal to be milked and the two central teat cups can be used for milking. The outer parts on the milker pail lid can be blocked off with rubber stoppers and the outside pulsator hoses can be shut off by joining them together. Narrow bore inflations under tension and narrow bore teat cup shells should be used. Vacuum in the milking system should not exceed 12 inches and 10 inches of vacuum is the author's preference. Pulsations should be set at 55 per minute at 10 inches of vacuum and 65 per minute at 12 inches of vacuum.

A used small rotary pump or piston pump sufficient to operate 3 or 4 units can usually be found at milking machine dealers at a reasonable price.

Vacuum lines should be 1¼ inch galvanized pipe and stall cocks can be set into the line at 36-inch intervals. An adequate vacuum regulator should be placed between the pump and the stall cock nearest the pump. The milker unit is operated with a three foot milker hose.

Each animal is prepared for milking by washing the udder with warm detergent solution using individual paper towels. As each animal is milked, the milker unit is slid under the next animal and attached. Using the suspended-type pail without actually trying to suspend it, the animal being milked learns very quickly to move backward and thus pull down the teat cups and prevent their "crawling" upward, thus facilitating rapid milk out. The average animal will milk out very well in three minutes using this system. By sitting alongside the animals as they are milked and sliding the unit under the next animal in the milking succession it is relatively easy to work out a very good system of managed milking. Using the 35 lb. pail, milk can be weighed for each animal or the milk from several animals can be collected before dumping through a strainer into a milk can.

The Milk House — The milk house shown contains the standard essentials for dairy cow herds. A milk cooler using cans is a relatively cheap practical way of cooling milk rapidly and holding it at a low temperature. A used ice bank bulk tank or a spray-type can cooler can usually be purchased relatively cheaply from a dairy equipment dealer. The coolers used for the smaller dairy herds 20 years ago are obsolete for large modern dairy cow herds today, but they will do an excellent job in a goat dairy of 30 to 60 milking does. Those who plan milking parlors and milk houses should check with local and state dairy sanitarians to be sure sanitary and construction requirements for the milk shed area are met. The plans shown provide an acceptable cleanable milking parlor and milk house for a Pennsylvania milk market where dairy cow herd requirements are relatively strict and often difficult to meet.

5. Keyhole Feeders (Figure III-4)

Keyhole feeders provide sanitary feeding with minimal loss. Those placed outside should be covered by a roof large enough to keep out rain and provide shade. Keyhole feeders used on a deep bedded manure pack should be bolted to posts on each end and raised as necessary when the bedded pack becomes deeper. Open hay racks not only encourage excessive waste of hay, they provide conditions ideal for build up of internal parasite burdens in the animals.

6. Baby Kid Housing

Open or partially open shed-type housing with raised wooden slat-floored pens off the floor at least fifteen inches provides dry draft-free quarters for kids. Pens should have three solid sides with the front side opening to the stall floor. Feeding, nursing and watering facilities should be placed outside the pen, accessible through keyholes for sanitation, necessary to prevent parasite and other disease problems caused or aided by contaminated feed. Bedding provided baby kids should be of inedible or unpalatable material such as sawdust, shavings, shredded fodder, shredded straw, or sugar cane bagasse. Pens for new-born kids should be provided with heat lamps in cold climates. These can be used until new-born kids are thoroughly dry and they have been given a few feedings of colostrum.

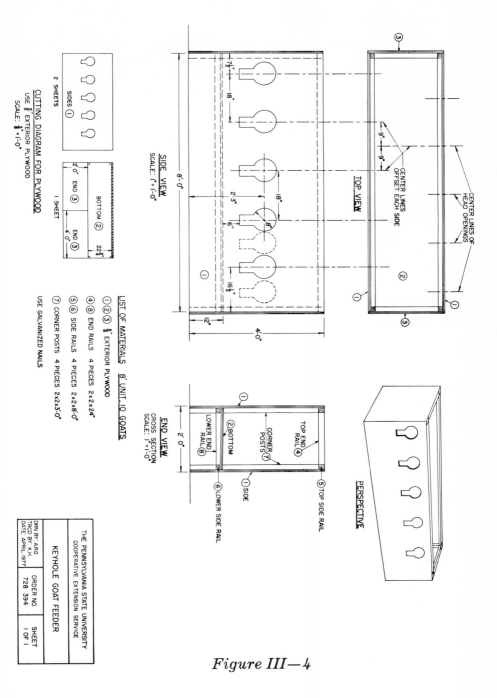

CUTTING DIAGRAM FOR PLYWOOD
USE ⅜" EXTERIOR PLYWOOD
SCALE: ¾"=1'-0"

2 SHEETS

SIDES ①

BOTTOM ②

END ③   END ③

1 SHEET

LIST OF MATERIALS 8' UNIT, 10 GOATS

① ② ③ ⅜" EXTERIOR PLYWOOD

④ ⑧ END RAILS 4 PIECES 2x2x24"

⑤ ⑥ SIDE RAILS 4 PIECES 2x2x8'-0"

⑦ CORNER POSTS 4 PIECES 2x2x3'-0"

USE GALVANIZED NAILS

SIDE VIEW
SCALE: 1"=1'-0"

TOP VIEW

CENTER LINES
OFFSET EACH SIDE

CENTER LINES OF
HEAD OPENINGS

END VIEW
CROSS SECTION
SCALE: 1"=1'-0"

⑧ LOWER END RAIL
② BOTTOM
⑦ CORNER POSTS
④ TOP END RAIL
⑥ LOWER SIDE RAIL
① SIDE
⑤ TOP SIDE RAIL

PERSPECTIVE

DRN BY: A.R.G TRCD BY: K.H. DATE: APRIL 1977		
THE PENNSYLVANIA STATE UNIVERSITY COOPERATIVE EXTENSION SERVICE		
KEYHOLE GOAT FEEDER		
ORDER NO. 728 394		SHEET 1 OF 1

Figure III—4

7. Herd Sire Housing (Figure III-5)

The most important requirement for housing buck dairy goats is complete separation from the female members of the herd. Open shed housing with drop-down panels for summer weather is best. Bucks require only shelter from rain and a dry place to lie down. Several bucks can share the same area if at least 40 square feet of pen space and 100 square feet of yard space is allotted for each. For housing one mature buck, the use of an open shed six feet by eight feet is adequate. Plans in this chapter provide housing for individual bucks with several distinct advantages. The tethering arrangement allows the buck to exercise and at the same time keeps him under constant control. Bucks with horns may be held by a collar. Hornless bucks should be held with a sturdy heavy leather halter. A simple open-fronted shade with a drop down panel on the rear wall for better summer ventilation will provide adequate shelter.

Deep bedding should be used inside the shed. A heavy utility pole guy wire should be stretched close to the surface of the ground between the building and an automobile axle driven its' entire length into the ground at a point distant from the building. The length of wire can be as long as 200 feet and the longer the better. A turnbuckle should be used on the wire to keep it stretched tightly. A small bull ring to which is attached a swivel and about 6 feet of light chain should slide along the wire. If the tether wire is placed close to the ground surface, it is easy to mow the grass around and over it to keep the yard in good shape.

The feeding facility provides for water, grain and hay feeding from the side away from access to the buck. This feeding facility should be placed so that the buck will have access to it but will not be able to move around it or get into it. Lengths of pipe keep the buck out of grain and water buckets and the hay rack is also made out of pipe to prevent the buck from chewing it. This buck housing arrangement is ideal for large fractious bucks. Opportunity for exercise and observation will keep bucks healthier and more contented.

8. Pastures, Dry Lots

Goats are primarily browsing animals. They do not make good use of pasture and they are difficult to manage on improved pastures. When goats are given access to unimproved pasture containing weeds, shrubs, and trees, they will graze the wild plants rather than the grasses and legumes normally eaten by cattle and sheep. Goats are much less selective than are cattle and sheep in the plants they eat. Many plants

33

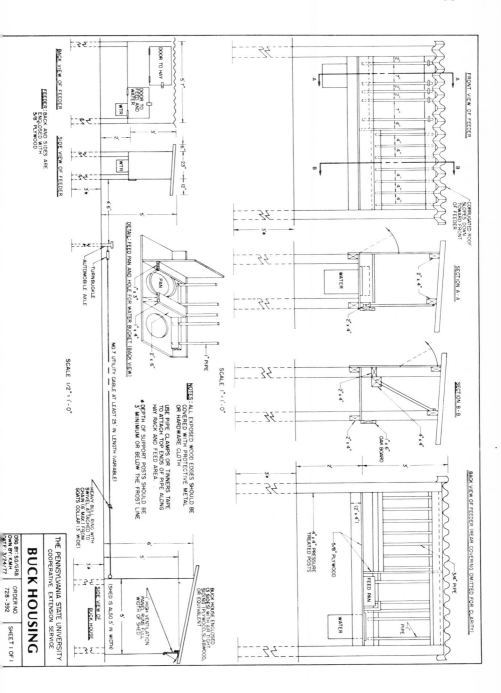

Figure III—5

which produce undesirable flavors in milk are eaten. These include goldenrod, honeysuckle, pokeweed, wild asters, and many others.

The best way to utilize fresh forage for a milking herd is to cut the green forage for the animals and feed it to them in a hay or forage feeder in the barn or dry lot. Most perennial grasses and annual grasses, if cut in the prebloom stage, are readily eaten and highly digestible when cut and fed to goats. Most of the legume forages commonly grown for dairy cow feeding are readily eaten by goats when fed. Comfrey is a very popular plant for green feeding. It is very high in crude protein. Some samples will test as high as 30% crude protein on a dry matter basis. Comfrey may contain excessive nitrate levels when the plants are stressed by cool dark weather or hot dry weather. Red clover pastured, cut green or fed as hay is relished by goats. It is an excellent feed for them provided that it is entirely free from mold. Kudzu is readily eaten by goats. It may be wise to watch goats as they browse kudzu vines, if vines are growing off the ground in shrubs and trees. The author has seen several situations where goats strangled themselves when caught in the climbing vines.

Summing up recommendations for use of pasture for goats: put young stock and dry stock on unimproved pastures and shrubby or weedy lots; they will make good use of this material. As long as they are not forced by starvation to eat poisonous plants, they will usually avoid them. Coarse woody forage is excellent for young animals to develop good rumen function. After milking does have completed a lactation in which they were fed relatively large amounts of grain and highly digestible hay, browse of any kind is highly desirable to restore both rumen capacity and function to prepare them for the next lactation.

When goats are placed in improved pastures, they waste much more feed than they eat. It is much better to harvest the material daily and feed it to the herd in a feeder which will prevent the animals from contaminating the forage.

Goats will accept as green feed many kinds of forage they might ignore when they are expected to consume it as pasture. Young perennial and annual grasses cut before the bloom stage, most legumes, and comfrey are readily accepted and utilized as green feed by milking animals. From the milk flavor standpoint, all other green feeds are hazardous.

9. Fencing

Use of a weed-cutter-type electric fence is a great boon to economical confinement of dairy goats. Four wires, 12, 18, 24, and 32 inches off the ground, fastened by insulators onto posts, will keep all goats in and dogs out. Once goats discover an electric fence, they will give it the greatest respect. The four-wire fence is best installed inside of permanent paddock fencing. Two wires, 12 and 28 inches from the ground, are sufficient to restrain goats accustomed to an electric fence when larger areas are fenced. Use of two-wire fence makes possible confinement of groups of bucks, dry does, or young stock in brushy or woodland areas where they can utilize the browse and get plenty of exercise. There is almost no other practical economical fencing available for goats. It is virtually impossible to confine bucks with any other fence less than six feet high unless it is unclimbable.

10. Available Building Resources

Most states have agricultural engineering and dairy science extension staff people who can be extremely helpful to dairy goat owners considering new or remodeled housing for their herds. Many of these people deny any knowledge of housing for goats, but all of them have resources and experience in animal housing which can be very helpful for dairy goat owners.

B.   The Herd

1. Managing Milking Animals

Although many dairy goat owners would hotly deny it, management of a herd of milking does is not much different from the management of a herd of milking cows.

In every herd or group of dairy goats, there is a definite arrangement of dominance or "peck order." Arrangements for feeding, bedding, exercise lots, and holding areas where animals wait to be milked, should eliminate as much as possible, opportunities for fighting. Horns or scurs should be removed from all animals. Those possessing them will often inflict severe injuries on their hornless herdmates.

Milking dairy goats are almost fanatic creatures of habit. They are happiest and they milk best when a regular daily routine is established with rigid adherence to a time schedule. Any departure from routine upsets the "will to milk" much more than it does for dairy cows. Any abrupt changes in grain or forage should be avoided. All ration changes should be made gradually over a period of not less than one week. Where maximum milk production is the goal, it is especially important that grain, forage, and watering facilities be kept scrupulously clean. One fecal pellet in a water trough may eliminate water consumption for the day with disastrous effect on milk production.

Milking order is much more important for dairy goats than for dairy cows. They become very much upset when they lose their place in the milking order. In a small herd, the milking order can match the "peck order" for minimal confusion and fighting at milking time. This is especially true where the herd is held in a holding pen or holding area just before milking.

Milk should be weighed at regular times (preferably at each milking) and small increments or withdrawals of grain can be made as necessary. For maximum milk production, challenge feeding is recommended. Essentially, challenge feeding is feeding a slight excess of grain until daily milk production peaks. This is followed by withdrawing grain gradually to maintain production, and preventing excessive weight gains. This is discussed further in the section on **Nutrition**.

The milking herd should be fed the most highly digestible, most palatable forage available. Four or five forage feedings each day of amounts which will be consumed within a half hour are infinitely better than one or two feedings daily. Goats will consume more and waste less forage. Availability of more than one palatable forage will result in greater intake when each forage is fed at alternate times. For example: if good early-cut alfalfa hay is fed alternately with green-cut sudan grass, the animals will consume much more total forage than if either one were fed exclusively.

Milking does respond to gentle quiet handling with minimal commotion. Strange dogs, goats, or other animals should be kept away from the milking herd. Visitors should be kept from close access to the herd at milking time. Anything which annoys milking animals at milking time manifests itself in less milk as a direct result of its effect on milk let-down.

2. Care of the Dry and Kidding Doe

Drying Off Milking Does — It is imperative that pregnant does have a dry period of at least 50 days before kidding. There are a number of good reasons for this. During the last 60 days of gestation, the foetuses grow rapidly and the requirements for nutrients increase. The udder tissue should undergo normal involution and quiescence before new secretory tissue develops for the next lactation. Depleted stores of muscle glycogen, a very important source of energy immediately following kidding, need to be replenished.

It should be the dairy goat owner's goal to improve the animal's condition (her meatiness) and at the same time avoid getting the animal fat. Any gross evidence of fat on the surface beneath the skin is evidence of excessive fat accumulation in the abdominal cavity. This is very important from the standpoint of good health through freshening. Too much fat in the abdomen greatly limits capacity to eat. As the uterus rapidly takes up more and more abdominal space in the fat animal, capacity to handle adequate food decreases. The animal then is forced to meet energy needs from use of its stored fat. Ketosis is the usual result.

Effect of Drying Off on Subsequent Lactation — Numerous research experiments with dairy cows show a significant increase in milk production when at least a 50-day dry period is undergone before the next lactation begins. This is most certainly true for dairy goats.

Management and feeding of the late lactation and dry doe should be directed toward getting the animal in the best possible state of health to meet the stress associated with parturition (kidding). Not to be ignored is the necessity that the events of parturition do not adversely affect the condition of the reproductive tract at the next time the doe should be bred, six or seven months later.

A list of these goals follows:

- Dry off the udder and prevent mastitis.
- Have the doe in lean, active, healthy condition for kidding.
- Have the doe's digestive system restored to normal capacity and function so that she will have both the capacity and appetite for handling large amounts of concentrate feeds.
- Bring the doe through kidding with the least possible damage to her udder and reproductive tract and with minimal stress.
- Prevent pregnancy disease (ketosis) and milk fever before and after kidding.
- Prevent post-kidding reproductive tract infections.
- Prevent baby kid disease problems.

How To Dry Off the Udder — When animals are producing less than four pounds of milk daily, they can be dried off simply by ceasing milking. Higher producing animals demand more attention. Milk flow can often be drastically reduced by withholding grain for several feedings, feeding the animal on fair quality grass hay and cutting down water intake. After the amount of milk drops below two pounds at a milking, then milking can be safely stopped.

It should be understood that at drying off, it is just as essential to milk-out the udder every time milk let-down occurs as it is at any other time. First goal, therefore, in drying off a doe is to prevent milk let-down.

Things Which Help to Prevent Milk Let-Down — Goats are extremely sensitive to changes in milking regime. Goat owners should take advantage of this fact when drying animals off.

Putting animals to be dried off in a pen with dry animals or young animals just before milking time will often prevent milk let-down. Anything that will upset the animal just before and during milking time will usually make it impossible for her to let down milk. If, when you try to do this the first time and are unsuccessful, the udder should be completely milked out. Never milk the udder unless you milk it out completely. Once milk is forced out of the milk producing tissue (alveoli) into the collecting ducts, it is easier for mastitis bacteria to multiply and possibly cause clinical mastitis. Usually, if grain is withheld and the doe is put into a pen of other animals or turned out into a lot at milking time, she will be sufficiently upset to prevent strong milk let-down. After several milking periods pass without milking, milk let-down will not take place and normal care can be resumed.

Mastitis treatment — The following situations provide justification for using special dry mastitis treatment formulation:

- Positive CMT reaction (exceeding trace reaction) of the milk in an udder half or to the entire udder when tested at least 30 days previous to drying off.
- Laboratory culture of milk samples during the previous lactation which reveals the presence of mastitis causing streptococci or staphylococci bacteria.
- History of clinical mastitis during the previous lactation.

Dry treatment Available — FDA-approved mastitis formulations designed for treating dry cows are useful for treating dry does. Those which contain at least a million units of penicillin and one gram of dihydrostreptomycin per cow dose are recommended. *(Quartermaster-Norwich-Chem.)* Synthetic slow-dissolving penicillin **Cloxacillin/ Orbenin D C** *(Beechem-Massengill)* or **Boviclox** *(Squibb)* are also excellent. The latter product has the distinct advantage of being manufactured and packaged sterile.

The Proper Way to Treat a Dry Doe — First hand-strip all the secretion you can get from the udder. Wash your hands and the udder thoroughly with warm mild detergent or soap solution. Be sure that the teat ends have been thoroughly cleaned. Dry the udder and teats with a clean towel; then dry your hands carefully. Using cotton or gauze swabs saturated in 70% alcohol, wash off the teat ends and holding the teat in one hand, scrub off the teat end with the cotton or gauze swab in the other. Carefully remove the cap from the teat cannula end of the treatment syringe or tube. Wipe the cannula with a clean alcohol swab. Holding the teat with one hand and squeezing it to dilate the teat opening, gently pass the teat cannula through the teat canal at least 3/4 inch into the teat cistern. Inject ¼ to ½ of the cow dose into the gland. Thoroughly and gently massage the gland after removing the cannula and dip the teat in teat-dip (see **Mastitis** section). Before treating the other half of the udder, wipe off the teat cannula of the treatment syringe with an alcohol swab and repeat as before.

Hazards to Unsanitary Treatment Technique — The environment, the goat's skin, your hands, bedding, etc., are all contaminated with organisms which may resist penicillin or actually grow better in the presence of penicillin. Injection of these organisms at the same time penicillin is administered may be more dangerous for the future udder health of the doe than no treatment at all. Yeasts, molds, non-ag streptococci and some resistant staphylococci may gain entrance to the udder in this way and cause serious udder damage and mastitis. Yeasts (primarily *Candida albicans*) are not uncommon contaminents found in some dry cow mastitis preparations, and their use has ruined udders during the dry period.

Hazards of Dry Treatment — Even when dry treatment is done in a sterile manner and it is correctly administered into properly prepared teats, there is some evidence that its use may make the udder more susceptible to mastitis just before, during and following freshening. The currently approved preparations are highly effective for ridding the mammary glands of the common mastitis streptococci and staphylococci; however, at the same time this is accomplished, production and liberation of leucocytes (white blood cells) into the tissues of the gland is drastically decreased. When this occurs, the gland tissue is much more vulnerable to attack by both specific mastitis organisms and environmental organisms capable of causing mastitis. It is like sending an army home from a fort and leaving it susceptible to attack.

Normal Dry Udder Secretion — Buttermilk-like fluid obtained during the first week or two following cessation of milking is normal. During the remainder of the dry period, a small amount of honey-colored fluid, which may have the consistency of honey, is normal.

Teat Ends — It is very important that the skin and mucous membrane of the teat end and teat canal remain healthy. At least once a week the teats should be examined for evidence of chapping and injury. Use of 50% sulfathiazole ointment or cod liver oil ointment for several days will be helpful. When teats have been cut, bruised or otherwise injured, mastitis dry treatment is indicated.

A Conservative Approach of Mastitis Dry Treatment — In view of the expense and the possible hazards of dry treatment, a conservative approach to treatment of only those animals for which dry treatment may be helpful seems justified. Any doe which has had clinical mastitis or recent teat injury should be dry treated. Where laboratory culture or CMT testing clearly indicates that pathogens are present and active, dry treatment may be most helpful. Where there is no history or evidence of mastitis, dry treatment is not justified.

Feeding the Late Lactation, Dry and Freshening Doe — The late lactation and dry period provides ample time to restore normal stomach function. Correctly fed high-producing does should be fed large amounts of high-energy, small-particle size concentrate feeds and the very best quality legume forage. Many successful dairy goat breeders feed does in early lactation as much as one pound of high quality dairy grain concentrate (14-18% protein, 75%-TDN, low fiber) for each two pounds of milk daily. Withholding some of the best quality forage so that the heavy producer will eat maximum amounts of grain is worthwhile, but the condition of the four stomach compartments is adversely affected by this necessary feeding regimen. Feeding more forage and less grain during the late lactation period will prevent accumulation of excess body fat and help to restore the abomasum (true stomach) to its normal size (about $1/3$ smaller than it should be in maximum lactation). Feeding late lactation and dry does on browse alone, if it is available, as a source of forage is excellent for restoration of normal rumen function. The "scratch factor" of browse or coarse long-fiber hay is highly beneficial for restoration of the normal rumen mucosa (lining) and rumen musculature.

The whole objective of this program for feeding does during their dry period is to keep them lean and active, prevent their getting fat, and restore the normal tone, capacity and relative size of their stomach compartments. Does which are not fed correctly during this part of the lactation cycle, particularly those animals which have become fat, are **prone to pregnancy disease, poor appetite at freshening, ketosis, and impaired production in the next lactation.**

Regardless of whether or not the dry doe is fat, no attempt should be made to make her lose weight in the last month before kidding. (See **Pregnancy Disease**.) Even fat animals should be fed gradually increasing amounts of concentrate during the last three weeks of gestation so they will not be forced to use accumulated body fat to meet their needs and thus most certainly suffer ketosis. Many overfat animals appear to be doing well until a few days before they kid. Then they lose appetite and rapidly develop ketosis and other problems.

Starting three weeks before freshening, gradually increase the amount of concentrate fed to the dry doe until by the day the doe freshens, she should eat at least one pound of the milking-herd grain mixture and as much as she wants of the best available quality forage.

Preventing Milk Fever — The best way to prevent milk fever in dairy goat herds receiving alfalfa or other legume hay is to severely limit or eliminate altogether alfalfa or other calcium-rich legume forage for at least three weeks previous to kidding. This feeding program activates the calcium mobilization mechanism within the body and thus prepares the animal for mobilizing available calcium when the lactating udder demands it. The best alfalfa or other legume hay should be fed in rapidly increasing amounts beginning on the day the doe freshens.

Preventing Udder Congestion — A popular myth insists that feeding excess protein during the dry period causes udder congestion. Actually, just the opposite is true. Dry does require at least the same protein content in their feed as the milking herd receives except that the total amount fed should be less. When feeding coarse hay or browse, an 18% protein mix may be necessary.

Excess Dietary Sodium — Be sure that salt content of the concentrate fed dry does does not exceed 1%. Avoid feeding mineral mixtures or molasses salt blocks which contain appetizers to increase their intake.

Milk Weight in The Udder — The udder-supporting ligaments and elastic tissue attachments are often permanently damaged, stretched and weakened by failure to relieve the weight of a large congested udder before freshening occurs. Don't be afraid to milk a doe for a few days if she has a large amount of milk to relieve excessive udder weight. Save the first quart of colostrum for feeding the kids. Keep it refrigerated or freeze it.

Udder Supports — Animals with poor median suspensory ligaments (where the udder floor drops and the teats extend laterally) can often be greatly helped by using udder supports. A piece of burlap 12 inches by 18 inches, with cotton straps (at each corner) which are tied over the loin and hips, will provide excellent support and prevent teat injury for the last few critical days before freshening.

Warm Water Massage — Use of lukewarm water and gentle massage rubbing backward and upward may be helpful. Never use water hot enough to redden your hands. If the udder feels hot and sensitive, ice water may be helpful.

Worm Medication for Dry Does — Worming dry does two weeks before they are due to freshen may be necessary for both the welfare of the does and their newborn kids in herds where worms are a problem. Only one worm medicine currently available is safe enough for use at this time. That is Thiabendazole.

Other Medication for Dry Does —

Selenium — **Tocopheral Injection** — In the selenium-deficient areas of the United States, injection of sodium selenite solution 60 days before kidding is helpful for preventing white muscle disease in the kids and fostering good uterine involution following kidding (see **Selenium Deficiency**).

Enterotoxemia Booster Dose — Injection of a booster dose of bivalent (Type C-D) **Clostridium perfringens** toxoid-bacterin in the period from 45 to 15 days before kidding will be helpful for insuring that colostrum will contain high levels of enterotoxemia antibodies to protect the kids as long as they are receiving milk (see **Enterotoxemia**).

Tetanus Booster Dose — Injection of a single booster dose of tetanus toxoid in the period within 45 to 15 days before kidding will be helpful to insure adequate tetanus antibody levels in colostrum for the kids and support resistance in the doe for another year.

Preparation For Kidding — At least two days before does are due to kid, they should be placed in clean disinfected maternity pens (at least 5 feet square with three solid sides and one side open to the floor to provide adequate ventilation). The maternity stall should be made of material which can be scrubbed clean and sprayed with sanitizer or disinfectant. Use an iodophor or chlorine dairy sanitizer after the surfaces have been scrubbed clean. For larger operations, a steam jenny (delivering 300 lbs./sq. in.) with detergent sanitizer does an excellent job. Avoid odorous irritant disinfectants. Rely on cleaning rather than disinfection to get the job done. Clean bright straw is the best bedding material to use in the maternity stall. Both water buckets and grain box are best placed outside the maternity pen using key-holes for access. Kids may be dropped into water buckets when these are placed inside the maternity pen on the floor. Kids should be born in a **DRY** draft-free place. It is not necessary to provide supplementary heat for healthy kids.

Onset of Kidding — The doe should be observed for signs of imminent kidding (foot stamping, looking around at her side, dripping milk, and discharging vaginal fluids). If the amniotic sac (water bag) appears and ruptures, kidding should take place within a few minutes. Then if the doe begins labor without result, she should be examined. Wash the vulva with mild soap and warm water, and thoroughly wash your hands. If upon examination with two or three fingers, you feel the fluid sac intact, give the animal more time. If, however, you can find two feet with the nose between them, try assistance. Extend each fore leg and pull steadily downward and backward. This is the normal forward presentation of the kid. Equally normal is the backward presentation in which you can feel the hind legs, hocks and the rear of the kid. Extending the back legs with downward and backward traction should help delivery.

If you examine the doe and feel anything different from that described, veterinary assistance should be sought immediately. As long as fluid is present and the uterus doesn't contract closely around the kids, delivery is easy. When the uterus contracts and fluids are gone, delivery of only slightly abnormal presentations can be very difficult.

Caesarian Section — Because it is so difficult to manually examine kidding does, veterinarians should not hesitate to do Caesarian section when it is impossible to easily deliver kids the normal way. The birth canal membrane and walls are rather delicate and will tolerate trauma to the same degree that can be tolerated by manipulating lambing ewes. Halothane anesthesia, Xylacine, or Surritol can be used with excellent predictable results. Does recover with a minimum of stress and exhaustion following Caesarian section done early. If the kids are alive at Caesarian delivery, prognosis should be good.

Retained Placenta — Fortunately, retained placenta occurs much less commonly in dairy goats than it occurs in dairy cattle. The placenta (afterbirth) which is part of the fetus, not part of the dam, should be passed within several hours of birth of the kids. Many goat breeders believe that giving the freshened doe all of the very warm water she will drink hastens passage of the placenta. This may be helpful because there is a rather large loss of body heat involved with labor and aspiration of environmental air when straining. A common cause of retained placenta and pyometra (pus in the uterus) in Eastern United States may be selenium deficiency. (See section on **Selenium Deficiency**.)

If there is any possibility that the placenta may not have been passed within twelve hours following kidding, wash clean the vulva and your hands, and attempt to examine the birth canal. If you can get hold of placental membrane with your fingers, gently attempt to withdraw it. Often the placenta has been shed from its cotyledons and it collects at the internal end of the cervix. A small amount of traction will usually suffice to remove it. Where the placenta is obviously retained and it is not possible to remove it manually, uterine infusion with an antibiotic solution may be indicated. Some veterinarians use from 10-15 mgms. of diethylstilbestrol which is said to keep the cervix open and greatly aid expulsion of the membranes.

Milking at Kidding — The udder should be washed with soap and warm water and dried immediately, and the kids should be fed colostrum as soon as possible. For the sake of having the doe conditioned to hand or machine milking, milk at least 16 oz. of colostrum from her and feed it to the kids in a pan or nipple bottle. As soon as the doe has cleaned the kids, remove them from her. Dip the navel cords of the kids in mild tincture of iodine as soon as the kids are born. Use a baby food jar and soak the navel cord in the iodine as soon as the kids stand.

3. Starting Healthy Kids

The diseases of baby kids will be considered by themselves mainly for the purpose of presenting a management program for their prevention. Losses of baby kids vary tremendously among herds. The losses in small herds are generally very small; in large herds, they often approach 30 or 40 percent.

Preventing sickness and losses in baby kids demands attention to many basic factors which relate to their health and vigor at birth, their care within the first few hours after birth, and their environment and nutrition until weaning time.

Factors Which Influence the Number of Kids Born Per Doe — Most dairy goat breeders would much rather have multiple births of kids from their does. Single kids are often exceedingly large and usually result in difficult kidding. In yearling does, large single kids are often presented head first with both legs retained, or feet first with the head back as result of the excessive size of the kid. The number of kids per doe can greatly be influenced by management of the does at breeding time. Breeding does at the normal or best time of the breeding period is important. They produce more ova during the cool shorter days of October and November than they do early in the breeding period in late July and August or at the end of the breeding period in late January or February.

Does should be gaining weight on an ascending plane of nutrition at the time they are bred and for at least three weeks thereafter. This is an observation long recognized by the breeders of all multipara (animals which have multiple births). Sheep and swine breeders routinely "flush" females by increasing their feed intake at breeding time and significantly increase the number of offspring born.

In order to have 305-day lactation records, it is necessary to start breeding does after they have been milking more than 180 days. By this time they have passed the peak production of earlier lactation and the heavy producers have usually milked off much of their body condition. If they are relatively free of internal parasites, increasing the concentrate feed beyond their needs for milk production will result in rapid weight gain. After at least three weeks of this feeding, they will be in ideal condition to breed to influence the number of kids they will have. It is especially important to worm does, if they are anemic, before breeding them.

Nutrition during late lactation may have tremendous effect on the health of kids at birth. When does become excessively fat and are suffering from ketosis as a result of excessive fat and lack of exercise, the kids also become intoxicated or weak as a result of the ketones present. (See **Care of the Dry and Freshening Doe.**)

Injection of Vitamin A with D and E may be quite helpful within 30 to 15 days of kidding, to insure against deficiency of these important vitamins in both the doe and kids at kidding time. Where forage quality may not be the very best, intramuscular injection of 500,000 units of Vitamin A with D and E, using one of the available commercial preparations, is good insurance against weakness in newborn kids.

Care at Birth — Management of the doe to prevent excessive fatigue, damage to the birth canal, prevent undue stress for the doe and kids, and insure delivery of live kids is covered in the chapter on "**Care Of The Dry and Freshening Doe.**" As soon as each kid is born, the nose and mouth should be carefully cleaned off. If they show rattling breathing sounds and gasp for air, they should be held head down by their hind legs to aid expulsion of fluid in their respiratory tracts. Oxygen mask outfits available for saving lambs and calves may be useful for reviving kids which show reduced tendency to start breathing. Kids should be dried off with a rough towel while the doe is engaged in cleaning them.

Protecting the Newborn Kid Against Disease — Beyond having the kid born vigorous and healthy, it is necessary to protect him, from the beginning, against organisms in the environment capable of producing disease. The baby kid, like all other domestic animals excepting the dog, is born totally susceptible to disease. In nature, the doe instinctively does things which insure that disease exposure is limited. In domestication, however, she usually cannot seek out a relatively clean place for birth to take place. There are two or three portals of entrance for disease, the nose and mouth and the navel cord. In order to minimize the likelihood of infection at birth, it is necessary for the kids to be born in the cleanest possible place. This should be a cleaned, disinfected kidding stall or pen bedded with bright clean straw. No cats, dogs, or goats should be allowed access to the kidding pens before new kids arrive.

Dip The Navel — The navel cords should be cut with a scissors or preferably a small emasculator, about six inches from the belly wall. Then, holding the kid in the standing position, dip the navel cord in tincture of iodine its entire length. Use of a small baby food jar for this purpose is good. Many breeders dip the cords again the second day.

Feed Colostrum — Within twenty-four hours before birth, one of nature's most fascinating miracles takes place in the mammary glands of the doe. Resistance to all of the diseases to which she has immunity (antibody) is contained in the gamma globulin fraction of her blood. Shortly before freshening, the gamma globulin literally leaks into the alveoli (milk-producing sacs) of the gland and it becomes part of the super-rich colostrum being manufactured for the expected kids. Colostrum contains higher levels of total protein, milk solids, lactose, globulins and fat than normal milk. It is also very rich in Vitamin A.

At the expense of her own resistance to disease, the doe furnishes tremendous protection against disease in her first milk. It has been shown experimentally that if the young animal ingests disease-producing organisms before he gets colostrum, he may die of acute septicemia before he is 72 hours old. Much work has been done in this area with virulent E. coli, the cause of white scours in kids. If the kid ingests E. coli before he gets colostrum, he is almost sure to die of E. coli septicemia within 72 hours. If he gets colostrum first and has the same exposure to E. coli, he usually will show no evidence of the disease. It is extremely important that the kid be fed clean colostrum as soon as possible after birth.

The First Feeding — Wash the doe's udder and dry it. Be sure to get the teat ends clean. Milk the doe in a clean sanitized receptacle and give the kid four ounces of fresh warm colostrum via a nursing bottle, pan or by passing a tube into his stomach to administer it. This should preferably be done before the kid is fifteen minutes old, to give him maximum protection.

During the first two days of life, kids should receive at least three colostrum feedings each day. Young kids are able to absorb antibody protection very well at birth, but by the time they are three days old, their ability to absorb colostral antibody is just about gone.

The Kid's Health Bank Account — Those first feedings of colostrum can be compared to a bank account or gift of protection given the baby kid by his mother. This, in nature, amply protects him against disease for at least a month. When the kid is that old, it will have begun to develop its own antibody resistance to disease. However, in some dairy goat herds, kids experience far more exposure to disease in the environment than would be experienced in nature. When kids come down with scours or pneumonia, it is directly related to the amount of exposure and stress they endure. Under very unsanitary conditions with bad ventilation, this may be within a week. Better conditions may prevent appearance of disease until the kids are nearly one month old. Dairy goat breeders should study their kidding management and facilities carefully to see where they are interfering with nature's almost perfect system for protecting baby kids against disease.

Increasing the Protective Qualities of Colostrum — When certain diseases are endemic (resident) within the herd, administration of a specific bacterin, toxoid, or vaccine to the doe during pregnancy will usually enhance the levels of antibody transferred via the colostrum. Administration of **Clostridium perfringens bacterin-toxoid, type C and D** and tetanus toxoid should be routine procedure for most American dairy goat herds. When the annual booster dose of the biologic is administered in late pregnancy, there is a significant boost in colostral antibody against that disease.

Where **Pasteurella sp., Corynebacter sp.,** or **Hemophilus sp.** infections are endemic problems within the herd, two doses of specific or mixed bacterin given during pregnancy may greatly enhance resistance to these diseases in the doe during the stress period of freshening and for the newborn kids during their first month of life.

Preventing White Muscle Disease — (see **Selenium Deficiency**

White Muscle Disease) — In most of central and all of eastern USA, injection of pregnant does 30 to 15 days before kidding and injection of baby kids 3-4 weeks of age will effectively prevent this serious disease of robust, rapidly growing young animals.

Feeding Colostrum — Every dairy goat breeder should keep a small supply of colostrum in plastic pint containers in the freezer. These can make the difference between life and death, or at least between a bad start and a good start, for kids bereft of colostrum from their own dams.

Feeding Sour Colostrum — About ten years ago, the popular dairy press hailed a new "breakthrough" idea for saving baby calves — feeding sour colostrum. The idea was not new; this author has a "Stock Doctor" book published in 1862 which recommends feeding calves sour milk to prevent scours. However, revival of the idea has been highly successful in saving calves. In large dairy herds where calf losses in spite of medications of all kinds exceeded 40%, use of sour colostrum cut the losses to under 10% without the use of medicine. Dairy goat herd owners should try this idea. It will reduce the cost of feeding kids and reduce the incidence of scours.

All of the colostrum and milk not necessary to feed the kids for at least the first seven milkings is saved. Put it in a covered plastic bucket and keep it in a warm place at 60° to 80°F. After the first two days, stir the fermenting colostrum well and feed to kids at the rate of two parts sour colostrum to one part warm water. Kids may be reluctant to drink soured colostrum from an open feed pan as well as they will take it from a nursing bottle, but they usually have no trouble adjusting if they are fed the material from the beginning as it sours. Colostrum from several does can be mixed together and used. Little feeding value is lost until the material is 60 days old. Milk can be added to the sour colostrum if the supply is short of the kids' needs. Never use milk from does treated for mastitis. The slightest trace of antibiotic in milk will ruin the soured material. The secret of success for soured colostrum is its acidity. The bad actor organisms, **E. coli** and **Salmonellae** cannot survive at the pH of below 4.0 which is normal for the soured colostrum. Reconstituted antibiotic-free high-quality milk replacers (without soya flour and containing spray dried skim milk and top quality white animal fat) can be used for addition to the soured colostrum if additional material is necessary.

Feeding Milk Replacer to Kids — Excellent growth and health can be achieved in baby kids by feeding them one of the high-quality milk replacers produced for lambs and currently available from feed sources. These are fed in multiple nipple Lamb Saver feeders on an ad lib basis. Addition of 1.0 ml (cc.) of undiluted Formalin per gallon will prevent the milk replacer suspension from spoiling for several days and it is safe for the kids. Excellent quality kids and lambs can be started by this method. Where the herd owner has a good fluid milk market, great savings are possible starting good kids with no greater disease risk than when feeding fresh milk.

Feeding Grain and Forage to Baby Kids — From the first day, baby kids can be offered small amounts of calf starter feed if they will eat it. Kids can often be started eating grain by putting a small amount of the grain into their milk feeding pan. It is important that they begin to eat forage as soon as possible to aid in rumen development and to enable them to be weaned easily. Succulent forage like grape leaves, comfrey, vegetable leaves, and green grass will usually be accepted in preference to hay in the beginning. When feeding hay, try several kinds and feed the kind that the kids consume best. That is more important to get them started than attempting to feed them less palatable hay that may be of much higher quality. The object in feeding young kids should be to get them to develop rumens necessary to handle grain and forage. Too many dairy goat kids have middles like race horses because they are not started right. They never become efficient users of forage because they have never developed rumen function nor rumen capacity.

Precocious Milkers[1] — Kids which begin to produce milk as early as three months of age are not at all uncommon among dairy goats. The condition is hereditary and in some strains of dairy goat kids, it is common. Because precocious milkers are more subject to udder injury and invasion of pathogenic bacteria into their udders, goat owners who do not have the time nor interest in caring for the precocious milkers should consider culling them.

Precocious milkers require stripping out the glands at least twice a week or as often as they fill with secretion. It is a good rule of milking to always completely milk out a gland any time that milking is done at all. Once the let-down syndrome has occurred, all milk should be removed. Some yearling does will freshen (or come into milk) as much as two months before they kid. These animals usually become better than average milkers, and it is usually worth the effort, even in commercial herds, to milk them as often as twice daily if necessary. Care should be taken to be sure that they do not lose weight from inadequate grain

[1] *Arn Campbell, Dairy Goat Journal 39(5): 5, 1961*

feeding if they are producing more than a pound of milk at each milking. If early milking occurs more than several days before birth of the kids, colostrum should be saved and frozen and fed to the kids for at least a day following their birth. Often the early secretion is thin and watery and typical colostrum is not produced until a day or two before kidding. The important thing is to save it, if it is produced more than a day or two before the kids are born.

4. Care of Herd Sires

Most dairy goat bucks are sadly neglected individuals until the beginning of the breeding season. The herd sires should be fed an amount of the milking doe's ration which will keep them in lean vigorous condition. No animal is more pathetic than a dairy goat buck confined in a small pen or lot. Bucks should have maximum opportunity for exercise. A number of bucks of different ages can be confined in a large area of browse or pasture if they are away from close association with the female herd. Most of the obnoxious habits observed in dairy goat herd sires are the result of confinement and boredom. Given all the exercise they need and a balanced ration, they can be quite different animals than most of them are. (See **Electric Fencing** and **Housing For Bucks**).

C.   Nutrition

1. Special Feeding Requirements

Dairy goats, quite unlike their cousins devoted to clearing brush and gleaning refuse dumps, are fastidious feeders. It is virtually impossible to achieve good milk production from a herd unless the animals are offered clean feed and water. Both water and feeding facilities should be constructed so that neither goats nor other animals or birds will foul them (see plans in **Housing**).

Grain storage for goats must be in a clean dry well-ventilated odor-free place. Milking does will not eat sufficient amounts for their needs when grain or hay smells of contamination or molds. One of the best reasons for feeding milking does commercially available high-quality dairy (cow) feeds is that there is a constant turnover and replenishment of the supply at the feed warehouse or mill. Fresh clean sweet smelling feeds are relished by goats. Dairy cows, sheep and swine will much more readily accept dusty or slightly damaged feed than will dairy goats. Of course, one can force a herd to eat less than ideal feed, but their response in lower milk production will severely penalize the feeder for it.

Goats, like other animals or possibly more than other domestic animals, like variety in their diet and will eat 10 to 25% more forage if it is fed in smaller quantities at frequent intervals. Feeding a different kind of forage at least once daily will often increase appetite for the entire ration.

Feeding one feeding of green forage immediately following milking is usually a good idea if it is practical to do so. Feeding green browse, weeds, or forage plants at that time has the least effect on milk flavor and a good effect on appetite.

Appetite and milk production are influenced most by the digestibility of the total ration and the amount of energy and protein in it. Does in early lactation require the highest possible digestibility and energy content in their ration until they have been milking at least several weeks beyond their peak of production. Protein is an especially critical factor in milk production. Deficiency of protein manifests itself quickly in lowered digestibility of the entire ration and depressed milk production in direct relation to the extent of the protein deficiency. Testing of the forage consumed and formulation of a grain ration to balance the forage fed will provide for adequate protein and energy intake. Without forage testing, gradual addition of protein supplement to the grain ration fed until maximum milk yields occur is one way to adjust protein levels to the animals' needs.

Feeding excessive protein levels results in increased nitrogen loss through the urine, and in abnormal soft pasty feces. Ideal feces for milking does should tend toward the pasty side. In late lactation and during the dry period, fecal pellets should be relatively dry and well formed.

Water — Water is the most important of all foods consumed by most mammals. It is tremendously important for feeding animals capable of high production. In a study of fifteen high-producing relatively healthy Pennsylvania dairy cow herds, the one parameter common to all of those herds was excellent quality drinking water. Experience by those who investigate poor health, poor productibility, and infertility of dairy cow herds often reveals that the animals are drinking poor quality water. Dairy goats appear to be much more sensitive to water quality than are most other farm animals. Unless milking animals are offered clean high quality water to drink, it is impossible to produce milk efficiently.

2. Exercise and Appetite

Daily exercise is extremely important for the health and appetite of goats. Does in heavy lactation need the least exercise because they are working hard and expending enormous amounts of energy. Others will greatly benefit by daily exercise. There is less fighting and much more evident content in goat herds if they can be allowed to walk or climb about a hillside every day. Most small herds of dairy goats will look forward to and accompany their caretaker on a daily walk as eagerly as companion dogs do, and both caretaker and the goats are better as a result of it.

The best way to feed grain to milking does is to feed it according to their current milk production on an individual basis. Where animals are kept in loose housing, basic grain amounts may be fed in a common trough as long as all of the animals in the herd have access to it at the same time. Additional amounts of grain for animals in higher milk production can be fed at the time of milking. Feeding more than a pound of grain to a doe during milking may produce delay in the milking procedure, but it will pay off in increased milk production and better health for those animals which need it.

Forage Quality — There is no substitute for the highest possible forage quality when feeding a herd of does capable of high milk production. There is simply no way to get the necessary feed intake when feeding low quality (high fiber, relatively low TDN [Total Digestible Nutrients], poor digestibility, low protein and low energy) forage. When highly digestible, high quality forage is fed, milking animals will have greater appetite for both forage and grain, and this will be readily apparent in increased milk production. Ideally, where excellent forage is fed, the ratio of pounds of grain fed to pounds of milk produced can be as low as one pound of grain to three pounds of milk in early lactation to one pound of grain to five pounds of milk in late lactation.

Weighing Milk — There is no good substitute for regular weighing of each animal's daily milk production. In commercial dairy herds, this may be done on a once-a-week basis and grain feeding can be adjusted for the next period accordingly. For the purebred dairy goat herd aiming for maximum milk production records, milk weights should be noted and recorded at every milking.

3. Feed According to Needs

The rule for successful feeding of dairy animals for producing milk to their fullest potential, maintaining good health and regular annual production of young is to feed them according to their needs.

Those who manage cow dairy herds which are producing an average of over 16,000 lbs. of milk per cow in 305-day lactations, with calving intervals of less than thirteen months and herd turnover not over 30% per year have a good understanding of how feeding cows according to their needs is done. The dairy goat herd producing an average of more than 2200 lbs. of milk per doe in 305-day lactations with a kidding interval per doe of about one year and herd turnover rate not exceeding 25%, reveals that the owner understands the fundamentals of feeding dairy animals. Too often dairy goat owners buy well-bred purebred animals which never produce up to their genetic potential because they are not fed correctly. There can be no real basis for herd improvement from production testing and culling unless the milking animals are fed to produce up to their maximum genetic potential.

The foundation for good dairy goat feeding is an understanding of rumen function. The ruminant animal depends upon microorganism activity for the nutritional elements necessary for all life functions, including milk production. The rumen is a large sacculated muscular organ which holds large quantities (four to five gallons in the goat) of plant material and fluid to support the tremendous numbers (millions or organisms per drop) of microorganisms present.

The forage, grain, minerals and vitamins eaten by the goat are, in fact, consumed in the rumen by the microorganisms. Proteins eaten become amino acids in the cells of the microorganisms; cellulose, starch, and sugars become fatty acids, etc. Cud chewing is part of the process to break down fibrous material for maximum use by the rumen flora. After rumen digestion has taken place, the ingesta (suspension of microorganisms, digested and undigested material) moves through the remainder of the digestive tract in much the same way as it does in the simple stomached (monogastric) animal.

The digestive system of goats and all other ruminants is designed physiologically to handle forages with a minimum of grain, fruits, etc. Too many dairy goat owners feed their animals diets which would be more appropriate for pigs — too much grain and not enough forage.

The doe capable of producing 3,000 pounds of milk is genetically a quite different animal from a wild one which will produce barely enough milk to feed a pair of kids for two months; however, physiologically, she is the same. The record milk producer has a digestive system identical with that of her wild sister. Meeting the genetic needs of the heavy producer without ruining her digestive system is the big challenge in feeding.

The doe with the genetic potential to produce large quantities of milk must have a large, active, powerfully functional rumen on the day she freshens when demand of the milk-producing tissues for nutrients begins. In order to develop the kind of rumen necessary, the late lactation and dry animal should be fed a high proportion of long-fiber coarse (less digestible) material. The "scratch factor," bulk, and lower digestibility foster development of a larger, powerful rumen.

On the day the doe begins to produce milk, the coarse, less digestible ration must rapidly be replaced with a highly digestible, higher energy, finer particle ration. By the time full production is reached, there is almost no way that the amount of nutrients necessary to meet udder demands can be eaten by the animal. A cursory glance at nutrient needs would show that a 125 lb. doe milking 15 lbs. of 3.6% milk per day should be consuming 1.85 lbs. of total digestible nutrients for body maintenance and 4.73 lbs. TDN for milk production. At this point, body reserves stored as muscle and liver glycogen and fat come to the rescue. If a high-producing doe is to be fed as close as possible to her needs, it is obvious that she must have the best possible legume hay or green forage and the quantity of it may have to be limited to only about 2 or 3 lbs. per day to get the animal to consume maximum amounts of grain. Feeding a high-producing animal up to and through the maximum peak of milk production is as much "art" as it is "science." Where good milk production records are to be made, gradually increasing grain intake by feeding more grain at more frequent feedings without causing digestive upset is the "art" part of it; the quality and balance of ingredients in the feed is the "science" part of it. When peak production is reached in the top notch doe, she may be eating as much as ¾ lbs. of grain for each pound of milk produced. Another very important part of the "art" of grain feeding is getting the highest amount of grain intake without butterfat depression in the milk produced.

After peak production has been reached and milk production levels drop to the point where the level of feeding begins to exceed the need, the good dairyman begins to cut down on the amount of grain fed and increases the amount of forage fed to the animal. Later, poorer quality forage and less grain (by the fifth month of lactation as little as 1 lb. of grain for 4 to 5 lbs. of milk) may be fed. The degree of condition (not necessarily fat cover, but muscle evident) should dictate amount of grain to feed with maximum amounts of reasonably good forage. Many does may not require more than ½ lb. of grain at a feeding by the time they are ready to be dried off.

As soon as the doe is dried off, feeding woody browse of some kind is a great boon to restoring function and capacity to a digestive system which was altered tremendously by the feeding program during the period of highest production. The fine-particle, high-energy, highly digestible ration fed at that time causes profound changes in the rumen and abomasum. The rumen loses tone and muscular action. Its capacity may decrease 25%. Rumen contractions and cud chewing markedly decrease. The mucosa (lining) of the rumen is also affected by the unnatural diet. There are profound changes in the structure of the papillae and the surface of the rumen mucosa. At the same time, the abomasum or true stomach increases greatly in size, attaining a degree of importance and function close to that of the monogastric (single stomached) animal. Continuing the special diet for the most milk beyond the animal's needs produces excessive fat which is a real hazard to both restoring digestive capacity and bringing about ketosis in late pregnancy or at the beginning of the next lactation.

So the "back to normal" diet which more closely resembles the diet of the wild goat or the "brush goat" is a vital necessity for the doe capable of high production, if she is to perform as expected for the next lactation.

Some dairy goat owners feel strongly that the feeding system outlined above "burns out" the doe, causes mastitis, results in infertility, etc. Actually, all of those are related to stress beyond that demanded by udder activity. When animals are fed correctly and milking up to their genetic potential, all other areas of management must be at their best (disease prevention, housing, milking, parasite control, etc.). The fine points of management make feeding good dairy animals according to their needs possible. The high-producing dairy animal is doing almost unbelievably hard work. She cannot be given the same indifferent kind of management given to an animal clearing undergrowth from a hillside.

4. Feeding Forage

It is possible to develop a herd of dairy goats with gunbarrel middles, but it is not possible to produce milk economically with animals of this type. (See Figure III-6). Development of rumen capacity, capacity to eat, and the appetite to go with it should begin when kids are very young. A common feeding practice which prevents kids from learning to eat grain and forage is too frequent feeding of milk and feeding too much milk. Twice-daily feeding is adequate for kids after they are three days old and a practical maximum of two pounds of milk daily should be set for animals to be reared as herd replacements. As kids approach weaning age, gradually adding warm water to the milk they are fed will provide them with necessary fluids for rumen development and ease the stress of weaning them. Grain and hay fed to young kids should be selected for them mainly on the basis of palatability. Hay which may appear to the feeder to be the best quality may not be as palatable or acceptable as other hay. For example, the author has seen baby kids eat red clover hay or brome grass hay with relish at the same time they refused to eat top quality alfalfa. The same thing is true of grain mixtures for baby kids. They should be fed the kind of available grain mixture which they will eat best. Goats of any age will eat more feed and waste less feed if they are fed small quantities at frequent intervals.

a. Forage Quality

The best way to determine the quality or feeding value of any type of forage is to have it tested by a forage-testing laboratory. Agricultural extension agents throughout the country have educational materials which outline the various parameters involved when forages are tested and what they mean in terms of feeding

Figure III—6

value to animals. Those who produce their own forage should learn how to take samples of forage for testing. County agricultural extension agents can show you how to do it.

Hay and silage samples should be analyzed before they are fed and a grain ration should be formulated based on the quality of the forage. It will pay the owner of a herd of 50 or more goats, who produces his own forage, to avail himself of forage testing—feed formulation service available today from various sources. If the goat herd owners will accept and follow basic principles of feeding which have been used for the past twenty years by those who manage high-production dairy cattle herds, who knows what can be accomplished with a good herd of dairy goats.

b. Factors Which Influence Palatability of Forage

Storage and Age of Forage — Goats steadfastly refuse to eat musty or dusty hay. Such hay usually contains a tremendous amount of mold. Most molds in hay, if not downright toxic, are an irritant to the digestive tract or the respiratory tract when ingested.

Age of Cutting — All hays are most nutritious and most digestible when harvested in the vegetative early stage of growth rather than at the reproductive mature stage of growth. Both legume and grass hays rapidly deteriorate nutritionally when flower heads appear. Under most circumstances, it is not possible to harvest all the hay on a farm in its optimum state of maturity, but those who buy hay for milking animals should buy it on the basis of early harvest if forage analysis is not available.

Other Factors — There are undoubtedly many other factors which affect the acceptability of forages which are difficult to assess quantitatively. Succulence is one of these. There are many weeds and other wild plants which are eaten with relish by goats. Some adversely affect milk flavor. Many of these can be fed with little or no effect on milk flavor if goats are allowed to eat them immediately after milking and none of the material is fed for at least three or four hours before the next milking. Forage intake can often be greatly improved in goats being fed the best of hays if some supplementary green forage is fed at least once daily. Hand harvested green legumes, surplus vegetables from the garden, surplus fruits like apples or pears, comfrey, turnips, pumpkins, etc., are welcome additions to the daily diet as they apparently improve digestion and appetite for the staple diet. Effects of agronomic practices in production of forage often play a role in palatability.

When adequate nitrogen is applied to growing grass so that it is succulent and tender, goats will eat it in preference to other grass which appears to be similar. Phosphorus application apparently has a great effect on the palatability of grass hays. Where grass is given adequate phosphorus application, hay harvested is much more palatable than other grass hay grown without adequate available phosphate. Similarly, adequate magnesium content in grass appears to increase its acceptability.

It is a sad fact that too many winning animals shown at dairy goat shows have been winners in spite of lack of body capacity. If it is an accepted fact that goats are no different from all other ruminants in that they must have relatively large rumen capacity to be profitable producers, the show ring should not ignore that requirement. It is true that much of the abdominal capacity of ruminant animals is the result of the way young animals are fed during development. However, those that fail to develop adequate capacity should be culled out, both in the herd breeding program and in the show ring. The mature dairy goat in the show ring should show the large muzzle and large body capacity necessary to eat the maximum amounts of feed. Too often animals with antelope-like muzzles and middles are made winners because they are pretty, rather than utilitarian.

c. Hay Equivalent Intake

A most important consideration for anyone feeding milking ruminant animals, regardless of species, is hay equivalent intake. This should be about 2.5 pounds of hay per 100 pounds body weight. Green foods and silages contain as much as two to three times the water content of hay and should be considered on that basis. A good dairy goat reared on adequate forage should have the body capacity and rumen function to eat at least 2.5 pounds of hay daily per 100 pounds of body weight and still consume adequate grain for maximum milk production. When hay equivalent intake goes below 2.5 pounds per 100 pounds, butterfat depression may occur in milking animals. Grain feeding, therefore, should be adjusted to levels which the animal will consume above her hay equivalent intake. This offers a fairly good means of comparison between efficient milk-producing animals and those which deserve culling from the herd.

5. Feed Additives

Antibiotics and other drugs can be demonstrated to increase growth rate and feed efficiency when added to feeds consumed by diseased animals. Improved performance cannot be demonstrated in disease-free animals. The inclusion of 100 gms per ton of chlortetracycline (Aureomycin) or oxytetracycline (Terramycin) to grain fed to young animals up to first kidding may be helpful for prevention of abscesses in herds infected with **Corynebacter pyogenes** or **Corynebacter ovis**.

In the author's experience, their value can only be guessed at in herds where segregation of baby kids and improved sanitary practices (as described in **Abscesses**) are instituted.

Many other feed additives are available for which extravagent or unfounded claims are made. The dairy goat herd owner would do well to use only those commonly available in commercial feeds formulated for dairy cows.

6. Nutrition Resources for Dairy Goat Owners

Very little specific research work has been done regarding nutrition of dairy goats. Some nutrition work has been done on non-lactating goats, but it shows only that the findings are not applicable to milking animals. There are many misconceptions, speculations and false conclusions in dairy goat literature about nutrition. Let it suffice to say that dairy goats are ruminants as are cows and sheep. Nutrition research which applies to lambs and non-lactating sheep, to calves and non-lactating cattle can be applied with confidence to kids and non-lactating goats. Nutrition research which applies to milking dairy cattle is applicable for milking goats. There is no research or clinical evidence to show that goats are more efficient converters of energy than are any other ruminants. There is no research or clinical evidence to show that dairy goats require any vitamins, minerals, "organic" health food additives, or medicines that are not required for milking dairy cows. Many American dairy goat owners waste money for feed additives touted by advertisers as necessary for goats. These may do more harm than good for the animals.

Unless one is managing a dairy goat herd of at least several hundred animals, feed formulations designed for feeding high-producing dairy cow herds should be chosen. Special requirements in concentrate rations for dairy goats are entirely related to palatability. These are freedom from dust, light bulky flaky grains with a minimum of fines, preferably no urea and minimal amounts of animal fat. All of these requirements are met in the better quality feeds widely available from feed suppliers for dairy cow herds. Dairy goat herd owners can buy smaller quantities of fresher feeds with less danger of mold problems when they buy better quality dairy cow feeds. Horse feeds have many undesirable qualities when used as feeds for milking does. Many have excessive quantities of molasses (which has an adverse effect on rumen flora); many have excessive fiber from large amounts of oats (over 25%) which seriously affects rumen digestion; few have adequate protein levels for milking does; and all of them contain excessive calcium supplementation for milking does being fed alfalfa hay. Where the owner of a single large herd of goats or owners of several herds can get together to buy and use large quantities of concentrate feeds, it might be economical and otherwise desirable to have grain rations specifically designed for milking goat herds. These would contain all flaked or rolled grains, pellets containing linseed meal, soybean meal and brewers' grains, no supplemental calcium for alfalfa fed herds and 0.5% trace mineralized salt and 0.75% monosodium phosphate per ton. One of the major problems experienced by owners of small dairy goat herds is finding concentrate feeds that are palatable and free from molds. In the author's opinion, premium quality (cow) dairy feeds available from most suppliers offer the best solution to the problem.

How to Determine Protein, Energy and Mineral Requirements for Concentrate Mixes to be Fed to Dairy Goats — Many state universities, feed companies, and private animal nutrition laboratories offer forage analysis services for all segments of animal industry. The only way it is possible to determine what is best to feed goats (or any other forage-eating species) eating a particular forage or combination of forages is to have the forage analyzed for its feeding value. Most of the forage analysis services develop specific feeding programs to be used with the forage or forages being fed. Standard tests reported include Dry matter, Protein, Fiber, Digestible Protein, Available Protein, Total Digestible Nutrients (TDN) and/or Estimated Net Energy (ENE). The average owner of a small herd of dairy goats who shops around a little can usually find a supply of forage-tested hay which he can buy from a progressive cow dairyman and know what he is feeding.

Usually the same feed being fed to a good high-producing dairy cow herd eating that forage alone will be the best possible feed for a high-producing dairy goat herd, if it has the physical characteristics that make it palatable for goats.

Mineral Tests — The same services which are testing forages for standard feeding values are testing those forages for mineral content.

Most offer ten to fourteen mineral analyses.

Managers of top production dairy cow herds routinely have forages fed to the cows analyzed for both standard values and minerals and have their grain rations balanced accordingly. The easiest course for the dairy goat herd owner to follow would be to use the recommended dairy cow rations for the top dairy herds being fed the same forage in his area.

Water — Water is the most important of all feeds for animals. It is impossible to have production efficiency and healthy animals where water quality is poor. Production in low-producing, poor reproducing, health-problem dairy herds is often improved tremendously by providing a new or better source of water. Water is the cheapest of all feeds. In cold weather, heating water to at least 55°F. will often double the water intake and correspondingly increase milk production in dairy goat herds. Clean warm water provided for loose housed herds using electrically heated waterers available for dairy cattle is ideal for the dairy goat herd.

Electrically heated water fountains containing floats rather than pressure operated valves are available. They should be placed about twenty-eight inches off the floor for milking does and they should be set in a wooden frame or keyhole-type barrier to keep goats from getting their feet into or onto them. Goats are more fussy about fouled water than any other animal. Slightly fouled water can reduce water intake tremendously and correspondingly cut milk production. When this happens to a dairy goat herd in peak lactation, milk production levels may be irreversibly affected by as little as one day depression of water intake.

7. The Eye of The Master

Regardless of the feeding program used or the scientific assistance available to the feeder, the good dairyman knows his animals individually. He knows how much grain they will eat readily from the beginning of the lactation and carefully increases daily amounts fed until the animals are eating the maximum desired amount and producing accordingly. Animals which are carefully fed for highest production, with the highest quality feeds, are not only healthier but they have better reproduction and longer lifetime performance. Dairy goat owners could receive very valuable education by visiting and observing the feeding of the highest producing dairy cow herds in their areas. These herds are usually on official testing and their production levels are published. County agricultural extension advisers or agents can be very helpful for feeding, education and counsel and for assisting dairy goat herdsmen in meeting and visiting successful (cow) dairymen.

One of the best educational programs for a dairy goat club can be a visit to a top-notch (cow) dairy herd at feeding and milking time. Most top dairymen will enjoy the experience as much as the dairy goat owners will. Dairy goat owners should avail themselves of the excellent nutrition information through literature and meetings of the agricultural extension service and the dairy feed industry. Elsewhere in this book, the author has bewailed the fact that dairy goat nutrition is about thirty years behind dairy cow nutrition. The resources necessary to catch up are freely available.

CHAPTER IV

QUALITY MILK PRODUCTION

A.   Introduction..64
B.   Factors Which Influence Keeping Quality of Milk 64
      1.   Sanitation 64
            a.   Milking Area...............................64
            b.   Milking Animals............................64
            c.   Hand Milking 64
            d.   Milking Equipment 65
      2.   Off-Flavors in Milk.............................65
      3.   Milk Holding Temperatures 67
      4.   Somatic Cells in Milk...........................67
C.   Resources Available 67

A. Introduction

Milk is defined by the dairy industry as the normal lacteal secretion of a healthy udder. Healthy udders are never found on unhealthy animals. Mastitis in half a goat's udder may be sufficient reason to reject all of the secretion from the entire udder. When antibiotics are infused into an infected udder half or administered by any other route to a milking doe, careful adherence to label directions for withholding milk should be followed. When veterinarians, for any reason, exercise their prerogative to administer medication to milking animals in any other way than prescribed on the label, the goat owner should insist on written instruction for milk withdrawal. Regulatory agencies are under fire to eliminate antibiotics from milk for very good reasons and they are empowered to invoke severe penalties on offenders.

B. Factors Which Influence Keeping Quality of Goat Milk

Two important factors are involved in producing milk with good keeping qualities: cleanliness and low temperature.

High-quality raw goat milk should keep without noticeable deterioration in quality for at least a week. High-quality pasteurized goat milk should keep without appreciable loss of quality for two weeks.

1. Sanitation

a. Milking Area — Goats should be milked in a fly-free, dust-free environment which can be washed down after each milking. Non-porous concrete surfaces are best for milking parlors. Milking parlors should have adequate light and ventilation. There should be no odors present in the milking parlor at any time.

b. Milking Animals — Milking does should have the hair from their flanks, udders, and hind legs clipped using a No. 2 Oster clipping blade or its equivalent. Udders and teats should be washed with a **clean** detergent-sanitizer solution and dried with an individual clean cloth or paper towel before milking.

c. Hand Milking — Where hand milking is used, the hands should be kept scrupulously clean, washed with soap and dried with a towel before milking. Where the person milking the does engages in garden or other dirty work, nails should be kept trimmed and scrubbed well, with a brush, before milking.

d. Milking Equipment — Because milk protein is hardened onto equipment at temperatures above 125°F. and milk fat is hardened at cold water temperatures, all milking equipment should first be thoroughly rinsed with tepid (110-120°F.) water. Detergents used for cleaning should be determined on the basis of the minerals present in the water. Assistance should be sought from the local health department or local dairy equipment dealer regarding this point. All surfaces which will receive milk contact must be thoroughly cleaned and dried by drainage after each milking and all surfaces which receive milk contact should be rinsed with an approved sanitizer before milking. Only stainless steel, approved plastic, or glass surfaces are satisfactory for milk contact. These surfaces can be hand scrubbed with a nylon brush; abrasive scouring powders or metallic scouring pads should never be used. A frequent fault in family milk production is the ritual scalding of milking equipment and containers which have not been thoroughly cleaned first. Any metallic glint on milking equipment or containers is indication of hardened precipitated milk protein as a result of use of too hot water. Milkstone frequently fouls equipment where very hot water containing dissolved calcium or iron salts is used. There is absolutely no substitute for proper cleaning. Development of off-flavor in milk after even short time storage can usually be traced to poor cleaning.

2. Off-Flavors in Milk

The presence of buck odor anywhere near the milking herd will produce off-flavor in milk. Unfortunately, those who care for goat bucks are usually oblivious to the odor; it's like long term acquaintance with a skunk. There is no way to produce good-flavored goat milk (milk with little or no flavor) if there is a buck goat over three months of age anywhere near the milking does. Bucks should never be kept in the same building where the does are kept.

Some female goats have small areas of goat odor cells in the skin of their heads in the same area where these are found in bucks. These are believed to be the source of goaty flavor in milk of individual does. It is the author's opinion that goaty flavored milk of individual does is an inherited thing and it should be identified and eliminated by selective breeding in herds where it occurs.

Feed Flavors — Many weeds and woody plants produce undesirable off-flavor or bitter flavors in goats' milk. Ragweed, wild onion, goldenrod, honeysuckle, elderberry, grape leaves, and blackberry leaves are readily eaten by goats, but they do impart an undesirable flavor to milk. There are many other plants which do this. For this reason, unless one can be certain that a milking herd on pasture will have no access to such plants, the milking herd should be kept in a bare dry lot and fed either green feed, hay, or silage of known content. No feed of any kind should be fed to does within two hours before milking. This is especially true of green chopped forages and silage. Some ingredients in concentrate feeds will influence milk flavor if they are fed within two hours of milking. Usually, the same feeds can be fed while the doe is being milked without affecting milk flavor.

Oxidized Flavor — A cardboard-like objectionable flavor in milk is usually the result of one or both of two things: exposure of the milk to copper, or exposure of the milk to fluorescent light or sunlight. Milk is so sensitive to copper exposure that extreme care should be taken to prevent contact of copper or any copper-bearing metal (white metal, worn plated spoons). Exposure of milk to sunlight or fluorescent light for only a few minutes adversely affects the flavor.

Rancidity — This is an extremely important consideration in the production of high-quality goat milk. The lipid membrane of goats' milk fat globules is extremely fragile. When the lipid membrane is fractured by any means (violent agitation from machine or hand milking, risers in milk lines which agitate milk under vacuum, etc.), the milk fatty acids become exposed to lipase found in raw milk. The fatty acids in the milk fat are broken down into shorter chain fatty acids which have undesirable flavors and odors. In goat milk, these are capriolic and caprylic acids, and they give the milk a goaty or buck-like aroma and flavor.

The best way to prevent rancidity or fat breakdown flavor in goat milk is to milk it with the least possible agitation and pasteurize it (or at least heat it rapidly to 135°F.), before cooling. Heat above about 130°F. destroys the lipase enzyme and prevents rancidity. Large goat dairies using pipeline milking parlors should run the milk through rapid pasteurization first and then cool it. Without this precaution, rancidity problems are a continuous hazard, to at least some degree, to consumer acceptance of the product whether it be fluid milk or some manufactured milk product.

About the only products made from rancid milk which are actually better because the milk was rancid are chocolate products. It may be one of the reasons for the popularity of goat milk fudge.

For the goat owner who does not understand what rancidity is like, a simple experiment might be helpful: put one cup of fresh raw goat milk in a blender and agitate it violently for a few minutes. Allow it to stand for a few minutes at room temperature and then smell and taste the difference between it and the milk from which the blenderized sample was taken. Adding a small amount of homogenized milk to raw milk will produce a flavor characteristic of lipolytic rancidity.

3. Milk Holding Temperature

Milk is an extremely fragile product. Bacterial growth begins immediately at milking and its extent depends upon two things: the number of bacteria which contaminate the milk from the moment it leaves the teat, and the temperature at which the milk is held. Milk should be cooled as rapidly as possible to 36°F. Many milk markets require farm cooling of milk in bulk tanks to be accomplished at the rate of one degree per minute to 36°F.

When only a few goats are milked, putting the milk in one or two quart containers immersed in cold or ice water to the level of the milk is a desirable, efficient way to cool it. For larger quantities, use of a soft drink cooler where the bottles are immersed in circulated refrigerated water will do an excellent job. At the present time, when many small cow dairies are going out of existence in the United States, small bulk milk coolers or small can coolers can be bought cheaply. When these are operating properly, they do an excellent job of cooling milk and holding it at the desirable temperature — not exceeding 40°F.

4. Somatic Cells in Milk

Milk from normal healthy udders contains as many as 250,000 somatic cells (white blood cells, tissue cells) per milliliter (about fifteen drops). Milk from mammary glands irritated by infection or injury may contain up to ten million or more somatic cells per milliliter. It is usually grossly abnormal (watery, clotty, etc.) in appearance and it has a salty flavor.

It is often difficult to taste the difference between normal milk (250,000 cells/ml.) and abnormal milk (one million cells/ml.). There is a tremendous difference, however, in the productivity and longevity between healthy udders and udders from which high cell count milk is produced. That, alone, is a good reason for goat owners to be concerned about somatic cell count. (See Mastitis)

C.   Resources Available

Many books have been written on this subject and many full-time, well trained dairy fieldmen are thoroughly familiar with this subject. These men are employed by local, state, and national government in departments of health and agriculture. They are dedicated people who too often are regarded as policemen rather than resource people. They prefer the latter role, and most of them welcome requests for assistance on problems regarding milk quality. Most dairy manufacturing or distribution businesses have full-time quality control fieldmen who may be readily available to dairy goat owners who have quality problems.

Good-quality goat milk is a delicious product equal to, or better in flavor than the best cows' milk. Products manufactured from good goat milk have excellent flavor. There is simply no way to make milk any better than it is when it leaves the animal's udder. Unfortunately, the quality of goat milk offered for sale is often so bad that rather reckless medicinal claims have to be made to induce people to use it.

If goat milk indeed has the great value it is reputed to have for stomach disorders (and this author would not challenge that), then those who have to use it should be happy to continue to use it after their malady has improved. Too often goat milk is sold and used as medicine and customers cease using it when their problems improve because the milk they buy is so unpalatable.

CHAPTER V

NUTRITIONAL DEFICIENCY DISEASES

A.   Specific Deficiencies. 70
     1.   Calcium 70
     2.   Cobalt. 70
     3.   Copper-Molybdenum. 71
     4.   Energy 71
     5.   Iodine 72
     6.   Iron 72
     7.   Magnesium (Hypomagnesemia in Grass Tetany) 73
     8.   Phosphorus 74
     9.   Protein 75
     10.   Salt — Sodium Chloride. 75
     11.   Selenium (White Muscle Disease). 75
     12.   Sulfur 77
     13.   Vitamin Deficiencies 77
         a.   Avitaminosis A 77
         b.   Avitaminosis B 78
         c.   Avitaminosis C 78
         d.   Avitaminosis D (Rickets) 78
         e.   Avitaminosis E (White Muscle Disease) 79
     14.   Zinc 79

Nutritional Deficiencies in Dairy Goats

Although simple uncomplicated nutritional deficiencies are extremely rare in the field, they can easily be demonstrated in the research laboratory. Goats, like other ruminants, do not require additional B vitamins or Vitamin C because these are synthesized by rumen bacteria. No attempt will be made to detail all of the deficiency symptoms which have been demonstrated by nutrition research, but attempts will be made in this chapter to describe deficiencies evident under field conditions.

A.   Specific Deficiencies

1. Calcium

This element is found in teeth and bones (99%) and in soft tissues and body fluids (1%). All concentrate feeds and non-legume forages require calcium supplementation. Calcium deficiency in American dairy goat herds is rare because they are fed almost entirely on alfalfa hay. Excessive calcium in the diet of dairy goats during the dry period predisposes does to milk fever, and excessive calcium in the diet of kids and bucks of any age may initiate progressive osteopetrosis (see **Arthritis**).

Calcium deficiency would most likely occur in lactating dairy goats receiving grass forage or corn silage without calcium supplementation in the concentrate fed. Normally 1.0 to 1.5% dicalcium phosphate added to the concentrate fed with such forages will furnish adequate calcium intake. Other acceptable sources of calcium for dairy goats are ground limestone and good quality steamed bone meal.

Blood calcium levels in dairy goats should be from 9.0 to 10.5 mg/%.

2. Cobalt

This trace element is a dietary essential for goats and other ruminants. It is required for rumen synthesis of Vitamin B_{12}. Deficiency is manifested by anemia, loss of appetite, low milk production, poor hair coat and poor unthrifty condition. Extremely low levels of cobalt (below 0.07 parts per million) in forages, prevent deficiency symptoms. Use of trace mineralized salt containing 15 to 30 gm. of cobalt chloride per 100 lbs. of salt effectively prevents cobalt deficiency. In areas where cobalt deficiency is known to exist, it is important that only trace mineralized salt containing cobalt be used for salt in the concentrates fed and as free choice loose salt.

3. Copper and Molybdenum

Both of these elements are vitally necessary for normal body function, however, they act antagonistically to each other. Excess of one results in deficiency symptoms of the other, and deficiency of one may result in toxic symptoms produced by excessive intake of the other. In areas of the United States where molybdenum toxicity is prevalent in cattle, goats may be expected to suffer from it but not show the dramatic symptoms seen in cattle. Cattle show diarrhea, bleaching of the hair coat, anemia and emaciation from excess molybdenum.

Addition of 0.25 lbs. of copper sulfate per 100 lbs. of salt usually eliminates molybdenum poisoning symptoms. Inclusion of 0.5% copper sulfate in trace mineralized salt satisfies copper requirements where copper deficiency is suspected. Up to ten times this intake is necessary for development of toxicity symptoms.

Copper Toxicity — Copper toxicity is usually an insidious thing which may occur suddenly after long exposure to excessive copper intake or molybdenum deficiency, or it may occur acutely from sudden access to excessive copper. Copper poisoning is not as important or prevalent in goats as it is in sheep. As in other ruminants, whether or not animals show copper poisoning is determined by a number of factors: molybdenum, sulfate, zinc, iron, and protein in the diet. Copper poisoning is manifested by severe liver damage and severe anemia. The author has seen copper poisoning in both sheep and goats when the animals had access to swine feeds containing 200 ppm copper.

4. Energy

The modern dairy goat has enormous requirements for energy during the first four to six months of lactation. Her nutrition must be similar to that of a high producing dairy cow at this time. Highly digestible, high-energy, low-fiber feeds are necessary to meet the requirement for lactation. Unless the doe is managed through late lactation and the dry period so that she freshens in lean active condition with a large actively functional rumen, she simply will not have the appetite or capacity to eat enough to satisfy requirements for maximum milk production. Does which freshen in fat condition may suffer from mild-to-clinical ketosis until they have lost the fat and become thin. During this time normal milk production has suffered. The fat animal actually suffers from energy deficiency, not because it was unavailable, but because she has neither the appetite nor capacity to ingest adequate feed to meet the needs of the lactating udder. Under the conditions most dairy goats in the United States are kept, they suffer energy deficiencies even though they may be offered all of the grain they will eat. One of the principal factors limiting full utilization of energy from grain mixtures is the mistaken belief that dairy goat rations require high levels of oats. Any ration containing more than 25% oats seriously curtails digestibility. Forage should be tested to determine the total digestible nutrient value (TDN) or calorie content. Generally speaking, grass or legumes harvested at the first appearance of bloom have the lowest fiber content and the highest energy content. Lack of adequate energy and protein at the time of breeding impairs fertility, and development of fewer ova reduces the number of kids which may be conceived.

5. Iodine

Deficiency of iodine in the body is manifested entirely in disfunction of the thyroid hormone system. The primary iodine deficiency symptom found in dairy goats is goiter in baby kids at birth. Massive swelling of the thyroid gland may increase the diameter of the upper neck to one often larger than that of the head. The enlarged thyroid glands can easily be palpated.

Baby kids born with goiter usually die from dystocia (birth difficulty) or are very weak. The hair coat is very short or fuzzy. Goitrous kids given supplemental iodine (five drops Lugols solution in one ounce of water daily for four or five days) may recover normally. Certain plants are goitrogenic (cabbage, soybeans, and yellow turnips). They inhibit thyroxine production. The goitrogenic substance in soybeans is only partially destroyed in processing soybean meal. The best way to insure adequate iodine intake for dairy goats is feeding iodized salt containing 0.007% iodine. For some reason, many dairy goat owners feel that trace mineralized or iodized salt (both contain adequate iodine) are not adequate in iodine, so they feed kelp products made and advertised as iodine and other trace element sources. Kelp is not harmful, but it is very difficult to demonstrate that feeding it has any healthful or economic effects on dairy goat productivity. Few of the so-called "organic sources" of trace elements have ever been accepted by the bovine dairy industry. Their purveyors have much less trouble selling them to dairy goat owners.

6. Iron

Iron is necessary for production of hemoglobin, the oxygen-carrying element of red blood cells. Anemia is common in animals fed solely on milk. It is very difficult to produce anemia in baby kids on an all milk diet unless they are unable to eat forage, grain or soil. When grain and forage are offered to baby kids from birth, the possibility of iron deficiency does not exist even though the kids may eat very small quantities.

7. Magnesium (Hypomagnesemia in Grass Tetany)

In areas where grass tetany occurs in beef cattle and dairy cattle, it can also be expected to occur in milking does. Because the average milking doe is fed some mineral supplemented grain and at least a small amount of legume hay during the time of highest milk production, hypomagnesemia is much less common in goats and dairy cows than it is in beef cattle in the same area.

Hypomagnesemia can be expected to occur in milking animals when blood serum magnesium levels fall below 1.8 mg./%. Animals with blood serum mg. levels over 2.0 mg./% are considered safe from the possibility of hypomagnesemia.

Factors Which Affect Magnesium Intake — During cool spring weather, greater availability and uptake of potassium apparently restricts uptake of magnesium by plants. Small grains and grasses are affected to the greatest extent. Potassium fertilization of pastures where soil magnesium is even slightly deficient is the most important cause of hypomagnesemia. Use of dolomitic limestone is helpful for prevention, but it may take several years after initial application for effect. Excessive nitrogen also interferes with magnesium uptake by plants. Applications of nitrogen for early spring pasture are best given in several small applications rather than one large early application.

Symptoms — Sudden acute hypomagnesemia usually causes excitement and convulsions and quick death within one-half hour. Chronic hypomagnesemia causes nervousness and trembling especially at milking time. When milking does are fed solely on lush grass or small grain pasture early in spring or late in fall, outbreaks of grass tetany can be sudden and rapidly fatal for the animals producing the most milk in the herd.

Prevention and Treatment — Where grass tetany is known to exist in a specific area, potash fertilizer should be withheld from early pasture until it has been grazed for one month or until the first growth of grass has been removed. Dolomitic limestone should be used instead of magnesium free limestone to maintain adequate soil pH.

Feeding supplementary alfalfa hay and ordinary mineral supplemented dairy feed will effectively prevent grass tetany in dairy goat herds grazing lush small grain pasture. Addition of ten pounds per ton of magnesium oxide to the grain concentrate fed is also good insurance against grass tetany where there is reason to be concerned about it. Molasses blocks containing magnesium oxide have little value for dairy goat herds. Consumption is even more erratic than it is by cattle. Some of the animals, usually those milking the most, steadfastly refuse to consume any magnesium oxide mixture from the block. Grass tetany should not be of great concern where at least some good legume hay and mineral supplemented dairy feed is fed to milking does. Acute symptoms closely resembling grass tetany may occur under the same conditions from enterotoxemia when goats are first introduced to new lush early grass or small grain pasture and they consume a large amount of the forage.

8. Phosphorus

Seventy-five percent of body phosphorus is present in bones and teeth; the remainder is found in body proteins and hormone and enzyme systems. Deficiencies of phosphorus are rarely seen in animals receiving grain mixtures containing protein supplements. These feeds are rich in phosphorus. The only forages fed to dairy goats which would normally be low in phosphorus content and therefore require phosphorus supplementation are also low in calcium: grass pasture hays, silages and corn silage. Deficiency of phosphorus, according to textbooks, is usually indicated when animals chew wood. This may be true to at least some extent in other domestic animals, but goats love to chew on wood regardless of their phosphorus intake. Seeing dairy goats chew on wood should not be considered sufficient reason to add phosphorus or additional phosphorus to their rations. The ratio of calcium to phosphorus in the total diet is most important. Animals fed high quality legume forage usually receive excessive calcium over the 1.5:1 ratio most desirable; therefore, when forages composed entirely of legumes are fed, concentrate supplementation should exclude calcium and add only phosphorus.

Dairy cow feeds available throughout the country are manufactured with calcium supplementation when grass or corn silage is fed and with phosphorus supplements when legume forage is fed. Blood phosphorus levels in normal lactating dairy goats should be between 5.5 and 7.0 mg/%.

9. Protein

This frequently accompanies energy shortage. It is often the sole limiting factor to milk production when dairy goats are receiving poor forage. Lack of adequate protein lowers the digestibility of forages. When dairy goats show sluggish appetite, poor rumen mobility, and low milk production, the best course of action is to gradually raise protein content of the ration. If protein deficiency is responsible, results are quickly noticed and production improvement will continue up to the point where protein intake exceeds the needs of the animal. Vegetable proteins are preferred over protein substitutes (urea, biuret, etc.) for dairy goats for two important reasons: protein substitutes require energy for their metabolism while most protein supplements contribute to the energy content of the ration. When dairy goats in peak production are fed large amounts of grain containing non-protein nitrogen supplements, toxic amounts of ammonia may be released. To utilize non-protein nitrogen supplements in the ration of dairy goats safely, the animals must receive adequate energy amounts. Goats should not be fed more than one pound of grain per feeding, and at least four feedings should be given per day. Grain mixtures for goats should never contain more than 30 lbs./ton of the non-protein nitrogen supplement.

10. Salt — Sodium Chloride

Sodium chloride is essential for regulation of acid-base metabolism. Lack of salt is not likely to occur in dairy goats because most of the dairy feeds available contain one percent salt. To meet any additional needs, dairy goats should have access to loose trace mineralized salt. Salt blocks are not recommended. When animals are on pasture in summer, they cannot get enough salt from a salt block in hot dry weather to meet their needs.

11. Selenium (White Muscle Disease)

Lack of adequate selenium, a very poisonous but essential element, produces profound disturbances in muscle metabolism. Most of the eastern half of the United States and some areas in the far west are extremely low in selenium. Selenium deficiency is especially likely to appear when animals in deficient areas are fed concentrates and forage produced in that area. A dietary level of 0.1 ppm (parts per million) is adequate for ruminants.

There is an important relationship between selenium and Vitamin E that has not been clearly explained. Some pathological changes in muscles respond only to selenium, others respond only to Vitamin E and others respond only to both. Most of the work done on the inter-relationship of selenium and Vitamin E has been conducted using chickens and small laboratory animals. In goats, as with cattle and sheep, diagnosis is based on post-mortem findings. Treatment and prevention recognizes the need for Vitamin E and selenium supplementation.

Symptoms of Selenium Deficiency — Sudden death of young kids under two weeks of age may reveal post-mortem evidence of muscle degeneration (white muscle) in the heart muscle or the diaphragm. In healthy rapidly growing young kids up to two months of age, selenium-vitamin E deficiency may show up following sudden exercise, and the animals show bilateral stiffness, usually in their hind legs or their loins. (This in sheep is called stiff lamb disease.)

In mature milking does, selenium-vitamin E deficiency may primarily manifest itself in poor involution of the uterus with accompanying retained placenta and metritis or pyometra following kidding.

Where this difficulty is seen in milking herds, selenium-vitamin E prophylactic treatment often produces dramatic results. The United States Food and Drug Administration in 1974 permitted the addition of selenium to swine feeds, turkey feeds and broiler feeds. This has produced excellent results in handling selenium deficiency problems in these species. Deficiency problems remain in the nutrition of horses and all ruminant species.

Prevention — Intramuscular or oral administration of 5.0 mgm. of selenium given four weeks before kidding, or, preferably for eastern United States, injection of 5.0 mgm. of selenium with alphatocopherol (Vitamin E), will prevent selenium deficiency symptoms in freshening does and in baby kids for the first month of life. Baby kids two to four weeks of age should receive their first injection of 5.0 mgm. selenium with alphatocopherol. This can be repeated again at six months of age. Feeding linseed meal as a source of half of the protein in the concentrate mix, or feeding corn from the western corn belt area in the concentrate mix, is helpful for prevention of selenium deficiency. Both of these feed ingredients are produced on soils where selenium levels are adequate or even slightly excessive, and selenium levels in the feeds are valuable supplementation.

Where freshening does develop metritis or become "downers," these animals should be subjected to careful scrutiny by a qualified animal pathologist at post-mortem to determine whether or not selenium deficiency is involved. Detection is relatively easy in examining carcasses of dead kids. The muscles involved have a characteristic white chicken meat or blanched appearance. Identification of white muscle disease lesions in one or more animals justifies a routine program of selenium-alphatocopheral administration. Wheat germ is an excellent source of Vitamin E, as is wheat germ oil.

Treatment — Administration of a single 1000 unit capsule of Vitamin E (easily obtainable from many sources) will often produce dramatic recovery from "stiff muscle" in kids if given when the problem first appears. A small supply of Vitamin E capsules should be in the medicine chest of those who manage dairy goat herds in the selenium deficient areas.

12. Sulfur

Sulfur deficiency does not exist in diets adequate in natural proteins. Sulfur is necessary for synthesis of certain essential amino acids in the rumen. There is little, if any, likelihood that sulfur deficiency could occur in goats fed normal rations. It would only be expected where corn silage and grass hay were fed with non-protein nitrogen replacing natural protein in the ration. A nitrogen-to-sulfur ratio of 10:1 is recommended for cattle. This should be adequate for dairy goats.

13. Vitamin Deficiencies

a. Avitaminosis A — Vitamin A deficiency is not uncommon in dairy goats. Severe Vitamin A deficiency signs are rare, but signs of mild deficiency are rather common. Green forage, high quality hay with good green color and yellow corn are good sources of Vitamin A, but unless high-producing animals get the very best quality hay, they may show symptoms of mild Vitamin A deficiency.

The commonest symptom of early or mild Vitamin A deficiency is night blindness. When the herdsman approaches the animals in the dark, they show fear and panic. Turning on a bright light ends all of that immediately and the animals act normally. Moderate Vitamin A deficiency also produces other symptoms not so easily recognized or evaluated. Metritis following kidding may be an important result from damage to the integrity of the uterine mucosa from lack of Vitamin A. Excessive tear production and wet areas below the eyes is another symptom. Lack of Vitamin A has detrimental effects on germinal epithelium. It may produce temporary impaired fertility or permanent infertility in bucks.

Prevention and Treatment — Goats fed on fresh forage or good green hay for at least half the year should not suffer from Vitamin A deficiency. Most good quality dairy concentrate feeds available contain adequate additional amounts of both Vitamin A and Vitamin D for dairy goat needs. As an additional precaution at a very low cost, intramuscular administration of 250,000 units of Vitamin A with Vitamin D and E, in water emulsion base, currently available everywhere for use in dairy cows and calves, may be worthwhile for does in late pregnancy. This dosage will insure adequate Vitamin A reserve for kidding, and furnish good colostral levels of Vitamin A for baby kids. Carrot oil on the market for Vitamin A supplement is much more expensive than other Vitamin A sources and it may not be as readily available to the animal.

b. Avitaminosis B — Deficiencies of vitamins of the B vitamin complex do not occur in healthy ruminants. These vitamins are synthesized in adequate amounts by rumen bacteria. However, animals which have been off feed may suffer B vitamin deficiencies. Animals on very low protein diets or mineral-deficient diets may have rumen bacteria numbers so low that adequate B vitamins are not synthesized. The practice of administering B complex vitamins to goats which have been sick apparently speeds recovery and may even be justified. Ordinarily, money spent for B vitamin supplements for goats on pasture or ordinary nutritional status is wasted. (See **Polioencephalomalacia**)

c. Avitaminosis C — Vitamin C is synthesized in the rumen even in young kids. Deficiencies never occur and thus supplementation or administration of this vitamin is not necessary.

d. Avitaminosis D — **Rickets** — Vitamin D, calcium and phosphorus have a close relation in metabolism. While rickets rarely or never occurs in mature animals fed formulated feeds and legume forage, it can, and frequently does, occur in young kids fed the best of rations when they are kept inside. Typical bow legs so often described as the symptoms of rickets are rarely seen. The commonest sign of rickets in young kids is the one most often seen in rapidly growing young calves kept inside — a depression behind the withers and a "loosening" of the shoulder blades with a roachiness or convex surface of the loin area. It is usually seen in rapidly growing young kids. Exercise outside is usually sufficient to eliminate this appearance. Irradiated yeast in the feed which furnishes 200 IU of Vitamin D per day or a single intramuscular dose of 500 IU of Vitamin D will eliminate early rickets in kids. At six weeks to two months, intramuscular administration of 125,000 IU of Vitamin A with D and E (0.25 cc.) of one of the commonly available ADE injectibles will effectively prevent rickets.

 e. Avitaminosis E — (See **Selenium Deficiency, White Muscle Disease.**)

14. Zinc

Zinc deficiencies have been produced experimentally with highly specialized diet in sheep. In practice, zinc deficiency in cattle and sheep is uncommon. The most likely abnormality to look for in goats would be thickening of the skin of the flanks and escutcheon areas or particularly slow wound healing with accompanying unthriftiness. Where zinc deficiency is proven, zinc may be provided by adding it to trace mineralized salt fed with the grain mix and offered as free choice loose TM salt.

80

CHAPTER VI

METABOLIC DISEASES

A.   Indigestion...82
      1.   Acute — Bloat 82
      2.   Chronic — Rumen Impaction 83
      3.   Abomasal Ulceration 83
B.   Ketosis — Pregnancy Disease.......................83
C.   Laminitis (Founder)................................85
D.   Milk Fever (Hypocalcemia).........................86
E.   Osteopetrosis (Nutritional Arthritis).................88
F.   Polioencephalomalacia (Cerebrocortical Necrosis).....89

A.   Indigestion

1. Acute Indigestion — Bloat

Acute indigestion or bloat is not as commonly seen in dairy goats as it is in cattle and sheep. It occurs usually when some new source of green legume or new legume hay is fed. It also occurs from sudden access to grain where animals are usually fed small amounts or from access to aftermath cornfields.

The most commonly observed symptom of acute indigestion is bloat. The rumen fills with gas or frothy material and becomes atonic so that the animal is unable to belch. Usually it is not necessary to administer treatment as long as rumination can be observed and belching of excessive gas is accomplished. Any person who manages ruminant animals soon learns to habitually look at the left side of the animal's abdomens. If a regular rhythmical deep wave of movement moves upward above the left flank of the animals and they belch gas or chew their cuds, it can be assumed that rumen function is normal.

Treatment — Identification of the cause of the problem and its removal from the diet is the first essential. For simple bloat treatment, two to four ounces of poloxalene (Bloat Guard — Smith Kline) or twice that amount of heavy mineral oil is usually sufficient.

Testing rumen contents and finding a pH below 4.8 is a good way to establish a diagnosis of grain overload acidosis. This is a rather common result of ad-lib feeding or too rapid increase of grain fed daily to does in early lactation. It is one of the problems commonly seen when grain intake is not carefully controlled and when animals have not been prepared during the dry period for high levels of grain feeding in early lactation.

Enterotoxemia is an ever-present primary or secondary complicating factor in just about every form of acute indigestion. It is so important and so prevalent in dairy goats that a regular routine prophylactic program against it is a fundamental necessity for managing a good milking herd of goats. (See **Enterotoxemia.**)

Choke — Choke is another cause of bloat in goats much less commonly seen than it is in dairy cows. A wad of fibrous material or a piece of apple or carrot may become lodged in the esophagus. Passage of a small stomach tube and administration of two ounces of mineral oil at the site of the choke (if it will not move easily) is often helpful. Esophagostomy is relatively easy to perform and should be done in a choked goat if the cause of choke can be palpated in the neck.

2. Chronic Indigestion — Rumen Impaction

This problem is relatively common in dairy goat herds receiving inadequate protein and energy on a high fiber diet. The most common symptom is a large distended solid abdomen with weak or absent signs of rumination. Impaction may occur when does which have been receiving relatively large amounts of grain are turned out to browse or are put with dry stock receiving poor quality hay and grain containing relatively high levels of fiber.

Impaction of the rumen is often found in herds when horse feed containing more than 25% oats is fed with poor quality grass hay. The most common cause of both acute and chronic indigestion is failure of the herdsman to understand digestion in the ruminant. The rumen is a mixing fermentation vat which depends for its proper function on feeding the kind of diet (balanced ration) which will support the greatest population of rumen organisms and have the physical characteristics which will stimulate rumen action. For example: it is well known that excessive amounts of molasses (over 160-200 lbs. per ton) greatly interfere with normal rumen digestion and thus affect the amount of nutrients available to the animal. Many horse feeds contain excessive amounts of molasses which prevents good digestion in dairy goats. These can be fed to horses which have an entirely different digestive system. Horse feeds may be more palatable for goats than some dairy feeds, but the most nutritious dairy goat feeds for milking does should contain only enough molasses to control dustiness of the feed and improve its palatability. In most cases, 120-125 pounds per ton of molasses is adequate.

3. Abomasal Ulceration

This is the ultimate result of failure to feed dairy goats according to their needs. When excessive grain and little or inadequate forage is fed to does in early lactation, chronic acidosis and rumen statis predisposes them to development of abomasal ulcers. Animals with small superficial abomasal ulcers periodically go off feed. Those with perforating ulcers may die from hemorrhage or severe peritonitis. Diagnosis is often difficult unless the ulcers are large and hemorrhagic. The presence of small liver abscesses at necropsy is usually associated with a history of ulcers of the rumen and abomasum.

B.   Ketosis — Pregnancy Disease — Acetonemia

Ketosis is a toxemia produced by accumulation of the poisonous by-products which result from incomplete metabolism of fat. It occurs in dairy goats in two situations: as pregnancy disease within a month before kidding and as a primary ketosis within one month following kidding. In the former case, pregnancy disease is much more common in over-conditioned animals with little exercise. Accumulation of abdominal fat during late lactation and early pregnancy limits feed capacity. Then when demand by rapidly growing kids occurs, attempt is made to utilize stored body fat and ketosis occurs. Less commonly, pregnancy disease occurs in thin underfed does with multiple fetuses during the same period. Animals show depression and inappetence and wobbly gait. They may go down and become comatose within two days. Acute cases are not as common as the chronic cases. Both can result in high mortality rates if treatment is not prompt and adequate.

Ketosis may occur in fat does just before kidding and immediately afterward. The chief symptom observed in these animals is finicky appetite, lack of normal kidding activity, and lack of interest in the kids. Ketosis is common in does capable of high production but badly prepared for it. (See **Care of the Dry and Freshening Doe**). When inherited high production ability generates demand for a relatively large amount of highly nutritious feed, the digestive system (mainly the rumen and abomasum) are simply not conditioned to meet the animal's needs. It is virtually impossible then to feed the doe as much as she should normally eat. She is forced to draw upon body reserves and her milk production suffers. Accumulation of ketones then results in loss of appetite and further drop in production. Loss of potential milk production is a very serious consequence of poor management and feeding which may continue through to the dry period. In many dairy goat herds where ketosis is not recognized as a serious problem, does are fat when they kid and close to emaciated condition six weeks later. Good feeding and management is evidenced by lean active condition during the entire lactation cycle. No milking animals should ever be fat. Urine and milk ketone tests are strongly positive in ketosis and **negative in early enterotoxemia. This is a dependable tool for differential diagnosis. The characteristic breath, urine and milk odor is a good practical sign of this disease.**

Treatment — An early dose of six to eight ounces of propylene glycol by mouth will often be sufficient. Propylene glycol should be given at the above rate at two doses daily for no more than two days. Oral administration of sodium bicarbonate solution (one tablespoonful in four ounces of water) followed immediately by one cupful of dextrose or honey (never cane sugar) will result in closure of the esophagial groove in the reticulum and deliver the simple sugar solution for immediate absorption to the abomasum (true stomach). Intravenous injection of from 50 to 150 ml. of 50% dextrose solution is also good treatment. Cortisosteroid injection may be used in conjunction with dextrose therapy, but only for animals which have already kidded. Administrtion of cortisosteroid in late pregnancy usually results in immediate kidding with retained placenta and metritis complications. In the veterinarian's judgement, the use of cortisosteroid may be considered the lesser of two evils. Actually, if the doe is in serious condition from pregnancy disease, it is usually too late to save her or the kids. TDN requirement for does in late pregnancy and lactation is 1.77 lb. TDN/ 100 lb. body weight for does carrying single kids. For dairy goat does in late pregnancy, from 125% to 150% (2.2 to 2.7 lbs. TDN/100 lbs. body weight depending upon the amount of fleshing of the doe) is realistic.

C. Laminitis — Founder

This is an acute or chronic inflammation of the fleshy vascular tissue underlying the horny walls and soles of the feet. It occurs much more commonly in front feet than it does in the hind feet. Founder occurs in horses when they are chilled following hard work or from sudden changes in feed. It is a rare but dreaded sequel to foaling in the mare. In the goat, laminitis most often occurs at kidding, following sudden changes in feed or accompanying attacks of enterotoxemia, pneumonia, mastitis, metritis, or allergic manifestations.

Symptoms — In acute laminitis which usually occurs simultaneously with mastitis following kidding, the animal shows a high temperature (up to 107°F.) with evidence of great distress when forced to rise and walk. The feet may feel hot to the touch. This form of laminitis may occur less commonly simultaneously with pneumonia and with acute rather severe allergic attacks.

Much more common in dairy goats is chronic laminitis where the onset is often insidious. The fact that the animal has experienced laminitis is often unrecognized by owner or veterinarian until the animal develops abnormal feet and is reluctant to walk. It is a common reason why dairy goats in United States herds move around on their knees. Chronic laminitis most often results from excessive grain feeding, usually at or following kidding, sudden changes in feeding or following mild bouts of enterotoxemia. "Sled runner feet" with toes turned upward are good evidence of long-standing laminitis.

Treatment —   Acute laminitis is difficult to treat successfully.

Recent recommendations have rejected the time-honored ice pack treatment of the past in favor of warm water packs on the feet. A course of antihistamine therapy is indicated together with intravenous electrolyte therapy for detoxification. When uterine infection is involved, infusion of ten parts sterile isotonic saline to one part hydrogen peroxide solution may be helpful for evacuation of putrid material from the uterus, followed by antibiotic infusion. Use of Oxytocin immediately following prolonged kidding to aid uterine involution is helpful for prevention. Removal of retained placenta after 24-36 hours is also helpful.

When goats go off feed following changes in feed or overfeeding grain or highly nutritious forage, eight ounces of milk of magnesia and at least four ounces of mineral oil may be helpful to combat rumen acidosis and aid in evacuation of toxic material. A regular ongoing enterotoxemia vaccination program is helpful, but nothing will take the place of careful management. Founder is the bane of herds of goats bred for high production but managed poorly. Feeding and management of high-producing animals so that they reach their highest producing capability without the problem of chronic founder is more than a science; it is an art. When feet have become abnormal, the only thing of some value is regular trimming of the feet to let the hoof walls bear as much as possible of the animal's weight.

D. Milk Fever — Hypocalcemia

Milk fever is a manifestation of deficient calcium in the blood of dairy goats during the periparturient period (just before, during, and just after kidding). Normal blood levels of does during this period are between 9.0 and 10.5 mg./%. In milk fever, calcium levels may drop below 5.0 mg./%.

Symptoms — Milk fever is not as commonly seen in the severe comatose form in goats as it is seen in high-producing dairy cows. Much more frequently, dairy does show wobbly gait behind, constipation, and inability to undergo normal strong labor at kidding. Often the only symptom they show is hind foot dragging. Hind parts feel colder to the touch. Serum calcium levels usually range from 5.0 to 6.0 mg./%. Relatively few goats develop severe symptoms and go down, become comatose, and die. Those that do go down should be rolled to a sternal position with their heads pulled around to one side to minimize the opportunity to aspirate rumen ingesta forced back by bloating pressure. In acute cases, death can occur within a few hours.

Cause — The current explanation for milk fever stated simply is this: when the dry goat ingests excessive calcium beyond her needs and the needs of the developing kids, calcitonin-producing cells situated principally in the parathyroid gland secrete calcitonin. This hormone causes deposition of calcium in the bones and prevents mobilization of stored calcium. When demand for calcium is suddenly increased for milk production, the hormone system necessary for its removal from bone is not active because is has been depressed by the hormone calcitonin, and blood levels of calcium fall. Absorption of calcium from the intestinal contents at the same time may be prevented by a diet (most commonly alfalfa hay) which results in excessive alkalinity (pH over 6.5). Vitamin D and its metabolites in the body are also related to calcium absorption and mobilization. Milk fever is rarely the result of deficiency of calcium reserves, but rather a failure to activate calcium mobilization. Parathormone-producing cells in the parathyroid gland have this function, but excessive production of calcitonin effectively suppresses their production of parathormone.

Prevention — For all practical purposes, milk fever in goat dairy herds can be eliminated by lowering calcium intake for the last thirty days of pregnancy until just before kidding. In most herds this can be accomplished by eliminating alfalfa from the diet during this period. This is usually sufficient to put the body in a negative calcium balance state, and it results in activation of the hormone system which mobilizes calcium reserves. Where alfalfa is the only source of forage for feeding dry does, grain mixes containing no calcium supplementation should be fed. When dry does are fed solely on grass forage during the dry period, the grain mix should contain 0.5% dicalcium phosphate or its equivalent.

Treatment — Intravenous injection of from 50 to 100 ml. of 25% calcium borogluconate solution using an 18 gge. needle to administer the drug into the jugular vein is the treatment of choice. The calcium gluconate solution should be slowly administered at body temperature with constant monitoring of the heart with a stethoscope. Size of dose should depend upon size of animal and degree of depression.

Although complete milking out has little to do with recurrence, it is perhaps better not to strip the udder of milk for one day following treatment.

Infusion of oxygen into the udder via a teat catheter using a small oxygen tank and a rubber tube is indicated for repeat treatment as it is for cows. The danger from introducing environmental pathogens into the udder is equally great. In the author's experience, very mild milk fever is not at all rare in mature high-producing does. Failure to treat it may result in serious complications (enterotoxemia, mastitis, and retained placenta). Milk fever should be treated only by a veterinarian. Much of the success or failure of milk fever treatment depends upon careful examination before diagnosis is established and proper administration of the treatment.

E. Osteopetrosis — Nutritional Arthritis

This form of proliferative calcification around the joints is not uncommon in mature animals. It occurs in many bucks by the time they are four or five years of age and in does a few years later.

This problem was studied extensively in bulls by workers at Cornell University, and it has the same etiology and progressive pathology in buck goats. Excessive calcium intake which results from feeding alfalfa hay and concentrates supplemented with calcium produces hyperplastic calcitonin cell tissue in the parathyroid gland. This potent hormone causes calcium deposition in the bones and excessive calcium may be deposited in the bones by the time the animals are one year old. It is seen very commonly in good quality young animals which are excessively fed high quality feed for show and sale purposes.

Hyperplasia of calcitonin cells and excessive calcitonin secretion is an almost irreversible situation. Fortunately for does which kid at one year of age and thus have early demand for stored bone calcium, the final onset of osteopetrosis is delayed. Young bucks, however, continue to store calcium in the bones and in the periarticular areas and gradually show stiffness and crampiness until many are nearly immobilized by the time they are six years old.

Prevention — The prevention of this problem lies solely in prevention of excessive calcium intake in young animals under one year of age and in buck goats throughout their lives. If alfalfa hay is fed to kids under one year of age, no supplemental calcium should be provided in the concentrate fed. Mature bucks should be fed grass hay or browse and never more than a pound or two of good alfalfa hay daily.

When alfalfa hay is the sole forage fed to dairy goats, no supplemental calcium should be added in the concentrate fed. Up to 20 lbs./ton monosodium phosphate should be substituted for calcium supplements. When the forage fed is entirely grass, then at least 0.5% calcium in the form of dicalcium-phosphate, steamed bone meal, or ground limestone should be included in the concentrate fed. Where mixed hay is fed, supplementation with calcium should be made in proportion to the amount of legume present.

F. Polioencephalomalacia — (Cerebrocortical Necrosis)

Polioencephalomalacia occurs in ruminants suffering from depletion of thiamine (Vitamin B_1). This vitamin is usually normally synthesized in adequate amounts in the rumen, but enzymes or toxins produced by molds apparently destroy thiamine and prevent its further production. This problem is often confused with enterotoxemia. Enterotoxemia is characterized by depression and incoordination. Polioencephalomalacia is characterized initially in goats by stargazing, twitching, followed by recumbency and clonic convulsions before death occurs. Course of the disease is usually two or three days.

Prevention and Treatment — Avoid feeding moldy feed to goats. This is an important reason for dairy goat owners in areas where there are small numbers of dairy goats (with concurrent slow turnover of feed) to feed their animals coarse flaked or rolled or pelleted dairy cow feeds. The dairy cow feeds are moved through feed outlets in larger quantities and as a result are fresher and freer from molds. Excessive molasses content of some goat feeds and horse feeds fed to dairy goats may also contribute to depression of Vitamin B_1 activity in the rumen because molasses fosters mold growth.

Treatment is dramatic and effective early in the course of the disease. A treatment effective, when given before animals become recumbent, is intramuscular administration, over a two or three day period, of from 300 to 500 mg./day of thiamine hydrochlorine (amount depending upon size of the animal).

Polioencephalomalacia-like symptoms may occur in goats poisoned by eating the fruits of ground coyotilla, a shrub indigenous to southwestern United States. Symptoms occur after six to seven days of eating the fruits of this plant and rapidly progress to dragging of the rear legs and recumbency.

CHAPTER VII

CONTAGIOUS AND INFECTIOUS DISEASES

A.	Abscesses	92
B.	Anaplasmosis	97
C.	Anthrax	98
D.	Arthritis	99
	1. Non-suppurative Arthritis	99
	2. Suppurative Arthritis	100
	a. Navel Ill	101
E.	Bluetongue	101
F.	Brucellosis	101
G.	Coccidiosis	102
H.	Contagious Ecthyma	104
I.	Dermatomycosis (Ringworm)	106
J.	Enterotoxemia	106
K.	Foot Rot and Foot Abscesses	109
L.	Infectious Bovine Rhinotracheitis	110
M.	Infectious Keratoconjunctivitis	111
N.	Johnes' Disease	112
O.	Leukoencephalomyelitis (Progressive Paralysis of Kids)	113
P.	Listeriosis	114
Q.	Malignant Edema — Blackleg	116
R.	Mastitis	116
S.	Pneumonia	127
T.	Pox	128
U.	Toxoplasmosis	129
V.	Traumatic Testiculitis	129
W.	Neoplasias	131

A. Abscesses

T wo organisms are most commonly involved in abscesses found in dairy goats. **Corynebacterium ovis** is the specific cause of caseous lymphadenitis commonly referred to as "abscesses" by goat breeders. Another name for this disease is pseudotuberculosis. **Corynebacterium pyogenes** primarily causes skin abscesses, but the organism may be primary or secondary in many disease processes in dairy goats. It is found in a type of mastitis which is characterized by numerous abscesses within the mammary gland.

Caseous Lymphadenitis — Pseudotuberculosis

Cause — The organism responsible for this disease, **Corynebacterium ovis** (formerly C. Pseudotuberculosis) was first identified in the same disease of sheep in 1894, and it has been studied extensively in sheep in many countries ever since. It is a small gram-positive rod with the characteristic morphology and staining of the diphtheroids. It grows readily in beef infusion media. On beef infusion agar, a wrinkled grayish white dry growth on the surface is characteristic.

Occurrence — The disease occurs sporadically in sheep-producing areas around the world. In eastern United States, many purebred sheep flocks of all breeds are infected. In Pennsylvania, it is not rare in purebred sheep and rather rare in sheep flocks of western origin.

This is the major disease of dairy goats in the United States. At the 1976 National Dairy Goat Show, at least twenty individuals in ten show herds represented showed scars resulting from incised abscesses and a few showed developing abscesses. About half the questions in letters received by the author as a result of the Penn State University Correspondence Course in Dairy Goat Management and Diseases relate to this disease, and the questions have come from the entire United States.

Symptoms — Abscesses usually develop singly in parotid (in throat latch), prescapular (in front of shoulder blades), superficial inguinal (in flank) or popliteal (above hock) lymph glands. When first noticed, they are several centimeters in size, but they gradually enlarge to grapefruit size in many cases. The initial abscess usually develops a rather tough capsule and may never burst through the skin itself. Upon excision, a definite capsule is found and the cavity in early lesions is filled with thick greenish cheesy soft material. Excision of older lesions produces laminated layers of dry cottage cheese-like material that literally requires peeling out of the capsule. Ordinary excision with good drainage and antiseptic irrigation produces uneventful healing,

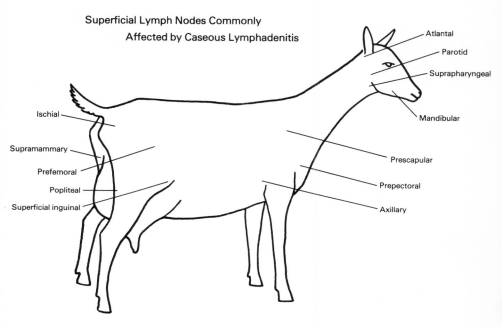

Superficial Lymph Nodes Commonly
Affected by Caseous Lymphadenitis

Atlantal

Parotid

Suprapharyngeal

Mandibular

Ischial

Supramammary

Prefemoral

Popliteal

Superficial inguinal

Prescapular

Prepectoral

Axillary

but by that time another superficial abscess usually appears. The first abscess rarely appears before the age of one year and the disease could be considered one of mature goats. However, it seems logical that animals become infected at an early age, and because the disease is a slow insidious process, goats rarely show lesions before they are mature. Evidence of surface abscesses reveals the possibility of deep abscesses which may be found in mediastinal (between the lungs), gastro-hepatic (between the liver and stomach) and mesenteric (in the intestinal attachment) lymph glands. They produce symptoms related to interference with function of the affected organs. The animal may become increasingly emaciated and weak. Mediastinal abscesses produce chronic cough and dyspnea (difficult breathing). When the animals become so weak they cannot rise, they are usually put down — too often without necropsy to reveal the cause of the disease. The typical clinical picture of internal caseous lymphadenitis can easily be confused with Johnes' Disease (paratuberculosis). When goats develop the above symptoms described for internal abscesses, and abscesses are not grossly observed at necropsy, Johnes' Disease should be suspected.

Transmission — In sheep, it is generally accepted that abscesses result from shearing wounds caused by contaminated shears, and this is certainly logical and proven possible. However, the possibility for shearing wound transmission in goats is not usual, and it is more likely that animals become infected from ingestion from an environment contaminated by the organism. Undoubtedly, blood-sucking lice and other external parasites could be involved. The primary source of infection, however, must be by ingestion from a contaminated environment.

Control — Because evidence and severity of the disease varies so much between herds, necessary control measures may vary. When an occasional abscess shows itself in a fairly large herd, it may be only necessary to segregate the affected animal, excise the abscess and treat the animal until the wound heals and all traces of exudation have ceased.

How To Treat Abscesses — Anytime after an abscess has sufficiently organized and become encapsulated, it should be incised. The incision should be made vertically, if possible, and as low as possible to secure good drainage. Pus should be carefully collected and buried or incinerated, and the wound should be thoroughly flushed with antiseptic solution. A favorite treatment of the author is — one part of Chlorhexidine solution (Nolvasan-Fort Dodge) in ten parts hydrogen peroxide. The cavity should be flushed daily until healed. The organism has been incriminated in mesenteric lesions in humans. The incision and treatment process demands strict attention to prevent contamination of other animals, the operator and the environment.

At the same time the abscess is incised and treated, four daily intramuscular injections of 100,000 units of penicillin with dihydrostreptomycin are indicated. During the treatment period, the affected animal should be kept from contact with any others. Before returning the treated animal to the herd, the entire area around and below the abscess should be washed with antiseptic detergent and dried.

The above treatment regime is quite different from the usual situation seen in infected herds by the author. Often abscesses are ignored until they rupture on the surface. A small incision may be made with a pen knife and the pus squeezed out with no further care or treatment given. This is the ideal way to develop a very high level of environmental contamination and increase the incidence and losses from the disease within a herd. An additional word of caution about excising abscesses: those which occur in the throat behind the jaw and under the ear require a veterinary surgeon's services. The area contains major blood vessels, cranial nerves and salivary gland tissue. Excising abscesses there requires professional expertise.

Justification For a Control Program

Caseous lymphadenitis can be eradicated from a herd, but the job is not easy. Eradication should be the goal of every herd owner who wants to show or sell goats. Sometime in the future when regulatory veterinary medicine becomes aware of the prevalence of this disease and the magnitude of losses from it, particularly in the purebred sheep industry, regulations may be forthcoming which will limit movement of animals from infected flocks and herds to shows and sales. The author has seen numerous herd problems develop when novice owners purchased purebred breeding stock to up-grade their herds from well-known breeders. If this disease is ignored or handled indifferently, sooner or later it assumes grave proportions and the owner is forced to try to eradicate it or go out of business.

Control Measures — Baby kids should be removed from their dams at birth and reared in a separate facility completely away from contact with the infected herd. Only milk from young does showing no lesions and having no history of the disease should be fed to baby kids. In severely affected herds, it may be better to feed kids a milk replacer formulated for lambs after they have had colostrum for three or four feedings.

Use of autogenous bacterin has been controversial, but in the author's clinical experience, it appears to have been most helpful in some herds. There is no specific commercial Corynebacterium ovis bacterin available at this writing. An autogenous bacterin can be custom made by veterinary biologics manufacturers, hospital, or veterinary diagnostic laboratories. Kids should be given two initial doses of bacterin at two-week intervals beginning at three weeks of age. Repeat doses should be given at three to six month intervals thereafter.

When the annual crop of doe kids has been reared to kidding age on this program, the owner must make the decision to totally depopulate the mature herd or selectively eliminate known infected individuals. Whatever decision is made, as soon as the known infected individuals or the whole mature herd is removed, the buildings and lots involved should be thoroughly cleaned and disinfected if possible. In most states, disinfectant detergent steam is used to clean and disinfect trucks, barns, etc. for eradication of other diseases. The services of an operator, the equipment and disinfectant are usually made available if one calls the Director of the Bureau of Animal Industry, or his equivalent, and asks for it. Where all of the mature animals in the infected herd are not eliminated immediately, all of those to be retained should be given at least two doses of autogenous bacterin at two week intervals at least one month before the young treated animals are introduced.

A regular booster shot program at three to six month intervals should be conducted until at least one year after all of the original infected herd have been replaced. One additional precaution has been recommended, but in the author's opinion, it is not backed by adequate research to justify it; that is, the inclusion of 100 gms. per ton of oxytetracycline (Terramycin) or Chlortetracycline (Auroemycin) to the concentrate feed fed to both the young herd and the infected herd. The above eradication program is expensive, time consuming and requires much work, but the advertising value and the economic value of an "abscess free" herd more than justifies it. Those who act now to control this disease will have taken the "stitch in time" if and when regulatory action is taken to stop its spread.

Other Abscess Problems

Corynebacterium pyogenes, a ubiquitous organism in the environment of many dairy goat herds, produces various problems. The pus produced by this organism is distinguished grossly from that produced by **Corynebacterium ovis**, the caseous lymphadenitis organism, by its yellow or greenish-yellow mayonnaise-like consistency. **C. pyogenes**

problems are often associated with poor hygiene. It is an organism which is apparently able to establish itself and build up its numbers in unsanitary situations. Then it appears to be ready to become involved in just about every pus-producing inflammatory process in the goat. It is commonly associated with **Pasteurella** organisms in pneumonia, with **streptococci** or **staphylococci** in mastitis where it causes multiple abscesses within the mammary gland. A particularly difficult problem caused by this organism is **udder impetigo.** In this situation, external parasites, chapping, small wounds, etc., of the skin of the udder become infected with **C. pyogenes** and small faruncles (abscesses) develop within the skin. These are very sensitive and painful to the touch. When they occur within or near the skin of the teats, milking is very difficult or impossible. Treatment of udder impetigo demands the use of a bactericidal ointment on the udder surface (Chlorhexadine, Tetracycline, sulfonamide, furacin, etc.) at least daily. Teats should be wiped with a paper towel or tissues and no udder wash should be used until the condition has abated.

Control Program for C. Pyogenes — Because this organism is so frequently involved with other infections in dairy goats, a control program based on a regular use of a bacterin containing **C. pyogenes** beginning with two initial doses at two-week intervals is indicated. Several commercial bacterins containing **C. pyogenes** with **pasteurella species** are available. In the author's experience, these appear to be helpful when a program of initial doses and annual booster doses are given. However, no biologic or treatment program can be expected to eliminate the need for a good general sanitation program for a dairy goat herd.

Melioidosis — Abscesses resulting from **M. Pseudomallei** infection are extremely rare in the U.S., but they commonly occur in other countries and can produce serious disease in man. Therefore, all abscesses should be handled with extreme caution.

B.   Anaplasmosis

This is an important disease of cattle which produces serious losses both as an acute disease with significant mortality and as a chronic disease. It occurs in goats in areas where it causes losses in cattle. A body in the red blood cell is associated with occurrence of the disease. It is transferred from wild carrier animals (deer and antelope in western United States) by ticks, blood-sucking flies, and mosquitoes to susceptible animals. Symptoms characteristic of the disease in cattle (high fever, anemia, jaundice, etc.) are not seen in goats, but the organism (anaplasma ovis) has been demonstrated in unthrifty animals in endemic areas in western United States.

A capillary antigen (CA) test is available which can be used by practitioners and diagnostic laboratories for detecting the presence of anaplasmosis infection. Stained blood smears usually reveal up to 50% of the red blood cells parasitized.

Prevention — The use of sterilized individual needles, syringes and instruments by livestock owners and veterinarians will eliminate an important means of spread in areas where anaplasmosis occurs. Regular control of flies and other blood-sucking parasites is important. A vaccine has been produced for protection of cattle.

Treatment — Where the presence of the disease can be established in a sick goat or a goat herd, individual sick animals can be given chlortetracycline orally at the rate of 50 mg/lb. daily for two repeated 5-7 day periods or the antibiotic can be administered intravenously or intramuscularly at the rate of 2 mg/lb. for similar periods.

Where the presence of anaplasmosis has been shown to exist in more than a few individuals in a herd, inclusion of 200 gms. of chlortetra-cycline per ton of grain fed may be helpful.

C. Anthrax

This disease of all animals and man is caused by a spore-forming bacterium, **Bacillus anthracis**. It is world-wide in distribution, but in the United States it causes significant mortality in Arkansas, California, Louisiana, Mississippi, Nebraska, South Dakota, and Texas. A few small areas exist in other states. The organism exists in the **sporalated** form in the soil during dry or cold weather conditions, but when weather conditions favor it, the vegetative form develops and multiplies rapidly. Anthrax outbreaks usually follow periods of sustained warm wet weather. Goats usually become infected when they graze areas contaminated with large numbers of anthrax spores, but infection is also possible via contaminated feed troughs.

Anthrax infection in goats is a peracute disease. Animals are rarely observed sick for more than a few hours and they are usually found dead. Temperatures taken early in the course of anthrax reveal very high fever (107-108°F.). Severe depression, labored breathing, and weakness are also seen. However, both sheep and goats are often found dead from anthrax without showing symptoms.

Diagnosis — At necropsy, diagnosis is usually not difficult, Carcasses frequently show no rigor mortis. Blood is dark, almost black, fails to clot, and small hemorrhagic effusions are frequently seen in serous and mucous membranes. The spleen, liver lymph nodes, and kidneys are usually enlarged. Because humans are susceptible to a chronic cutaneus form of anthrax, necropsy should be performed using surgical mask and gloves and proper disinfection of instruments and facilities should follow necropsy. Carcasses should be burned. Samples of blood should be collected aseptically from fresh carcasses and blood smears should be made. These should be taken, refrigerated, to an animal diagnostic laboratory immediately.

Anthrax is a reportable disease; the state veterinary regulatory official should be notified immediately when the disease is suspect. Fortunately, in the United States, where anthrax occurs, veterinarians and livestock owners are aware of it and they watch for outbreaks when weather conditions are right.

Prevention — Prevention is accomplished by use of anthrax vaccine, but this should only be used where it is permitted by state regulatory officials. Where the disease regularly occurs, state and federal officials move rapidly to contain it and they supervise disposal of carcasses and rigorous **disinfection** at all infected premises. Because anthrax is a spore-former, infected areas may go for years without an outbreak only to have disastrous outbreaks when conditions are right.

If anthrax is suspect in a dairy goat herd in an anthrax endemic area, removal of the animals from the infected lot or pasture, and treatment of any animals that show depression or fever, using large intramuscular doses of penicillin (1,000,000 IU/day) for several days, may prevent further losses. Administration of penicillin to the entire herd may be justified.

D.   Arthritis

1. Non-suppurative Arthritis

This condition appears to be relatively common in dairy goats in western United States. Usually one carpal (knee) joint is affected. It is characterized by a rather rapid painful swelling of the joint capsule early in the course of the disease. At first the goat carries the affected leg, or if both legs are affected, it refuses to walk. After the first week, pain apparently subsides, but the animals are permanently disfigured for show.

Chlamydial Arthritis can be considered one of the non-suppurative types. In California, this form commonly occurs following herd outbreaks of chlamydial abortion. Signs of arthritis appear about a month following abortion. Then hock, carpal, or stifle joints fill with a pale yellow fluid. Dr. Jackson of San Bernardino, California, frequently isolates chlamydia from this fluid. Treatment of the entire herd with tetracycline at the rate of 200 grams tetracycline per ton of grain mix for periods of at least two weeks may be helpful.

Treatment of Animals Showing Swollen Joints — Aseptic aspiration of joint fluid early in the course of the disease, followed by injection of corticosteroid and broad spectrum antibiotic, is commonly used by veterinarians. Joint fluid is rarely grossly abnormal in appearance, but its quantity is excessive. Application of a tight elastic bandage following injection is helpful for preventing a permanent big knee.

2. Suppurative Arthritis

Several kinds of bacteria may be responsible for suppurative arthritis in goats. When bacterial infections become systemic, organisms gain entrance to the synovial (joint capsule) fluids more readily than they can enter either the spinal fluids or the urine.

In mature animals, the most important and common cause of suppurative arthritis is **Corynebacterium pyogenes**. Infection by this organism commonly follows periods of stress. Hot swollen joints with severe lameness may appear a week to ten days following return from a show or a sale. The animal affected usually shows signs of "shipping fever" (depression, 104° to 107° fever temperature, inappetance) in the first few days following return home.

Treatment with broad spectrum antibiotics relieves those symptoms, but the joint involvements usually appear following cessation of treatment. Pure cultures of **C. pyogenes** can be aspirated from the joints. Systemic treatment is usually unsuccessful when the joint infections become established. Aspiration of pus and injection of tetracycline with corticosterioid may be helpful. Severe cases develop polyarthritis in which most of the joints of the limbs are affected.

Prevention — In areas where **C. pyogenes** arthritis commonly accompanies febrile disease following stress of shows and sales, sick animals should be given adequate antibiotic therapy for at least five days with a subsequent five-day course of treatment begun a week following the end of the first course of treatment.

a. Navel Ill Arthritis (see Navel Ill)

Baby kids are highly susceptible to navel ill which may kill them quickly from acute septicemia or it may become manifest weeks later in a hot joint. The organisms usually involved are hemolytic streptococci or staphlococci. Other organisms may be involved, e.g.: **Erysipelothrix rhusiopathiae, Corynebacterium pyogenes,** and **Corynebacterium ovis.**

E. Bluetongue

Bluetongue is an infectious virus disease which affects ruminant animals. It is infectious but not contagious; that is, it must be carried by a vector to a susceptible animal, but it will not spread from an infected animal to a susceptible one by simply exposing the susceptible animal to the infected one. For example, tuberculosis is a contagious disease which will spread from one animal to another without the necessity for an intermediate vector or host.

Bluetongue is a highly acute devastating disease of white-tailed deer, but it can and does produce disease in sheep, cattle, moose, bighorn sheep, goats and various African ruminants. Bluetongue was known and described in Africa many years before it was found anywhere else. Today, there are apparently many different strains of Bluetongue virus. Those in North America are far less virulent than those of the Middle East and Africa. The disease has never been found in South America, Australia, New Zealand or Northern Europe.

A small blood-sucking gnat, (**Cullicoides Varipennis** in the United States) is the most important vector. The female gnat feeds on an infected host and the virus multiplies rapidly in her salivary glands, reaching a peak of transmitting potential in ten to fourteen days.

Symptoms in Sheep — Panting, high fever, increased pulse, frothing at the mouth, and salivation appear in that order as the inflammation of the oral mucous membranes develops. The "blue" cyanotic color of the tongue may appear one day and disappear the next. Death may occur from the acute phase of the disease, but it usually follows as a result of secondary pneumonia.

Bluetongue virus, or laboratory evidence of its presence, has never been found in goats in the United States. Experimentally, however, goats have come down with mild evidence of the disease where exposed to virulent strains of the virus.

102

Precaution — Where Bluetongue in sheep or of white-tailed deer occurs in the vicinity of dairy goat herds, efforts to eliminate gnats from access to the herd may be worthwhile. The gnat responsible breeds in muddy areas. Keeping the herd inside and spraying the animals and immediate environment with an approved fly spray may be worthwhile.

F.   Brucellosis

Brucella melitensis is a strain of the brucellae specific for goats. It is the cause of Malta Fever in humans. It was named Malta Fever after widespread human infection was found on the island of Malta. On that island, an attenuated B. melitensis vaccine is administered to animals three to seven months of age. This apparently confers immunity for at least two and a half years. While localization of virulent vaccine organisms is known to occur in the regional lymph nodes of vaccinated animals, the vaccine does not produce a persistent titer.

In the United States, the incidence of brucellosis in goats is extremely low, almost non-existent. As is the case with tuberculosis, dairy goats are subjected to dairy cow regulations against brucellosis without adequate justification for it. Goats have developed blood reactions to the disease on exposure to infected cattle. Blood testing goats can only be justified in areas where goats may be exposed to infected cattle. Unfortunately, there are many areas in the United States not yet "brucellosis free" where regular annual blood testing may be prudent. Brucellosis may be just as readily transmitted to humans from infected goats as it is from infected cows. Where purebred animals are produced for show and sale, owners of dairy goat herds, at present, have no alternative but regular herd testing for both diseases. In Pennsylvania, more than 1,100 dairy goats have been tested annually for the past twenty years. Not a single brucellosis infected goat has been found. There is neither need nor justification for the use in goats of Strain 19 brucellosis vaccine, the vaccine commonly used to protect heifer calves.

G.   Coccidiosis

Coccidia of dairy goats are microscopic protozoa of at least three different species. These are host specific; that is, the coccidia of chickens, cattle, dogs, or cats are not infective for goats. However, goats do share three species of coccidia with sheep. Coccidia have highly complicated life cycles with both free-living stages, sexual and asexual reproduction and a cellular stage in which the parasite invades, reproduces, and severely damages cells in the intestinal mucosa of the host animal. Diagnosis of coccidiosis is usually made with the presence of typical oocysts which are found upon microscopic examination of feces by one of the flotation methods. The presence of oocysts in feces does not necessarily justify treatment. A few oocysts 200-500/gm. of feces may be more advantageous than none; through them, the host may acquire immunity.

Symptoms — In goat herds, coccidiosis problems are usually limited to kids under four months of age, but older animals previously not exposed to coccidial infection may show symptoms within two to four weeks after exposure. Mild infections in kids usually produce transient inappetance and soft stools similar to normal feces of calves. Fecal examination of apparently normal kids may reveal thousands of oocysts per gram of feces. Severe coccidiosis is characterized by bloody or tarry diarrhea with straining, rapid dehydration and death.

Control and Treatment — Two stages in the life cycle are important from the standpoint of control and treatment: the oocyst stage and the schizogenous stage (asexual reproductive stage). Oocysts are passed with the feces. Then microscopic round cysts sporulate asexually and form eight small banana-shaped sporozoites within the cyst capsule. At this stage, further development ceases if the cysts are not ingested by the goat. A single goat not showing symptoms of coccidiosis may shed millions of microscopic oocysts in its feces daily. These can blow about, attached to dust, and easily contaminate food and water. Coccidiosis build-up is aided by confinement, overcrowding, and poor sanitation. One of the best arguments for separating baby kids from the older animals in confined herds should be to protect the young kids from overwhelming exposure to coccidia oocysts.

Coccidiosis of kids, in the author's experience, has greater implications than intestinal disease alone. One of the stages of a coccidial parasite, **Toxoplasma**, is found outside the gut in the central nervous system and the respiratory tract. The author has often observed a simultaneous chronic cough in young goats showing symptoms of mild coccidiosis or at least large numbers fecal oocysts. This chronic respiratory problem predisposes them to pneumonia and often stunts their growth badly. Where young kids have a persistent chronic cough and the presence of lung worms cannot be demonstrated, toxoplasmosis (infection of the lung tissue by an intermediate coccidial stage) should be considered. Reduction of oocyst infection for young kids, or newly acquired susceptible animals, demands special sanitation effort to prevent ingestion of oocysts. Feeders designed to keep kids out of them are especially important. Keeping baby kids outside in a large dry lot is infinitely better for them than confinement in badly ventilated "warm" housing. Before the new crop of kids is born, the house and lots where they will be reared should be thoroughly cleaned and disinfected. This is a fundamental sanitation chore which will also help to protect the baby animals from overwhelming infection by numerous other pathogens.

Drugs used to combat coccidiosis owe their activity to inhibition of the schizogenous stage which occurs within the tissue cells. Sulfonamide drugs are coccidiostatic, not coccidiocidal; therefore, they allow the animal to develop resistance. Sulfaguanidine or sulfaquinoxaline are prescribed for treatment of intestinal coccidiosis because they are poorly absorbed and exert their activity in the intestinal mucosal cells. Treatment of coccidiosis in kids, in the author's opinion, demands the additional use of another systemic sulfonamide to attack the metazoite stages which commonly occur in the respiratory system and, more rarely, in the central nervous system.

Rational treatment for kids would appear to be administration of sulfaguanidine or sulfaquinoxaline at the rate of 0.6 gr. per lb. per day for at least four days. Then administer 0.5 to 1 gr./lb./day of sulfathiazole or sulfadimethoxine per day for four more days. This regime can be repeated if symptoms do not completely disappear. It is not realistic to attempt to eradicate coccidia from a herd of dairy goats. Far more sensible is development of a sanitation program which will minimize danger of severe infection in the baby kids born into the herd each year. Coccidiosis problems primarily occur when goats are kept in an environment far removed from that of their natural nomadic existence. Where it is possible, young goats will be infinitely healthier if they have minimal confinement and maximal opportunity for exercise and outdoor living.

H.   Contagious Ecthyma — Sore Mouth — Orf

This disease of sheep and goats is caused by a virus highly resistant to drying. The virus has remained viable in scabby material for as long as twelve years following an outbreak of the disease.

Symptoms — Small blisters develop principally on the lips and gums. These rupture and become scabby lesions underlain by inflamed sensitive areas. In baby kids, the lesions develop on the gum just below the incisor teeth. The kids often refuse to nurse normally and when they do, they usually spread the infection to the teats of the does. Those lesions become painful and if the virus invades the teat canal, severe mastitis (usually secondary and caused by **Corynebactium pyogenes** or staphylococci) is a common result. An outbreak of sore mouth in a herd of goats at a time when kids are not present and the herd is not in the height of lactation is usually a relatively mild problem. When young kids are present, it can be a very serious problem.

Transmission — Because the virus persists so long in scabby material, it should be taken for granted that one outbreak of sore mouth in a herd of goats guarantees the possibility of others later. Goats should not be exhibited in shows without prior protection against contagious ecthyma. Outbreaks in susceptible herds usually follow return of animals from shows or introduction of new animals.

Immunity — Goats which have experienced an attack of sore mouth are usually highly resistant to infection thereafter. A commercial vaccine containing finely powdered scabby material is used to protect animals. Its use it not necessary nor is it recommended for closed herds where animals are not shown, and bought and sold. However, in the author's experience, this is not the usual situation. Many dairy goat owners who have only a few dairy goats spend numerous weekends at goat shows with their animals. It appears that regulated or planned infection is the logical approach to prevention of sore mouth problems.

Vaccination Program — Initially, vaccine should be administered at a time when there are no nursing kids present. Unless it is known that certain animals have experienced contagious ecthyma, all animals should be vaccinated. The dry vaccine is reconstituted with diluent just before administration. It is administered using a brush over scarification made on the skin surface. The best site for innoculation is the bare skin surface under the tail about two inches from the base of the tail. After the initial administration, it is necessary only to vaccinate the annual kid crop after they are weaned and at least one month before any are shown. (See **Precautions** under **Treatment**.)

Treatment — Treatment of sore mouth is aimed toward preventing invasion of bacteria into the lesions. When this occurs, lesions become very sore and necrotic ulcers may develop. Scabby material can be gently removed using hydrogen peroxide and cotton or gauze swab. Antiseptic astringent lotion, Chlorhexidine solution, pyotannic blue lotion, or sulfonamide urea solutions, etc., should then be applied to the lesions.

Precautions — Whether administering vaccine or treating the lesions, precaution against becoming infected with the virus should be taken. Wear rubber or plastic gloves. Breaks in the skin may allow penetration by the virus. Painful lesions and inflammation of the hand, arm and axillary lymph gland occur in human infection, and discomfort may persist for weeks.

I. Dermatomycosis — Ringworm

Ringworm is a rather common problem in goats housed during the winter in dark, poorly ventilated housing. The scabby elevated lesions of ringworm so often seen in cattle are rarely seen in goats. The usual picture of ringworm in a dairy goat is a thickened gray scaley skin with a thinned hair coat. The animals show no evidence of itching unless they are concurrently infected with lice, and this is commonly the situation. The hair coat is dry and lifeless in appearance.

Prevention and Treatment — While treatment for ringworm is generally satisfactory, it is usually of no avail unless the housing conditions which foster it are corrected, and the lice which spread it are eliminated. Thorough scrubbing, or high pressure spraying of the animals with a solution containing 30 gms. of Captan per five gallons of cold water, is highly effective against the ringworm fungus. Good supportive treatment would include intramuscular injection of at least 200,000 IU of Vitamin A for mature goats.

Caution — Ringworm of goats, like ringworm in other domestic animal species, may be infectious to man. Handling animals with any dermatomycoses should be followed by thorough washing of the hands.

J. Enterotoxemia
Overeating Disease, Toxic Indigestion

Enterotoxemia in goats is caused by toxin produced by the organism **Clostridium perfringens, type C and type D.** Enterotoxemia occurs in sheep and goats throughout the world. Sheep are most susceptible to type D toxin, but goats are highly susceptible to both C and D types. Under normal conditions of management and feeding of dairy goats, the possibility of enterotoxemia of dairy goats of any age is ever present. Under management and feeding conditions throughout the United States, it is impossible to manage a herd of dairy goats without experience with this disease.

The exact conditions for the growth of the organism and absorption of the toxin within the intestine are not understood. The toxin, like other toxins produced by Clostridial organisms, (tetanus, botulism, etc.), is deadly poisonous. Symptoms produced depend upon the age of the animal, previous exposure, and the amount of toxin absorbed. The organism is commonly found in the environment and the digestive tracts of animals.

Symptoms — Evidence of depression, intoxication, and incoordination is indicative of enterotoxemia, regardless of age. In baby kids, excess feeding or sudden access to palatable feed, changes in feed, or feeding following an unusual period of hunger, may cause acute enterotoxemia with sudden death. Less violent digestive upset may cause depression, wobbling gait, recumbency, or coma. In older animals, enterotoxemia causes more subtle symptoms. Animals may show only transient listlessness and diarrhea, or, with more absorption of toxin, may show the severe depression or sudden death as seen in susceptible kids. Predisposing factors in adults are changes in concentrate feed, excessive feeding of concentrates to animals with digestive tracts not in condition to handle it, sudden changes in forage, sudden access to highly palatable forage, sudden access to food and overeating in very hungry animals, gastrointestinal stress for a host of reasons (excessive fiber intake, calcium deficiency, acidosis, etc.). The possiblity of enterotoxemia should always be considered when goats show evidence of intoxication, whatever the circumstances.

Prevention and Control — It is the author's opinion that it is unrealistic and quite foolish to attempt to manage a dairy goat herd under conditions in the United States without a good program to prevent losses from enterotoxemia. In spite of the fact that good commercial vaccines are available for improving the animals' resistance against the enterotoxemia organism and its toxins, reliance on vaccination alone will not prevent problems or losses. It is imperative, when raising kids, to feed small amounts at frequent intervals, or give kids constant access to milk, grain and forage. Use of a lamb-saver feeder where kids can nurse frequently is much safer than giving kids large feedings two or three times daily. Changes in feed for animals of any age should be gradual. In goats of any age, changes from one type of grain or forage to another should take place gradually over a period of at least ten days to two weeks. Changes in protein and energy levels in concentrates fed should be gradual. For example, if forage analysis reveals that the protein and/or energy content of the concentrate fed should be increased or lowered, at least two weeks of gradual adjustment should be taken to reach the desired level. If 14% protein has been fed and the new forage requires 18% protein in the grain mix, increase the protein level at the rate of not more than 2% per week until the desired level is attained.

If it becomes necessary for economy reasons to start to feed urea or other non-protein nitrogen rather than protein from a vegetable source, not less than three weeks should be taken to make the complete change and no more than thirty pounds per ton of urea should ever be used as a substitute for protein.

Dry Period Feeding — Restore good rumen function by feeding browse or other long fiber coarse forage. (See **Feeding the Dry Doe**.)

Vaccination Program to Control Enterotoxemia — All the animals in the herd should be given two initial doses of Clostridium perfringens type C and D bacterintoxoid at at least a two-week interval. An annual booster dose to does in late pregnancy increases antibody levels in colostrum and, in addition, helps protect nursing kids through lactogenic immunity. Kids should receive their first dose of toxoid-bacterin at three to four weeks of age, followed by a second dose two weeks later. All animals in the herd, including the bucks, should receive at least two doses of toxoid-bacterin annually: one when does are in late pregnancy, and another about the time kids are four to five months old.

Diagnosis and Treatment — The best practical way to make a presumptive diagnosis is to administer a large dose of Clostridium perfringens C and D antitoxin (40-100 ml.) as soon as possible after the appearance of symptoms. Prompt recovery, even though it might be only temporary, should be considered diagnostic. Positive urine glucose is also good diagnostic evidence of enterotoxemia.

At post-mortem, examination of the duodenum just below the abomasal pylorus may reveal slight hemmorrhage or reddening of the mucosa. Pulpy kidney is usually considered diagnostic, but the author has never necropsied a dead goat for any reason without finding "pulpy kidney." Diagnostic laboratories frequently inject intestinal ingesta into mice to demonstrate toxin but the author has not found any procedure more useful than the prompt use of antitoxin when symptoms first appear. Veterinarians should have the antitoxin available for that purpose. Repeated doses of antitoxin at four to eight hour intervals may be necessary to save animals which have absorbed a large amount of toxin. Administration of two ounces of magnesium sulfate in a pint of water, followed by 1/8 to 1/4 dairy cow dose of magnesium hydroxide — activated charcoal — ruminatoric mixture commercially available for dairy cow use, may be helpful for mature goats. Caffeine or other stimulants may also be helpful.

K.   Foot Rot and Foot Abscesses

Foot Rot (Virulent Foot Rot, Contagious Foot Rot)

Foot rot is a specific disease of sheep and goats caused by a combination of two infecting organisms: **Fusobacterium necrophorum** and **Fusiformis nodosus. F. necrophorum** is a normal resident of soils of livestock farms. **F. nodosus** cannot survive in the soil more than a few days. Neither organism can cause the disease alone.

Foot rot begins as an interdigital dermatitis but it quickly spreads to the horny structures of the hoof and sole. Transmission of the disease is aided by a warm moist environment. Goats are more resistant to it than are sheep, but serious problems can occur under overcrowded wet conditions. The appearance of foot rot in a herd usually follows exposure to a new animal or return to the herd of show animals.

Symptoms — Lameness varying from very mild to severe is the obvious symptom seen. Upon examination of the interdigital space (between the toes) of the affected foot or feet, dermatitis is commonly seen. The disease progresses into the hoof, often causing slight separation of the wall at the corium (skin-hoof wall junction). Separation of the hoof from the diseased skin rapidly spreads to the sole and heels. By this time, the animals usually move around on their knees if the front feet are involved, or they remain recumbent if more than one back foot is involved. Removal of the necrotic (dead) tissue using a knife or foot shears reveals a characteristic rotten foot odor.

Eradication — Initially, every animal in the herd should have its feet trimmed. All necrotic tissue must be removed. In severe cases, this demands radical trimming down to living tissue. Feet of all animals in the herd should dipped in 10% formalin solution as they are trimmed. Trimming instruments should be disinfected in the formalin solution between animals. Animals with known lesions should be segregated. The infected feet, in addition to the formalin treatment, should be injected in the interdigital space with 300,000 units of penicillin with dihydrostreptomycin in a water emulsion base. Goats without foot lesions should be moved to clean ground or a clean pen. All animals' feet should be examined once each week and trimmed and treated if necessary. If the infected animals are removed from the infected lot or pasture for at least a week, the clean and recovered animals can be returned there, after the area has been kept free of all animals for at least that amount of time. A few chronic infections which are refractory to several treatments may require sacrifice of the animals. For several weeks following a foot rot outbreak, it may be advisable to walk the herd through a narrow trough (two inches deep and at least six feet long and eighteen inches wide) containing 10% formalin solution once each week. Care should be taken to prevent concentration of the formalin solution by excessive evaporation. Concentrations exceeding 10% may severely damage the skin. A safer, equally effective solution can be made by dissolving a pound of commercial blue stone (copper sulfate) in five gallons of water. Use of wood chips, excelsior or peat moss helps to prevent spattering of the animals' bellies and udders with foot bath solution. Needless to say, new animals brought into the herd from whatever source should have their feet trimmed and should be carefully examined for foot rot.

Foot Abscesses

These result from **F. necrophorum** infection of bruises of the skin above the hoof or the softer tissue of the heels. There is considerable swelling, inflammation and pain. Early treatment prevents involvement of the deeper tissues and joints. Intramuscular injection of 100,000 to 500,000 units of penicillin streptomycin suspension is the treatment of choice for early cases. Chronic cases may require extensive local treatment in addition to repeated antibiotic therapy.

Removal of the source of foot injury and regular trimming of hooves to prevent trauma to the softer tissue of the heels is most important for foot abscess prevention. The presence of sharp stones or sharp gravel in wet places is the usual source of injury. Filling and draining the wet places may entirely eliminate the problem in a herd where it regularly occurs.

L.   Infectious Bovine Rhinotracheitis (IBR)

Although research workers have not been able to experimentally infect goats with IBR virus and produce the disease, virus has been recovered by Dehanty at the University of Maryland in two goats. Goats appear to be highly resistant to IBR infection, but the animals in the

Maryland situation had been given a five-day treatment of corticosteroid which eliminates resistance to the IBR herpes type virus. The author has seen a single goat, in close association with a dairy herd, which was sick for nearly three months with IBR as a result of similar ill-advised treatment. The goat developed a fever temperature (104.5°F.) mucopurulent nasal and conjunctival exudate about two and one-half months after the onset of the disease in the dairy herd. There seems to be no justification for prophylactic vaccination of dairy goat herds against this disease. Where sick goats could possibly have been exposed to IBR, corticosteroids of any kind should not be administered for treatment.

M. Infectious Keratoconjunctivitis (Pink Eye)

This infectious disease of goats is commonly associated with showing the animals in hot dry weather. In cattle, the cause of pink eye, **Moraxella bovis**, has been definitely established. Little research has been done on the disease in goats, but a **Rickettsia** is believed to be the primary cause.

In spite of lack of information about the specific cause of pink eye in goats, the fundamental environmental factors which predispose animals to the infection and the basic approach to treatment must be the same for a herd of goats infected with pink eye as it is for a herd of cattle with the problem. While most references insist that the causes of the disease are species specific, this author has felt that association with sheep at shows is commonly part of the history of outbreaks.

Prevention — No vaccines are available for pink eye in any species. Bright sunlight, dust, and lack of protection from wind when hauling animals, are important predisposing factors. Hay fed to goats at home or at shows should be fed in low keyhole-type feeders and it should be free from dust. Overhead hay racks are particularly bad at shows because they release dust, etc., as the goats feed. This may irritate the eyes and thus predispose the animal to more specific infection.

Symptoms — Early symptoms of pink eye are excessive production of tears, wet streaks below the eyes, and reddened conjunctiva. Within a day or two, opacity of the cornea develops and by the end of several days, corneal ulceration may occur.

Treatment — Herd Prevention — when any evidence of pink eye is discovered at a show, all animals which were there should be treated with broad spectrum antibiotic opthalmic powder, spray or ointment, and segregated from the home herd for at least one week. Any evidence of pink eye in a herd of dairy goats is more than indication of infection in the affected animal; it is evidence of a herd problem. It has been shown in cattle, and the same observation is appropriate in goats, that many animals not showing symptoms of the disease may be resistant carriers of the infection. Flies and lice may be important vectors to spread the organism to infect or reinfect susceptible animals. Close contact may be sufficient to spread pink eye in goats. From the very beginning of an outbreak, every animal in the herd should be treated until no more cases are found. Local treatment with broad spectrum antibiotics is the best. Where indicated, large doses (100,000 IV/animal) of Vitamin A administered intramuscularly might be helpful. Animals should be kept inside in darkened quarters for at least a few days after the recovery of the latest case. It is especially important to prevent dust, pollen, etc., from getting into the eyes.

N.   Johnes' Disease — Paratuberculosis

This chronic disease of cattle, sheep and goats caused by **Mycobacterium paratuberculosis** produces a thickening of the intestinal wall which greatly interferes with absorption of water and nutrients through it. In cattle, Johnes' Disease is characterized by chronic recurring diarrhea that is progressively fatal. Cattle, goats, and sheep most often begin to show symptoms following unusual stress at parturition (calving, kidding, lambing). However, diarrhea is not a common symptom of Johnes' Disease in goats. Lesions produced by the organism are found higher in the digestive tract and there is usually no evidence of diarrhea until a few days before the animal dies. Infection apparently takes place up to seven or eight months of age in goats and sheep. Older animals may still be susceptible but resistant enough that they do not show symptoms. Typically, Johnes' Disease in goats is characterized by progressive emaciation and weakness over as much as six months' time until the animals become recumbent and die. The disease must be differentiated at post-mortem between internal parasitism and **Corynebacterium ovis** or **C. pyogenes** internal abscesses. Characteristic Johnes' Disease findings in the goat at post-mortem include marked thickening of the mucosa of the duodenum, jejunum, and ileum of the small intestine and caecum. Acid-fast **M. paratuberculosis** organisms can easily be demonstrated from acid-fast staining of affected mucosa scrapings.

Diagnosis in the Living Animal — A new fecal culture method for diagnosing the disease is the best laboratory detection tool to date. Five grams of fresh feces are collected from the rectum and sent refrigerated or frozen to an animal disease diagnostic laboratory. Most central animal disease diagnostic laboratories and all veterinary college diagnostic laboratories have this capacity. The sample is subjected to a fecal culture technique which requires ten to fourteen weeks to make a diagnosis. Positive diagnoses are reliable. Some of the negative ones are not.

Intradermal injection of Johnin or avian tuberculin has been used for detection of Johnes' carriers. It has little value. Animals showing clinical symptoms are usually negative to the test.

Johnes' Disease Control Program — Not enough is known about Johnes' Disease to recommend a fool-proof detection, control and eradication program. The disease has become more prevalent in eastern United States in the past twenty years. The new fecal testing procedure justifies sending to a laboratory fecal samples of all new mature animals before they are introduced into a herd.

Where Johnes' Disease has been diagnosed in a dairy goat herd, there is an additional good reason for isolating newborn kids from the herd until they are at least one year of age. Some of them may still come down with Johnes' Disease later as a result of intra-uterine or at-birth exposure, but the incidence of the disease can be greatly reduced by this means alone. No drugs or biologic weapons have been found to prevent or treat Johnes' Disease. There is some evidence reported by French veterinarians that supplying adequate phosphorus in the ration will prevent severe symptoms and help animals resist Johnes' infection.

The grain mixture fed to Johnes' Disease infected herds should contain at least 1% monosodium phosphate in addition to whatever calcium supplementation may be necessary. The possibility of Johnes' Disease should not be ignored when occasional older numbers of a dairy goat herd become progressively emaciated and weak. Early diagnosis of the disease may save years of frustration trying to eliminate it. In Pennsylvania, Johnes' Disease is a reportable disease subject to state regulatory action. This should be the case everywhere.

O. Leukoencephalomyelitis
(Progressive Paralysis of Kids)

This virus disease of three to sixteen week old dairy goat kids was first described by workers at Washington State University. It is believed to be caused by a virus which slowly attacks the white tissue of the brain and spinal cord. Affected kids first show slight hind leg incoordination which progresses until they have difficulty walking and they finally go down and become totally paralyzed. Some studies have indicated that the dam may act as carrier of the virus to her kids. Cases have been recognized in Washington, Oregon, Connecticut, Pennsylvania and California. The disease occurs only in goats and it is of great interest to those studying multiple sclerosis and encephalitides in humans which sometimes follow childhood viral diseases. Because transmission of the virus is not understood, affected herds should be held under quarantine. This disease can be confused with enterotoxemia. The presence of enterotoxemia or polioencephalomalcia should always be ruled out before attempts are made to establish the presence of leukoencephalomyelitis.

P.   Listeriosis — Circling Disease — Listerellosis

Listeriosis is caused by a bacterium, **Listeria monocytogenes,** a ubiquitous organism found in many animals and birds, water, feeds and soils. It is a small gram-positive rod which does not form spores, but is extremely resistant to effects of the environment.

In goats, listeriosis is primarily a wintertime disease. A common source of the disease is improperly fermented corn silage, where the pH of the silage exceeds 4.5. Outbreaks usually occur after a sudden drop in temperature in the wintertime. Up to 35% of a herd may come down with symptoms following the right combination of circumstances. However, these have not been clearly established.

There are two forms of the disease: the encephalitic form and the abortion form.

Encephalitic Form

The encephalitic form is the predominant form in goats. Early in the disease, affected animals show depression and listlessness with fever temperatures from 104° to 107°F. Within a few hours, an ear droops and the lip on the same side shows paralysis and the animal begins to circle. The course of the encephalitis is rapidly fatal. Few goats last more than 24 hours after development of circling symptoms. Circling is always in the same direction. It is not a constant symptom and some goats may show only incoordination and involuntary movement. In dairy goats, this disease is often difficult to differentiate from enterotoxemia. In enterotoxemia, however, the symptoms are primarily those of toxic depression. Circling, paralysis of a side of the face, and/or an ear and involuntary movements are not usually seen. Brain abscesses may produce similar symptoms to listeriosis, but the course of the disease is usually much slower.

Abortion Form

This form may be more common than is generally suspected. Where brucellosis-negative newly purchased does abort in late pregnancy, listeriosis should be suspected. The dam rarely shows any symptoms, but metritis and secondary septicemia occasionally occur. Listeria organisms can usually be isolated from the uterine discharges and from the milk for long periods following abortion. The organism can usually be recovered from the placenta and various internal organs of the fetus. It is important that listeriosis be ruled out when abortion occurs in a goat herd. It is another good reason for pasteurization of goat milk.

Prevention and Treatment — Corn silage is an excellent feed for milking does, providing that it is clean, has fermented properly and can be fed in a clean manner. The disease has occurred in beef cattle herds where a few goats were able to jump onto the silage bulk feeder and contaminate it with soil from their feet. Corn silage made at the proper time in the early dough-stage, packed tightly in airtight storage, fermented at least three weeks, and fed fast enough to prevent spoilage, is entirely safe feed which is an excellent succulent source of energy. It, however, is not a very practical feed to feed unless one has a large herd of milking does or a herd of cattle being fed silage at the same time.

Animals which develop true encephalitic symptoms rarely live, but animals given massive doses of penicillin early during the incubation stage (when they are listless and show high fever) may respond to treatment. When a clearly recognizable case of circling disease appears in a herd, all animals should be carefully checked for early symptoms (high temperature and listlessness) and given at least 1,000,000 units of penicillin intramuscularly daily for three days. Attention should be directed to feeding sanitation. The commonest cause observed by the author results from animals (usually young kids) with muddy feet getting into hay feeders. When listeriosis is suspected, the affected animal should be submitted to a veterinary diagnostic laboratory for positive diagnosis of the disease via bacteriological culture. Positive diagnosis immediately rules out other problems which may have similar symptoms (poisonings, enterotoxemia, brain abscesses). Sometimes it is difficult to establish diagnosis in aborted fetuses but the great value of diagnosis is certainly worth the effort. No biologics are available for prevention of listeriosis.

Q. Malignant Edema and Blackleg

Malignant edema is caused by **Clostridium hemolyticum,** a spore-forming soil organism which causes gas gangrene when it contaminates wounds. It is commonly found in soils of livestock farms, but it should not be of concern on a farm until it causes disease there.

It is far less common than is blackleg (caused by **Clostridium chaveii**). Goats appear to be very resistant to both. In the author's practice in Virginia where blackleg was prevalent and malignant edema not at all rare, neither blackleg nor malignant edema were observed in goats which occupied farms where both diseases were observed in other animals. Unless either disease has been diagnosed in goats in a particular area, bacterin vaccination available against them does not appear to be justified. Certainly, another Clostridial disease, tetanus, caused by **Clostridium tetani,** is more important than malignant edema.

Malignant edema affects more species of animals. Cattle, horses, sheep, goats, swine and man are susceptible. Blackleg usually appears as a rapidly fatal, more localized gangrene of a group of muscles with a characteristic black appearance and a peculiar sweetish necrotic odor. It rarely affects goats and swine, and it never affects horses and man.

Prevention — Where either disease can be established as a cause of death in dairy goats, commercial bacterin-toxoids are available for prophylaxis. They are available for these and several other Clostridial species (**novii** and **sordelli**) found in cattle and lamb feed lot problems.

Good surgical technique with minimal wound contamination, antibiotic treatment and good drainage minimize the rather small danger of these two Clostridial diseases.

R. Mastitis

Mastitis is inflammation of the mammary gland. It is characterized by swelling, heat, sensitivity or pain, and congestion of the tissue. In addition, abnormal milk is characteristic of mastitis.

It is reasonable to assume that one cannot expect to have healthy udders and good milk from an unhealthy herd of goats. Mastitis prevention is even more important for dairy goat herds than it is for dairy cow herds. The milk from dairy goat herds is often used without pasteurization and it is often consumed by infants and chronically ill people. Several of the organisms involved in mastitis of goats (**Staphylococci, Corynebacter, E. coli** etc.) may also cause disease in susceptible humans; therefore, those who own and milk dairy goat herds should be greatly concerned about prevention and control of mastitis.

This is justified from an economic standpoint, because it is well known that subclinical mastitis infection can reduce production by as much as 25%. But it is even more important for the dairy goat herdsman to offer for sale good milk from healthy udders.

Causes

Many bacteriologists simplify mastitis by listing the organisms found in either acute clinical cases (when all of the symptoms above are obvious) and from subclinical cases where the only findings are the presence of pathogenic bacteria and excessive somatic cells, leukocytes or white blood cells and other tissue cells in the milk.

Two primary factors in herd mastitis problems must be recognized: the resistance of the animals to infection, and the virulence or ability of the organisms involved to cause disease. The most important single stressor which lowers resistance to mastitis infection is injury to the udder and teats. The slightest injury of the end of the teat at the external orifice of the teat canal predisposes the animal to acute mastitis attack.

Organisms Involved in Dairy Goat Mastitis

Streptococci — The commonest pathogen involved in dairy cow mastitis is **Streptococcus agalactiae.** This also occurs in dairy goats but it is not nearly so widespread and common, and it is apparently not as easily spread. **Streptococcus uberis** and **S. dysgalacticae** are environmental streptococci that are encountered in bacteriological culture of goat milk samples, but they are rarely involved in clinical cases. Clinical streptococcus mastitis cases are characterized by swelling and tenderness of the udder. Small white flakes and watery milk are the usual secretions found. The animal usually has a temperature of 104°-105°F. at the beginning of an acute clinical attack. Repeat attacks result in destruction of milk-producing tissue and its replacement by fibrous (scar) tissue.

Staphylococci — Hemolytic staphylococci are involved in most cases of acute gangrenous mastitis. The onset and course of the disease is rapid. The animal shows severe depression, swelling and pain in the affected gland and a yellow clotty secretion. Rapid progression in the affected gland to development of a gangrenous area is the usual situation. These cases are almost always the result of severe injury to the udder.

Non-hemolytic staphylococci — Organisms of this class are almost universally ignored by dairy cow mastitis laboratories. This group of organisms causes an insidious progressive mastitis in dairy goats and is of major importance in some herds. Early cases may show only a slight thickness and tenderness at the base of the gland near its rear attachment to the body wall. The animal may show reluctance to let down her milk. The milk usually shows no gross abnormality but a Direct-Somatic Cell Count (done in a dairy laboratory or animal disease laboratory) or the California Mastitis Test (see California Mastitis Test in this chapter) reveals abnormally high cell content of the milk. The greatest difficulty with this form of mastitis is the difficulty of detection. Because the course is rather slow and insidious, it is often not recognized until the affected gland has been ruined.

Coliform Mastitis — Two organisms involved in these cases are common environmental contaminants. They most commonly cause severe septic (toxic) mastitis early in lactation. Teat end injury and routine use of mastitis dry treatment appear to influence the number of cases of coliform mastitis. Typically, in **Klebsiella** mastitis of dairy goats, there is an extremely severe reaction. The affected gland becomes very hot and congested and only a very small amount of clear yellow fluid may be removable. The doe's temperature may be as high as 108°F. This organism releases endotoxins which may kill the animal even when antibiotic treatment effectively destroys the organism. Few early lactation does survive **Klebsiella** mastitis and they do it only after long periods of nursing care. When animals do survive, no effect of the attack is evident in the mammary tissue, or in production from the previously affected gland, during the following lactation. **Klebsiella** organisms grow in astronomical numbers in fresh sawdust used as bedding. The fresh sawdust right from the sawmill is usually contaminated with **Klebsiellae**. These rapidly increase in numbers when the sawdust is used as bedding. In Pennsylvania, new oak sawdust has been the type of bedding most commonly involved in dairy cow **Klebsiella** mastitis problems. It is not found in sawdust of kiln-dried wood, or planing mill shavings.

The other organism, **E. coli,** is found in the lower intestinal tract and the environment of all animals, including man. It commonly causes mastitis in cows and goats when teat ends are injured and the animals are forced to lie down in filthy wet bedding or when they walk through mud or water contaminated with manure.

E. Coli cases show severe depression from the onset, severe cold swelling of the affected gland, a small amount of dark or bloody discharge with a characteristic dead tissue odor. Lowered blood calcium with milk fever symptoms are characteristic of this form of mastitis. Prognosis is poor. Surgical removal of the affected gland may be the most logical approach to treatment.

Corynebacter Mastitis — Mastitis involving **Corynebacterium Pyogenes** and occasionally **C. ovis** is not rare in dairy goat herds where these infections are otherwise manifested. **C. pyogenes** commonly causes thickened milk secretion and the development of multiple abscesses within the udder. **C. ovis** usually produces hard encapsulated abscesses of the supramammary lymph glands (behind and above the mammary glands). Milk from udders with **C. ovis** abscesses is markedly reduced in volume and watery. Neither one of these infections justifies attempts at treatment. Affected animals should be culled from the herd.

Management for Mastitis Prevention

Facilities — It is most important that buildings and facilities for dairy goats contain nothing that will injure udders. Dairy goats naturally like to climb onto anything, crawl over, under or through fences. Any building, fencing, brush clearing or pasture development should be carefully considered as to its effect on udders. Damage to teat ends is especially important. High door sills, grain, browse, or pasture stubble (briars, thorns, etc.) can cause small-to-severe injury to teat ends and be responsible for serious mastitis outbreaks.

Fighting — Udder injuries sustained as a result of the constant re-establishment of the "peck order" are a common source of mastitis. Crowding at feeders leaves animals subject to attack from behind. Using keyhole feeders to prevent butting injury is well worth the effort for animals fed outside of their own tie stalls.

Management of the Freshening Doe's Udder

Careful management of the freshening doe to minimize udder injury and damage to the suspensory ligaments of the udder greatly affects future susceptibility to injury and the circulation of blood and fluids through the milking gland (see **Care of the Dry and Kidding Doe**). This includes proper care at drying off the udder, too.

Milking Injury — This is undoubtedly the underlying cause of most dairy goat herd mastitis problems. In order to understand all of the implications involved here, the herd owner must understand the mechanism and importance of milk let-down and the mechanism and sources of injury for both hand milking and machine milking.

Milk Let-down — Receptor nerves in the udder floor, teats, the ears, eyes and nose carry stimuli to the hypothalamus nerve center in the base of the brain. This activates the pituitary gland (the master hormone gland of the body) to produce oxytocin. Oxytocin is absorbed into the blood stream and carried to the capillaries surrounding the microscopic milk-producing sacs of the mammary gland (alveoli). Small neuromuscular fibers surrounding the alveoli contract on exposure to oxytocin, and this contraction, multiplied millions of times in similar neuromuscular fibers in the remainder of the gland forces milk into the collecting ducts and teat cistern under pressure. This lasts no more than six minutes in the average mammary gland. It is a conditioned reflex. Therefore, it must be carefully developed and continually nurtured to produce good strong milk let-down for relatively complete evacuation of the gland and rapid milking.

However, there is a compensatory mechanism which effectively stops or prevents milk let-down. When does are frightened, angry or upset in any way, the same receptors carry stimuli which cause secretion of adrenalin by the adrenal glands. Adrenalin paralyzes the neuromuscular fibers of the mammary gland alveoli so that they relax and this shuts off milk let-down immediately. Other actions of adrenalin increase aereation of the lungs, increase blood supply to the muscles, etc., and prepare the animal to react to the unfavorable or dangerous stimuli.

From the above, it is extremely important that first freshening does be taught from the beginning to like and enjoy every aspect of milking. Sight alone of the good milker at milking time will cause milk let-down in many does. The atmosphere for milking must be calm and pleasant for the milking does, otherwise milk let-down, milk production, and udder health will be affected. The good dairy herdsman recognizes the importance of good milk let-down, and concentrates on learning the fine art of perfecting it in his herd. Milk let-down is aided tremendously by preparation of the udder for milking. So is the quality of the milk produced.

Preparation of the Udder for Milking — First of all, long hairs of the udder should be clipped off. This will improve cleanability of the udder skin and prevent hair-pulling discomfort during udder preparation and milking. It is impossible to produce clean milk from goats which have not had their udders and flanks clipped.

The udder should be thoroughly washed with a piece of cotton towel or paper towel immersed in warm sanitizer or sanitizer detergent solution. Washing should include massaging and care to thoroughly clean the teat ends. This should be followed by thorough drying of the udder and teats and the milker's hands before milking begins. From one half to one minute should elapse between the beginning of udder preparation and the beginning of milking.

Hand Milking — Full hand milking should be done as gently as possible and as quickly as possible. Udder washes which cause chapping and hardening of the teat skin and the milker's hands hinder rather than help good milking. The author's preference for udder preparation would be the use of a gentle detergent widely used for hand dish-washing rather than a dessicating iodophor-phosphoric acid or chlorine sanitizer detergent usually used for dairy cows. Anything which in any way damages the ends of the teats or irritates the udder skin and interferes with good milking is taboo for milking goats. Hand milking should never exceed five minutes per goat, and it should be reasonable and not excessive. After the udder is milked, one should be able to go back to the doe immediately and milk at least one full stream out of each teat. Trying to milk them "bone dry" is responsible for much of the injury which occurs with hand or machine milking.

Machine Milking — It is not the author's intention to write a long discussion about the mechanics and operation of milking systems. A basic understanding of the parts of a milking system and how they work is essential. Much good information on machine milking systems and how to operate them is available from all manufacturers of dairy cow milking systems, from the National Mastitis Council, and from state agricultural extension publications. The milking machine pump removes air out of the system and produces rarified air (vacuum) within it. Manufacturers and state university extension bulletins specify pump capacities necessary for the types of systems used. A sanitary trap is placed next to the pump to prevent moisture or milk from getting into the pump. It also furnishes a supply of rarified air which is available for sudden needs during operation. The vacuum regulator is placed in the milk line between the sanitary trap and the first stall cock to keep the vacuum level for milking constant at all times. This is an extremely important component of the milking system. It should be kept clean and free from dust so that it responds quickly and smoothly to vacuum changes. Close by the regulator should be a vacuum gauge which will show at a glance that vacuum levels remain constant with no variation during the entire milking process.

Vacuum Lines — These should be 1¼ to 1½ inches in diameter for the smallest of systems. **The pulsator** is a device which alternately and regularly allows the pump to evacuate the air in the space between the inflation and the teat cup to dilate the inflation and the teat. This is the "milking" phase. This is followed by the "rest" phase which allows atmospheric air to move into the space between the teat cup and inflation, collapsing the inflation, massaging the teat (to remove the effect of the milking phase or blood circulation in the teat tissue) and allowing the teat to refill with milk.

A relatively constant level of vacuum should exist in the teat cups, the milker claw (if there is one), the milking receptacle and the milk lines. The same basic criteria essential for the correct operation of the older bucket milkers are necessary for the operation of the most modern sophisticated milking systems. Most dairy goat herds in the United States are milked with simple bucket systems, but any of the pipeline systems can be adapted for them. Two of the teat cups are removed and two pulsator ports blocked, so that the machine has a single action (milks both teats at once) pulsator or a double action (milks one side at a time) pulsator.

Vacuum Levels for Milking Goats — Goats can be milked out very well using two to three inches lower vacuum level than is generally required for milking cows. Pulsation rate generally used for milking goats is 55 pulsations per minute.

Applying and Removing a Milker Unit — When udder preparation and milk let-down has occurred, two full hand squirts of milk should be milked into a strip cup or strip plate and examined for abnormality under good light. The teat cups are then applied, taking care that they do not pick up extraneous material on the floor or the goat's belly. The machine is adjusted, if possible, so that teat cups pull downward and do not move upward to the base of the teats. Most goats will milk out quickly in less than four minutes so the operator should stay in attendance and pull down gently on the teat cups toward the completion of milking. Cessation of milk flow can easily be determined by feeling the teat cistern or the inflation tubes. Machine stripping should be minimal and hardly be necessary if the teat cups are not allowed to "crawl" upward toward the udder. It is especially important that goats should not be overmilked. The milking machine is capable of producing severe teat-end damage and internal mammary tissue damage if teat cups are allowed to remain on the teats after milk flow ceases.

How to Check Milking Machine Performance — A simple milking system tester can be made using a vacuum gauge, a gate valve, a short piece of milker hose, and a 3/8 inch tee as illustrated. If the milking system has a number of milking locations, cleanliness and patency of the vacuum lines should be tested at regular (monthly) intervals. Put the tester on the stall cock nearest the pump. Start the vacuum pump. Open the gate valve on the tester so that the vacuum level on the tester gauge drops at least five inches. Then move away from the pump to each stall cock and attach the tester **without changing the gate valve adjustment.** Lower vacuum found at any location shows that there is an obstruction to air flow somewhere between that location and the last normal reading. This might also be in the stall cock itself.

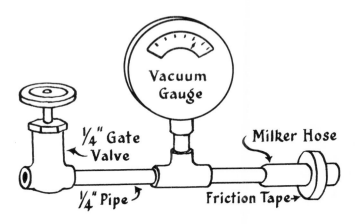

THE MILKING MACHINE TESTER

This simple gadget can be used in several different ways to check vacuum lines, vacuum output, and the milker units themselves. A short length of milker hose, a standard milking-system vacuum gauge, and a ¼" gate valve are attached, as illustrated, to a TEE made of ¼" pipe. Wrap enough friction tape around the milker hose at one end to make it fit snugly into the teat cup of the milker (this is usually about 1-½" in overall diameter).

Testing the Pulsator — Attach the teat cup end of the pulsator tube (between the teat cup shell and the pulsator) to the tester. Observation of the gauge should show regular metronome-like operation with alternation between the desired milking vacuum level and zero inches of vacuum. Leaking pulsators and sticking defective pulsators will readily be revealed by this simple test.

Checking the Milking Vacuum in the Teat Cup — While milking an animal, remove one teat cup and insert the tester in it. Vacuum fluctuation of more than one-half inch in the teat cup is not desirable. For pipeline milking systems, this test reveals lack of capacity or other flaws obstructing milk and air flow.

How to Check Herds for Mastitis

Bulk Sample Tests — If you sell milk to a market where regular somatic cell tests are performed, you will be given (or you should ask for it if you don't receive it) a regular monthly report of the somatic cell count of the milk sample taken from your bulk tank. This is usually reported as a DMSCC (Direct Microscopic Somatic Cell Count). For healthy dairy goat herds, DMSCC should be less than 500,000. The count may be expressed as WMT (Wisconsin Mastitis Test). For healthy dairy goat herds, the WMT should be under 17. In a few states, the somatic cell count may be reported as MWT (Modified Whiteside Test). For healthy dairy goat herds, this test should not exceed **Trace** classification.

A Good Barn Test for Udder Health

The **California Mastitis Test** is a simple test which can be run using a clean white china saucer or a CMT test paddle and the CMT reagent which is available from veterinarians and farm supply sources everywhere.

Before taking a sample from your bulk milk tank or from individual cans of milk, agitate by stirring gently for at least a minute. Take a teaspoonful of the stirred milk with a similar amount of the reagent and mix it with a gently rotating motion for fifteen seconds. A light lavender solution with no suggestion of flocculence is negative (normal) milk.

Trace reactions show a slight thickening and a tendency to stick to the saucer. A Number One (CMT 1) reaction shows a definite tendency to jell. A Number Two (CMT 2) reaction shows marked thickening and cohesion of the mass. A Number Three (CMT 3) reaction actually peaks in the center and it stays together as a definite mass. CMT reactions for healthy goat herds' bulk milk should never exceed a CMT trace reaction.

The CMT can be a useful tool for regular monthly surveillance of udder health and for determining whether or not to treat does for mastitis when they are dried off. Some goat dairymen check individual udder halves at two-week or monthly intervals and keep a record of reactions noted. This may not be necessary, but it may be especially valuable in herds where non-hemolytic staphylococci infection exists. In that situation, weekly CMTs of all milking glands may be worthwhile. The CMT is extremely valuable for checking animals at least a month before turning them dry to determine whether or not mastitis dry treatment should be used. Routine treatment of all udders when they are turned dry is expensive and it may actually be undesirable. Some evidence indicates that routine dry treatment increases susceptibility of dairy cow udders to coliform types of mastitis at, or shortly after, freshening.

The CMT is a valuable tool to use to check an udder which might have had mastitis attack or injury during the current lactation, to determine whether or not to use dry treatment.

Mastitis Dry Treatment

Currently, slowly soluble or slowly available penicillin dry treatment formulations are highly effective for removal of the common mastitis pathogens from udders. Correctly used where indicated, and in a sanitary manner, they are the best new development in mastitis elimination in recent years. It is imperative that they are used correctly.

How to Treat Dry Udders — It is important that very careful sanitary procedure be used for infusing dry teats. Many environmental organisms (yeasts, molds, non-ag streptococci) can be introduced using faulty technique. These are resistant to penicillin, or they may actually grow better in the presence of penicillin, making the dry treatment harmful rather than helpful.

After the doe has been dried off four or five days, milk out all of the coagulated milk in her udder. Then wash the udder carefully with warm water and soap. Be especially careful to get the teat ends clean. Dry the udder, teats, and your hands with a clean towel. Using 70% alcohol and a gauze pad or cotton swab, grasp the teat with one hand and thoroughly scrub the teat end with the alcohol pad. Wipe the infusion canula of the mastitis preparation with another alcohol pad and inject one quarter of the usual dairy cow dose into each half of the dry doe's udder. Gentle massage for several minutes may facilitate penetration of the infused material throughout the gland. Check the udder for several days after treatment for signs of inflammation. If these occur, strip out the mastitis treatment and treat again.

Teat Dipping

Dipping teats in a germicidal solution immediately after milking has been demonstrated to prevent the spread of mastitis streptococci and staphylococci in dairy cattle herds. However, the teat dips generally used for dairy cows (iodophor, chorine, and chlorhexidine solutions) are much too dessicating and irritant for the teats of dairy goats. The author has found only two germicidal dips that will do the job without irritating the teat skin. They are TD-34 (manufactured by Babson Bros. and available from Surge dealers) and Butter T-Dip (manufactured by Schuyler Research Associates and sold by New Holland Supply Co., Lancaster, PA). Both of these products are effective germicides and they keep the teat skin and the milker's hands in excellent condition.

Mastitis Treatment

The best way to treat mastitis is to evacuate the gland as much as possible before infusing anything into it. Gentle massage using warm water and a towel and repeated effort to hand milk will successfully remove a large amount of secretion.

It is better to withhold any infusion of mastitis antibiotic until the entire udder has been thoroughly milked out, even if it requires a half dozen attempts at two-hour intervals. If inflammation and pain prevent milking out the udder on the first attempt, systemic treatment, that is, intravenous or intramuscular injection of antibiotic, is indicated. The use of small repeated intramuscular doses of oxytocin is often quite helpful for evacuating milk from an inflamed gland. Infusion of antibiotics directly into the gland via the teat canal should be done in the same manner as outlined under **How to Treat Dry Udders.**

What Antibiotics to Use — For streptococci or staphylococci mastitis, no antibiotics available offer more promise for treatment than simple penicillin-streptomycin formulations. Infuse at least 10,000 units of penicillin per udder half for not less than two consecutive milkings in lactating udders. Corynebacter and coliform mastitis are usually treated systematically and by infusion with broad spectrum antibiotics (tetracycline, tylosin, erythromycin, neomycin, etc.).

Good nursing, giving special attention to see that the sick animal is eating and drinking and is not bullied by other aggressive animals in the herd is a most important part of treatment.

Laboratory Culture of Milk Samples for Mastitis Detection — This procedure is the best time-honored way of detecting the kinds of organisms present in the udders of the herd, and for determining the most useful antibiotics to use to treat mastitis. Samples should be collected in sterile milk sample bottles from clean alcohol swabbed teats just before milking and carried to a mastitis laboratory under refrigeration immediately. Where high somatic cell counts are encountered, this is the best way to determine whether or not a specific infectious organism is involved and what to use to eliminate it after the basic source of stress or injury is eliminated.

How to Go About Correction of Abnormal Milk Problem Herds

Where monthly milk market reports, laboratory culture, clinical cases, or CMT testing indicate that the herd is suffering from mastitis infection, it is very important that efforts to eliminate the problem be kept in proper perspective. Obviously, indiscriminate or specific treatment of udders cannot be justified unless the underlying sources of stress or injury are first found and eliminated.

For example, it will do little good to treat infected quarters if a few animals with horns or scurs are brutally injuring udders every day. No antibiotics can eliminate the need to remove sources of injury from milking does. Milking equipment (if machine milking is used), milking technique and milking sanitation should be thoroughly examined and deficiencies corrected before any treatment program is begun. Clean environment, clean udders, good milking technique and prevention of injury are infinitely more important than medication for prevention of mastitis.

Those who produce raw goat milk for infants or chronically ill patients should be very careful to ensure that the product they sell comes only from healthy udders.

S.   Pneumonia

In dairy goat herds, the primary cause of pneumonia in both summer and wintertime is stress from bad ventilation. In summertime, particularly at shows or in transit to shows, overcrowding and overheating and dust often furnish sufficient respiratory stress for one of the **Pasteurella** or **Hemophilus** species of organisms to set up pneumonia with typical "shipping fever" septicemia. In eastern and central United States, many dairy goats are confined in closed loose housing. It is impossible to prevent recurrent wintertime outbreaks of pneumonia where attempt is made under those conditions to keep inside temperatures above outside temperatures. In any situation where condensation occurs on windows, walls, or bedding, conditions are ideal for pneumonia. (See **Housing**.)

In the author's experience, there is only one situation more likely to produce pneumonia than the above situation; that is hauling goats in an uncovered truck in cold wet weather. Where goats are assembled for show in summertime, protection from the hot sun should be provided and pens should have cross ventilation to the floor. Aisles and alleyways between pens should be sprinkled with water to keep down the dust.

Treatment — The tetracyclines, the long acting sulfonamides, or Tylosin are the author's choice for treatment. Either antibiotic should be given in adequate dosage intravenously or intramuscularly to maintain adequate blood levels for not less than four days. Good nursing is especially important for dairy goats with pneumonia.

Effort should be made to keep the animal eating and drinking and protected from harrassment by other members of the herd. Treatment should be continued as long as respiratory sounds are detected, and repeated for another course of four days, if they reappear. Chronic lobular pneumonia is a frequent sequel to inadequate treatment.

Verminous pneumonia frequently complicates lungworm infection in animals under one year old and newly exposed older animals. Elimination of the lungworms using levamisole (Tramisol-American Cyanamid) is necessary before secondary treatment is begun. Mortality is quite high when severe lungworm infection is complicated by pneumonia. (See **Lungworm Control**.)

T.   Pox

This virus disease of goats is spread by contact by external parasites, or via the milker's hands. Lesions are smaller than those of cow pox and swine pox and they are usually confined to the bare skin areas of the body. Male kids and milking does are most commonly affected. Lesions appear from five to ten days after infection. Animals first show a mild transient fever up to 103.5°F. Few signs other than the small grayish vesicles are noted. These rupture, and typical pox scabs remain. Animals showing lesions should be milked last. Do not wash udders with detergents or disinfectants. Use carbolized vaseline or chlorhexidine ointment on the lesions and wipe off the ointment from the teats with clean paper tissues or towels before milking. Reapply ointment after milking. Kids should not be allowed to nurse does showing lesions. If effort is made to treat the lesions with the viricidal ointment, this usually effectively stops the spread of pox and the problem will disappear in a short time.

U. Toxoplasmosis

Toxoplasmosis in the goat has the same source as the disease in other animals, **Toxoplasma gondii**, isosporal coccidia of cats. The disease has widespread distribution in animal industry, and it is a problem of increasing human health significance.

In sheep, some research work has been done which can be used as reference until investigation in goats corroborates or refutes it. Free-living stages of the cat coccidium are ingested and they migrate throughout the body setting up small foci of necrotic infection. When these occur in the central nervous system, they produce incoordination and other symptoms of encephalomyelitis. Infection during late pregnancy results in placentitis and metritis with abortion or birth of weak or stupid kids.

Toxoplasmosis is diagnosed in the laboratory using the complement-fixation test of blood serum and microscopic study of placental smears. Prevention is accomplished by keeping cats and cat feces from contaminating goat feed. Recommended treatment for positive animals is sulfadiazine or sulfamethazine. (See **Coccidiosis — Internal Parasites.**)

V. Traumatic Testiculitis —(Traumatic Epididymitis)

Traumatic testiculitis is one of the most important causes of infertility in male goats. Two important sources of injury are physical facilities (feeders, partitions, fences) and severe blows from behind by other bucks. Most of the injuries occur before bucks are one year old. The butting injuries often occur when buck kids are penned together and they share common hay feeders or grain troughs. The usual lesion found is a hard lobular swelling at the proximal end of the testis or in the body or tail of the epididymis.

Awareness of the problem is the best way to prevent it. When an aggressive buck kid begins to fight his pen mates, he should be removed before serious damage is inflicted. The testicles of all young bucks should be carefully examined at purchase for evidence of injury. In sheep, semen from the damaged testis is not only inferior but it causes deterioration of the semen from the normal testis. Unilateral castration or vasectomy has been used to improve the semen quality in that species. It undoubtedly would be of value for buck goats.

Ref: Pulsford, Aust. Vet. J. 43 (3): 99-101, 1967.

W. Neoplasia In Goats

By James Wadsworth, V.M.D., M.S.
Department of Animal Pathology
University of Vermont, Burlington

Since the dawn of civilization, man and beast alike have been victims of tumors. A tumor is a neoplasm (neo = new + plasm = formation). It is an abnormal parasitic mass of tissue. Tumors grow at the expense of the host's tissues as autonomous, lawless growths. As such, they are immune to the restraints and controls characteristic of normal tissues. Tumors are functionless and many survive on a minimum blood supply.

Neoplasms are classified as benign (harmless) or malignant (deadly). Benign tumors essentially occupy space, but can cause complications, such as pressure, strangulation or occlusion of organs, hormonal imbalances, and infection.[1] Malignant tumors invade tissues. They infiltrate and destroy tissue locally and elsewhere in the body by spreading and forming new tumors. The term "cancer" today refers to any type of malignant tumor.

Tumors can be effectively classified on a histological basis. The following classification has been compiled from several texts.

Classification Of Tumors[2]	Benign	Malignant
Tumors of Connective Tissues	fibroma lipoma myxoma chondroma osteoma	fibrosarcoma liposarcoma myxosarcoma chondrosarcoma osteosarcoma
Tumors of Muscle	leiomyoma no benign form	leiomyosarcoma rhabdomyosarcoma
Tumors of Endothelium	hemangioma lymphangioma meningioma	hemangiosarcoma
Tumors of Hematopoietic & Reticuloendothelial System	lymphoma no benign form	lymphosarcoma myeloma
Tumors of Pigment Cells	melanoma	malignant melanoma

Tumors of Nervous System	neurocytoma neuroma glioma	neuroblastoma neurosarcoma gliosarcoma
Tumors of Epithelium	papilloma adenoma	epidermoid carcinoma adenocarcinoma

Benign and malignant tumors possess specific differential features useful in the diagnosis of neoplasia, as follows:

Benign Tumor	Malignant Tumor
Slow growing	Rapid growing
Greater cellular differentiation	Anaplasia evident
Usually encapsulated	Usually invasive
Mitotic figures rare or absent	Abundant mitoses
Expand and encroach adjacent tissue	Infiltate and invade
Never metastasize	Spread via lymph and blood
Tend to be less vascular	Often vascular and necrotic
Inclined to be nodular or spheroid	Tend to be amorphic
Highly variable in color	Reddish if vascular; yellow if necrotic
Often firm with abundant stroma	Usually soft and friable
Not fatal, except due to location	Fatal, if untreated
Systemic changes not common	May cause anemia, loss of weight, cachexia, etc.

The goat is not especially prone to tumors. yet, almost a half century ago, skin cancer was reported in the Angora goat.[5] These malignant skin lesions affected the perineum of the females for the most part, but also occurred on the ears, at the base of the horns, and on other areas of the epidermis. Native and Boer goats were generally free of these lesions, even when kept in the same flock. Apparently, this tumor-type existed since the early days of the introduction of the angora goat into South Africa. Female goats were most often affected, castrated males rarely, and entire males never. The incidence of skin cancer was estimated as up to 1% in adult or aged goats. These pedunculated tumors found on the side of the vulva or under the tail were moist, pink, grey or black masses. Many were complicated by secondary bacterial infection, blowfly strike, gangrene, and hemorrhages. Of sixteen examined histologically, three were prickle-cell carcinomas, eight basal cell carcinomas and the rest were combined forms. Many contained melanin. No evidence of spread by contact or coitus was found. It was noted, in passing, that the angora goat is highly refractory to the carcinogenic action of coal tar.

Angora goats from South Africa imported to Sudan likewise presented skin cancer. In one herd of 42 animals, six cases were noted in one year.[4]

One report exists in the literature of a thymoma in a goat.[5]

Skin warts or papillomata are known to affect Saanen milch goats.[6] This type of tumor occurred in a herd of 200 Saanen goats. The warts were found mainly on milking goats, not on dry animals. No lesions were noted on the udders or teats, but affected the head, neck, shoulders, and forelegs above the knees. The number of warts per animal varied from one to twelve. No warts were seen on the hands of the caretakers or attendants, and there was no contact with cattle. A probable viral origin was suggested. The lesions consisted of papillary fibrous projections covered with cornified epithelium.

On the other hand, cutaneous papillomata do occur on the udder and teats of milking goats.[7] In a herd of 200 Saanen goats, 50 out of 150 lactating animals showed cutaneous papillomatosis. Only white animals were affected. The lesions were limited to the skin of the udder and teats, interfering with milking. Of five animals from which biopsy material was examined, three showed papillomas and two skin carcinoma. Two goats were autopsied. One revealed three squamous cell carcinomas without lymph nodal metastasis; the other showed one papilloma and two carcinomas with one metastasis in the supramammary lymph node. A viral origin seemed to be indicated.

A lymphosarcoma of the thymus has been reported in a five year old female goat as well as a reticulosarcoma of the liver in a four year old individual.[8] A prominent English pathologist has also reported lymphosarcoma in goats.[9]

It is apparent that the male goat is quite susceptible to tumors of the adrenal gland. One study has shown that 169 out of 770 adrenals from castrated male goats had cortical adenomata, while 244 glands from male goats were free of neoplasia.[10] Furthermore, only two of 273 glands from females were involved. Unfortunately, goats are not often subject to detailed necropsy studies. Since castration may incite pituitary tumors, it would have been interesting to examine the pituitaries of these male goats.

Under the United States Department of Agriculture, the slaughter of meat-producing animals provides valuable data on disease, including neoplasia. During an eight-year survey, 800,000 goats were slaughtered, of which only 70 were affected with tumors.[11]

Tumors of the nervous system in animals are not common. However, a neuro-ectodermal tumor and a spongioblastoma have been reported in the goat.[12]

A giant cell sarcoma was reported in a goat, which involved the maxillary sinus.[13] Also, the pigmented tumor, the melanoma, occurs in goats.[14]

In a necropsy series of 2500 goats, 500 adrenal cortical adenomata were found in 316 goats, of which 314 were castrated males and two females.[15] This indicated over 12% of the goats had tumors in one or both adrenal glands.

Two tumor-types have been reported in the goat from observers in India. One was a bile duct carcinoma with metastasis to the lungs.[16] The other was a cholangio-cellular carcinoma with pulmonary metastasis.[17]

Finally, primary pulmonary mucoepidermoid tumors have been reported in the goat.[18]

There is a serious deficiency of pertinent data on environmental causations of cancers in animals. Yet, we know that cancers occur universally in all animals, regardless of their natural habitat. Therefore, when we consider the phenomenon of environmental carcinogenesis, we may correctly conclude that the goat, like other mammals, is indeed susceptible to the adverse effects of environmental carcinogens.

Abstracts of Other Relevant Tumor References

Tumors in Dairy Goats — Both benign and malignant neoplasms are rare in goats. A squamous-celled low grade carcinoma was found in ten of 1600 animals completely necropsied at the Army Chemical Center, none of which were diagnosed clinically. All occurred in the diaphragmatic lobes of the lungs. There were no signs of malignancy or metastasis in any of them. A few malignant lymphosarcomas have been reported and osterosarcoma in one animal was reported in an English study. *(E. Cotchin, Vet. Rec. 72 (40) 816-822, 1960)*

Neoplasms of Goats and Sheep — Only eleven neoplasms in goats and three in sheep were observed out of 1385 neoplasms examined in animal disease diagnostic laboratory in India. Incidence of neoplasms in goats was only 0.8% of those encountered in domestic animals. Ten of the eleven cases were cutaneous neoplasms, five of epithelial origin, two of connective tissue origin and three melanomas. *(S. Damodaran and K. Palathasaratny, Ind. Vet. J.)*

References:

1 Moulton, J.E.: *Tumors in Domestic Animals, University of California Press, Berkeley, 1961.*

2 Wadsworth, J.R. and Bolton, W.D.: *Some Clinico Pathologic Considerations in Veterinary Oncology. J.A.V.M.A. 128: 233, 1956.*

3 Thomas, A.D.: *Skin Cancer of the Angora Goat in South Africa. 15th Rep. Dir. Vet. Serv. S. Afr. 659, 1929.*

4 Curasson, G.: *Le cancer cutané de la chèvre Angora. Bull. Acad. Vet. Fr. 6: 346, 1933.*

5 Jackson, C.: *The incidence and pathology of tumors of domesticated animals in South Africa. A study of the Onderstepoort collection of neoplasms with special reference to their histopathology. Onderstepoort Jr. Vet. Sci. 6: 3, 1936.*

6 Davis, C.L. and Kemper, H.E.: *Common Warts (papillomata) in Goats. J. Amer. Vet. Med. Assoc. 88: 175, 1936.*

7 Moulton, J.E.: *Cutaneous Papillomas on the Udders of Milk Goats. N. Amer. Vet. 35: 29, 1954.*

8 Honeker: *Geschwulste bei Ziegen. Dtsch. tierarztl. Wschr. 61: 427, 1954.*

9   Cotchin, E.: Neoplasms of the Domesticated Animals. Review Series No. 4 of the Commonwealth Bureau of Animal Health, 1956. (Farnham Royal Bucks, England)

10 Richter, W.R.: Adrenal Cortical Adenomata in the Goat. Amer. J. Vet. Res. 19: 895, 1958.

11 Brandly, P.J. and Migaki, G.: Types of tumors found by federal meat inspectors in an eight-year survey. Epizootiology of cancer in animals. Annals of the N.Y. Academy of Science 108: 872, 1963.

12 Luginbuhl, H.: Comparative Aspects of Tumors of the Nervous System. Epizootiology of cancer in animals. Annals of the N.Y. Academy of Science 108: 702, 1963.

13 Andreev, A.: Giant-cell Sarcoma of the Maxillary Sinus in a Goat. Vet. Sbir. Suf. 63: 22, 1966.

14 Mustafa, I.E. Cerna, J. and Cerny, L: Melanoma in Goats. Sudan Med. J. 4: 113, 1966.

15 Altman, N.H., Street, C.W. and Terner, J.Y.: Castration and Its Relationship to Tumors of the Adrenal Gland in the Goat. Ame. J. Vet. Res. 30: 583, 1969.

16 Chauham, H.V.S. and Singh, C.M.: Bile duct carcinoma in a goat, with metastasis in the lungs. Indian Vet. J. 46: 945, 1969.

17 Paikne, D.L.: Cholangiocellular Carcinoma with pulmonary metastasis in goat. Indian Vet. J. 47: 1043, 1970.

18 Altman, N.H. et al.: Primary Pulmonary Mucoepidermoid Tumors in the Goat. Cancer 26: 726, 1970.

CHAPTER VIII

DISEASES OF KIDS

A. Colibacillosis, E. coli Septicemia, Diarrhea, Scours ... 138
B. Hypoglycemia — Birth Chilling 139
C. Navel Ill — Omphalitis, Arthritis of Kids 140
D. Salmonellosis — Bloody Scours, Black Scours 141
E. Stressors Which Lower Disease 141
    Resistance of Baby Kids 141
    1. Environmental 141
    2. Erratic Feeding 142
    3. Lack of Space 142
    4. Lack of Attention 142

A.   Colibacillosis — E. coli Septicemia, Diarrhea, Scours

A number of organisms singly or combined are responsible for septicemia, rapid dehydration and death in baby kids. Of these organisms, **Escherichia coli**, **Salmonellae**, and **Chlamydia** are important in that order. Enteropathogenic strains of E. coli build up numbers in a contaminated environment. Unless a sanitation program is developed for the area where does freshen and where baby kids are kept until weaning, E. coli and other organisms build up both in numbers and virulence. Several factors enable E. coli to infect kids and cause severe early losses: physiologic immaturity of kids when the doe is fed inadequately during gestation, birth in a contaminated environment, failure of the kids to get or absorb colostral antibody after birth, feeding excessive amounts of milk or other feed causing indigestion, and feeding inferior quality milk replacers. **E. coli** septicemia causes rapid dehydration, coma and death in kids under three or four days of age. It is caused by ingestion of virulent E. coli before the kid has ingested colostrum or when the kid has ingested colostrum which has little or no antibody content for the particular virulent strain of organism. It often occurs in weaker kids which are slow about nursing the first time. The course of E. coli septicemia is so rapid in the very young kid that treatment is usually of no avail. **E. coli** scours or diarrhea usually occurs between seven days and one month of age depending upon the amount of exposure to the organism and stressors which affect resistance. Affected kids develop brown-yellowish to grayish-white diarrhea. Temperatures initially rise to 105°F. in acute cases, but rapidly fall as the kids become weak and dehydrated. In the acute cases, death results from dehydration and shock.

Treatment — Any rational approach to treatment must first be directed toward restoring electrolyte balance and overcoming shock. Fortunately, the necessary materials to do this are found in every kitchen.

Hypotonic Electrolyte Treatment for Scours — Electrolytes given by mouth should be approximately half the concentration in which they are found in blood. These materials must be used exactly according to directions. The author has seen several situations where excessive quantities of electrolyte salts were administered, "because they are inexpensive," with disastrous results.

Electrolyte solution to be given by mouth — A Hypotonic Electrolyte Solution —
- 2 teaspoonfuls common table salt
- 1 teaspoonful baking soda (sodium bicarbonate)
- 8 tablespoonfuls of crystalline dextrose, honey or white corn syrup **(Never Use Cane Sugar)**
- Mix in 1 gallon of warm water

Administer to kids via stomach tube (this is the easiest way — have your veterinarian show you how to do this), or by nursing bottle or syringe. Give eight ounces to one pint for every ten pounds body weight per day. Withhold milk during the time electrolyte solution is administered. Neomycin, nitrofurazone, chloramphenicol, or virginiamycin can be added or administered by mouth at the same time the electrolyte solution is given.

Most drug companies manufacturing animal drugs have electrolyte formulations which are more complete. They are equally effective as the above and they are available from veterinarians and drug supply sources.

Veterinarians frequently administer isotonic electrolyte solutions with dextrose (isotonic — contains electrolytes in the same concentration as in the blood) by continuous slow drip intravenous administration. This, too, is excellent treatment and is quite effective. Recovery from dehydration and shock is rapid and uneventful. This treatment should be tried for animals which are comatose and close to death. The author has seen kids close to death in which it was difficult to find evidence of heart beat, rise and move around within a half-hour following administration of hypotonic electrolyte solution via a stomach tube.

B. Hypoglycemia — Birth Chilling

The blood of new born kids contains about fifty milligrams percent of glucose (dextrose). This is the only immediately available source of energy and body heat. Kids born during very cold weather, weak kids born in normal weather, kids born to does which for some reason have no milk, or the occasional kids born to does which refuse to let them nurse, rapidly become depleted of blood glucose. As glucose levels fall, the animals shiver, hair stands on end, they arch their backs, move stiffly, finally lie down in a curled up manner, then quickly become comatose and die. Many kids and lambs with hypoglycemia are given up for dead by owners who do not understand the cause of the problem.

Treatment — Take the kids into a warm place (80-90°F.). Administer by mouth at least 25 milliliters of 5.0% glucose solution using a hypodermic syringe and small rubber stomach tube. The solution can be effectively administered using a high enema. (Pass the tube about eight to ten inches before injecting the solution.) As soon as the kids have revived sufficiently, administer two ounces of warm colostrum with the tube by mouth or let them nurse if they will. Return them to the normal environment as soon as they are active.

C.   Navel III — Omphalitis — Arthritis of Kids

Navel ill may be caused by several environmental organisms (**Erysipelothrix rhusiopathiae, streptococci, E. coli, staphylococci, chlamydia, C. ovis, C. pyogenes**) which gain their way into the body via the umbilical cord. Kids born into a filthy environment are especially prone to navel ill.

Early infection by massive exposure to organisms which rapidly ascend the umbilical cord into the liver or the arterial circulation usually results in a sudden or at least rapid death from septicemia, within the first few days of life. Less severe exposure may result in formation of an abscess at the umbilicus which results in depression, high fever and the usual symptoms of inflammation. These abscesses may weaken the belly wall and predispose the kids to umbilical hernias. More subtle and often more serious are umbilical infections which may be undetected until liver or other internal abscesses develop or arthritis develops on one or more joints of the legs. These may not appear for four to six weeks. The kid usually refuses to support his weight on the affected leg. The affected joint frequently feels hot to the touch and the animal develops a chronic fever (103 - 105°F.).

Prevention and Treatment — Prevention is fairly sure and easy when kids are born in pens which have previously been cleaned and disinfected, and umbilical cords are dipped in tincture of iodine or other antiseptic as soon as possible after birth. Some breeders redip the kids' cord on the second day and this is recommended when the problem has occurred frequently. Many breeders and veterinarians tie off the cord about two inches from the belly wall after dipping the cord or injecting tincture of iodine or Lugol's solution into the cord itself.

At the age of four or five days, the umbilicus should be examined for the possibility of localized infection. This can be done when the kids are dehorned. Evidence of inflammation at that time should justify local antiseptic treatment and an intramuscular dose of penicillin with streptomycin (at least 100,000 units of penicillin).

Arthritis cases are difficult to treat successfully. Joint fluid should be aspirated and subjected to laboratory culture for identification of the causative agent and indication for specific antibiotic treatment. Some veterinarians have treated these cases successfully by intensive systemic administration of the antibiotic indicated, together with aseptic aspiration of fluid from the affected joint and intra-articular infusion of the antibiotic. This treatment is expensive but it may be justified for valuable purebred kids.

D.   Salmonellosis — Bloody Scours — Black Scours

Salmonellae are ubiquitous organisms present in the environment and capable of causing rapidly progressive gastroenteritis when resistance of kids is lowered by stressors. It is characterized by initial high fever (105 - 107°F.), severe watery black or bloody diarrhea with a putrid odor. Often masses of clear mucous and shreds of tissue are passed.

Treatment — Treatment is effective only if given early in the course of the disease. In very young kids, mortality is very high. Administration of large quantities of electrolyte with large doses of broad spectrum antibiotics is indicated (see **Colibacillosis**). Chloramphenicol, tetracyclines, and sulfonamides are most often given intravenously to treat the salmonellae septicemia. Nitrofuran is given by mouth to treat the intestinal infection. Treatment should be continued for at least five days.

A chronic carrier state of infection may persist in recovered animals for many months. These serve as a source of infection for other young animals which may be exposed to them.

Salmonellosis rarely occurs in older animals, but has occurred in herds when new carrier animals are introduced or following stress related to shows or shipment.

E.   Stressors Which Lower Disease
Resistance of Baby Kids

1. Environmental Stressors

Baby kids are able to withstand very cold temperatures if they are fed adequately on milk or high-quality milk replacer. They need protection from wind, rain, and drafts, but they do not need supplemental heat. They must have a dry bed. Nothing makes them more susceptible to sickness than a wet bed. Heat lamps may be used in severe weather, but they are really not necessary.

Excessive environmental moisture and foul odors are sure sources of respiratory problems in kids. Owners who close up the barns to keep animals warm, and thus limit access to fresh air, contribute more to pneumonia problems than does any other single thing.

2. Erratic Feeding

Erratic feeding is another source of stress for kids. When they are excessively hungry, they gorge themselves, develop indigestion and enteric (gut) pathogens quickly take advantage of this situation. If milk replacers are used for feeding baby kids, only the best quality milk replacers should be considered. Spray-dried non-scorched skim milk powder and the best quality white animal fat are necessary ingredients. Severe salmonellosis problems in baby kids, calves, and lambs have resulted from attempts to feed them overheated roller-dried milk or milk derivations, soya flour, starch and poor quality fat.

3. Lack of Sufficient Space

Lack of sufficient space is a very important source of stress for baby kids. Very early in the life of a group of kids, a peck order is established. Timid animals may require individual feeding and a safe place to get away from more aggressive kids. Buck kids should be separated from doe kids by the time they reach six weeks of age.

4. Lack of Attention

Lack of attention and opportunity to exercise and play has a deleterious effect on the health and appetite of young kids. They are best kept outside in nice weather with ample room to play. Rocks, tree limbs, or something of the sort should be provided for their climbing and playing. They like nothing better than a large, dry, sunny lot. Nothing is worse for their development and health than crowded, wet, dark pens.

CHAPTER IX

INTERNAL PARASITE CONTROL

A.		Herd Worm Problems	147
	1.	Blood Sucking Worms	147
	2.	Tapeworms	147
	3.	Lungworms	148
B.		Symptoms of Excessive Worm Burdens	149
C.		Diagnosis of Worm Infections	149
D.		Management and Facilities to Prevent Ingestion of Worms	150
E.		Management During Tapeworm Treatment	152
F.		Management to Control Lungworms	152
G.		Medication	153
H.		Drugs Available for Treatment	154
I.		Liver Fluke Disease	156
J.		Cysticercosis (Bladderworm Disease)	157
K.		Nose Bots, Head Grubs, Oestrus-ovis Infection	158
L.		Herd Parasite Control — A Challenge to Veterinarians	158

The feral goat in its normal habitat is a nomadic browsing animal. Normal environment for feral goats throughout the world is relatively dry, and forage is sparse, consisting mostly of shrubs and trees with very little grass. Removal of goats from their normal dry barren habitat to regions of the world which are humid and temperate with relatively abundant pasture has greatly affected the normal relationship between goats and their internal parasites. It should be understood that parasites are normal inhabitants of the digestive tracts of animals. In feral goats living in their natural environment, a host-parasite relationship exists in a state of equilibrium where neither the parasite nor the host suffers because of the presence of the other. There is some evidence that there are benefits derived from the normal host-parasite association as it occurs in nature.

Factors in the management and environment of goats under domestication upset the normal host-parasite relationship, enabling the parasites to increase in number and affect the health, growth and productivity of their hosts. It is logical that goats, sheep and horses, which, in the wild, inhabit dry barren regions, should be especially susceptible to internal parasite problems in domestication to a greater extent than are cattle or swine which, in the wild, live in more humid regions. Cattle and swine, as they reach maturity, are much more resistant to internal worm infections than are horses, sheep, and goats. The life cycle of a typical blood-sucking worm (see Figure IX-1) might help to clarify this: the adult worm lives in the intestine, attached to a blood capillary in the wall of the intestine. Male and female worms copulate in the intestinal lumen and prodigious numbers of microscopic-sized thin walled eggs (ova) are produced. These pass with the feces and hatch within hours to several days if they receive adequate moisture, warmth and protection from the sun. The microscopic larvae move away from the feces when moisture and shade permit it. During their pre-living period outside the host, the larvae undergo progressive stages of maturation for a period of several weeks until they reach the infective stage. Then, when they are eaten along with the host's food and they reach the proper area of the digestive tract, they may complete the life cycle in either of two important ways: as the late stage larvae arrive in the digestive tract, they may become adults immediately, or they may enter the gut or stomach mucous membrane lining and remain there sequestered and relatively dormant (the histiotropic phase). Two natural phenomena arouse them from their dormancy to mature as adults and suck blood and begin reproduction. These are the beginning of lactation and the lengthening of hours of daylight. New light on the life cycles of internal worms now shows that

Direct Life Cycle of a Typical Blood-sucking Roundworm

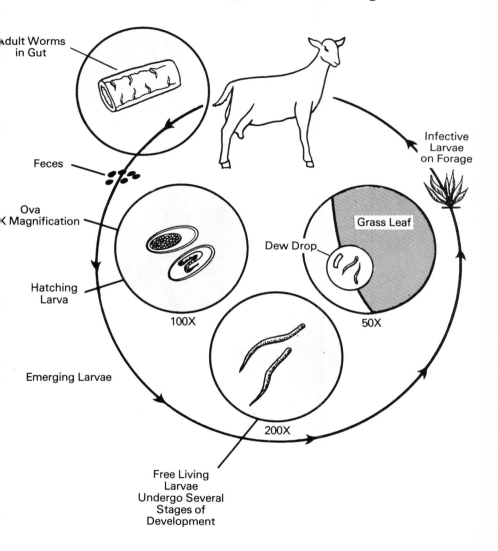

Figure IX—1

most blood-sucking worms have only one or two generations each season. The number of dormant larvae which remain in the host animals over winter and the number of larvae which contaminate the environment play a dual role in favor of the parasite.

Another important recent finding is that for some reason, lactating animals are apparently not able to reject adult worms even though they may be old enough to have developed immunity to the worms.

Control of internal parasites therefore demands a management and medication program which will prevent ingestion of worm larvae, and in addition to that, will kill the maximum number of larvae and adults in the animal. Most of the newer worm medicines available today are highly efficient against the adult worms. Few have any effect on the dormant larvae buried in the digestive tract walls.

It is obvious that the hazards against completion of such a simple life cycle in the goats' wild habitat are infinitely greater than they would be under domestication and typical management circumstances. In the wild state, the host animals may be forced to move to new browsing areas almost daily and the hot desert sun may destroy most of the millions of worm eggs produced each day. In domestic management, larvae may survive for long periods in the moist shelter of bedding and pasture forage, and the build-up in numbers of larvae under normal pasture conditions such as those found in the eastern United States may be enormous. Freezing and thawing under the most severe conditions have no harmful effect on worm larvae. The goat under usual domestic conditions may be confined most of the year within a limited pasture area, unlike its wild relative which may be forced to move continuously to find adequate sustenance. Preventing excessive worm burdens in domestic dairy goats demands that the life cycle of their internal parasites be understood and management measures be taken to keep the number of worms under control. This is accomplished by removal of the adult parasites from the gut using specific drugs which kill the worms without killing the goats, and by managing the animals and their pastures so that there will be minimal numbers of infective larvae present.

How Worms Harm Goats — Blood-sucking worms chiefly cause anemia which has many bad side effects. Anemia adversely affects growth, strength, productivity, production, and reproduction. Blood-sucking worms damage the mucosal surface lining of the intestinal tract. This interferes with digestion and absorption of food. Lung worms in their life cycle, migrate through the liver and lungs and cause extensive damage to those and other vital organs. Tapeworms selectively absorb digested nutrients from the gut and literally starve their hosts when their numbers are excessive. Worm larvae of all kinds may migrate into the brain or spinal cord and cause serious, usually fatal neurological disturbances.

A.   Herd Worm Problems

1. Blood Sucking Worms

These live primarily in the true stomach (abomasum), the small intestine, caecum and the large intestine. Various species live in specific areas and they vary greatly in size and manner of attachment.

Stomach Worms — Three species predóminate. **Haemonchus** (large stomach worms) are very important where there is abundant summer rainfall. **Ostertagia** (brown stomach worms) and **Trichostrongylus species** are most important in areas where there is winter rainfall and pasture. These species greatly intensify egg production at their favored time of year. In Pennsylvania, **Haemonchus** egg production is at its height in early summer while the other two species produce more eggs in late summer and autumn months.

Worms of the Intestinal Tract — A number of **Trichostrongylus species** (small wire worms), **Hematodirus, Bunostomum** (hookworm), and **Oesophagostomum** (nodular worms) are important intestinal parasites of goats. All of them cause anemia and weakness. In addition, nodular worms cause severe damage to the gut wall where they encase themselves in small nodules. This causes irreparable loss of absorptive capacity. The diarrhea characteristic of nodular worm infection may remain and continue to adversely affect goats long after the parasites have been destroyed by use of vermicidal drugs. **Trichuris sp.** (whipworms) commonly are found in the lower intestinal tract. They produce ova and larvae which have higher resistance to the effects of the sun and dryness than do other blood-sucking species.

2. Tapeworms

The common tapeworm of sheep and goats (Monezia expansa), the large tapeworm, lives in the intestine. In addition to causing emaciation in young animals supporting a large number of parasites, these worms may be an important factor in causing enterotoxemia. At least 50 Monezia tapeworms are necessary to produce noticeable injury or effect on growth of kids, but when this tapeworm infection is established in a herd, it is not unusual for a few individuals to harbor hundreds of the worms in numbers which may occlude the intestinal lumen. Monezia tapeworms live in the intestine and daily shed segments which are filled with eggs containing microscopic embryonal tapeworms. These are passed with the feces. The segments are broken open and the embryonal tapeworm larvae are eaten by at least two common species of mites which live in the soil. After a six week period in the intermediate host, the immature tapeworms reach an infective stage. They are released and rapidly develop to maturity when mites are ingested by the goats as they consume mite-infested forage. Goats acquire resistance to infection by these worms. Young kids are usually the only animals in the herd seriously affected by their presence.

Thysanosoma actinoides, the fringed tapeworm, occurs in sheep and goats in western United States. It often causes condemnation of sheep livers at slaughter. The fringed tapeworm is smaller than Monezia and the fringed segments passed with the feces are white and pill-shaped. The life cycle is unknown. There appears to be no economic importance in the presence of this parasite in a dairy goat herd.

3. Lung Worms

Two species of lung worm may affect goats in eastern North America. **Dictyocaulus filaria,** the most common species, has a direct life cycle. The adult worms live in the large bronchi (air passages) of the lungs. The produce embryonated eggs which are expelled from the trachea by coughing. Most of them are swallowed but a few may be expelled from the mouth. Hatching usually occurs in the intestinal tract and the larvae are expelled with the feces. The free living larvae are relatively resistant to the weather. After undergoing several molts, they reach the infective stage within six to seven days. Following their ingestion, they migrate from the intestinal tract via the bloodstream through the liver to the lungs. There they penetrate the capillary walls, enter the air sacs and move into the air passages. They cause extensive damage to lung tissue and pneumonia is a common problem where lung damage is extensive.

The lungworm, **Mullerius capillaris,** of sheep and goats rarely causes severe problems in sheep, but it can cause verminous pneumonia in goats. The life cycle of this worm is complicated by the necessity for an intermediate host — slugs or snails. The larvae which pass in the feces are ingested by the intermediate host and the goat must eat an infected snail or slug in water or forage in order to become infected. This would appear to be difficult. In fact, it is quite easy when goats are maintained in swampy or wet pasture area.

Protostrongylus rufescens is another important lungworm of goats which is cosmopolitan in distribution. Like **M. capillaris** it requires an intermediate snail or slug host. Larvae of the two species are extremely difficult to differentiate. Guralp, Kavanaugh and Baker of Cornell found **P. rufescens** to be highly refractive to treatment with 0.15 ml. of 1% solution of Emetine Hydrochloride, a drug highly effective against **M capillaris**. However, Emetine Hydrochloride has a very narrow margin of safety, too narrow to justify its use.

B.   Symptoms of Excessive Worm Burdens

Anemia is a common symptom of excessive blood-sucking worm burden. Examination of the mucous lining of the lips, conjunctiva, anus or vulva reveals abnormally pale color. Severe anemia often produces swelling of the lower jaw (bottle jaw). Diarrhea with black liquid or tarry feces is commonly associated with nodular worm infection, but it is not a reliable symptom of worm infection. Reduced milk production, poor appetite and poor growth are good symptoms of worm infection. The presence of tapeworms can usually be detected by the small white noodle or maggot-like segments which are passed with the feces. Lungworm infections are characterized by a chronic persistent deep cough. The British call lungworm disease "husk." The word very well describes the characteristic lungworm cough.

C.   Diagnosis of Worm Infections

In order to develop a sound medication program or when symptoms suggest the possibility of worm infection, the assistance of a veterinarian will be most helpful. Worms can be identified by the physicial characteristics of their eggs in fresh feces.

Taking Fecal Samples — A few fecal pellets should be collected as they are passed by the animal. When checking herds for worm infection, it is best to take composite samples from representative groups of animals in the herd. Samples should be collected from young kids (under two months of age) for coccidiosis examination, and from weaned kids, yearlings, the mature milking animals and the bucks. A composite sample should be made up of at least twelve pellets containing four pellets from each of at least three animals. The fresh material should be placed in a labelled small clean jar (baby food jars are excellent) and chilled immediately in a refrigerator. The cold samples should be taken to a veterinarian for microscopic examination. Using a simple flotation technique, the worm eggs can be collected from the samples and species identification made. Because worms shed varying numbers of eggs at different times, and the presence of some species is far more serious than others, the professional judgment of the veterinarian is most important. As previously mentioned, the goal should be control, not complete eradication, of all internal parasites. The object of fecal examinations done at least several times each year is to develop a sound management and treatment program which will furnish good control with minimal levels of reinfection.

Necropsy — Dairy goats of all ages which die from any cause should be carefully examined for internal parasites. Severely parasitized animals which die of worm infection frequently reveal no worms on post mortem necropsy or fecal examination. When post mortem examination reveals severe anemia and submandibular edema, a presumptive diagnosis of severe blood-sucking worm infection should be made. The author has been involved in several herd problems where treatment of the herd was delayed because neither worms nor their eggs were found when a veterinarian or veterinary pathologist examined several dead animals.

"Worm-free" Herds of Goats — It should be understood that a goal of "worm-free" status is possible but not practical and rather hazardous for a herd of dairy goats. When "worm-free" status is attained, lack of any exposure to parasites soon renders the animals extremely susceptible to parasite infections. Bringing in new animals or bringing in worm eggs on contaminated footwear can then produce explosive parasite problems. Selling animals from a worm-free herd can be hazardous, too. The worm-free animals are "sitting ducks" for severe parasitism when introduced to herds not free of worms.

Methods of Worm Control — Two methods for achieving good control of worms are apparent: management and facilities which minimize exposure to infective larvae, and medication which destroys adult worms in the animals' bodies.

D. Management and Facilities for Preventing Ingestion of Worm Larvae

It is most important that goats live in a dry, clean environment. If they are forced to lie down in their own manure or manure-contaminated bedding, they obviously get larvae into their mouths as they groom themselves. A bedded manure pack is usually satisfactory if its surface is kept dry. Under winter conditions, any attempt to raise the ambient temperature inside a building containing a built-up bedded manure pack by closing windows or doors results in condensation and dampness of the pack surface. This, together with warmth generated by the manure beneath, provides excellent conditions for worm larvae survival and migration. Under these conditions, wintertime parasite problems can be severe.

Bedding — Inedible or unpalatable bedding is to be preferred over edible types. Sawdust, mill shavings, peanut hulls, shredded corn fodder, sugar cane bagasse, straw or poor quality hay are desirable forms. The drier the bedding materials are, the better.

Free Stalls — Free stalls which provide deep bedding and some privacy and protection from dominant animals help to provide worm control. They should be narrow enough so that goats are unable to turn around in them. The curb behind the stalls should be not less than eight inches above floor level and bedding should be at least four inches higher in front of the stalls. Goats prefer to lie on an up-hill or level surface; they refuse to lie in holes or downhill surfaces. Dairy goat free stalls should have partitions at least 36 inches above the bedding level.

Pasture Management — Permanent grass pastures are exceedingly difficult to manage for prevention of internal parasite problems. Rotation of animals using small areas which will furnish two-week periods of grazing is infinitely better than allowing animals continuous use of a large area. The individual areas can be managed using strip grazing with an electric fence. After animals are moved to a new area, the grazed area should be mown as short as possible and soil and grass stubble given full exposure to the sun. This effectively destroys worm larvae and provides new growth of fresh succulent forage for the next grazing period. The size and number of paddocks for grazing will be determined by the species of forage, the usual rainfall, and the number of animals. If pasture growth exceeds the need for grazing, nearly mature material can be removed for hay.

Dry Lot — Unless there is at least one-half acre per animal available for pasture, the herd should be kept in a dry lot with no forage for grazing.

Young Animals — From the beginning, young animals should be kept separate from other animals. This is especially true for use of pasture.

Forage Feeding — Forage feeding for goats in a dry lot should be accomplished using fence line feeders which prevent or minimize any edible material being trampled by the animals.

Annual Forages — Use of annual grasses (Piper sudan grass, annual brome grss, etc.), cow peas, and clovers are excellent means for furnishing goats palatable nutritious forage. Feeding them as green forage results in much less waste than allowing the animals to graze. Comfrey, kudzu and other perennial forage crops can best be utilized by hand harvesting them and feeding them in fence line feeders. When feeding green forage and especially broad-leaved species such as comfrey, be cautious about feeding large amounts during periods when the weather may interfere with normal growth of the plants. Periods of cold dark wet weather or periods of hot dry weather may sufficiently alter the nitrate levels or produce other toxic nonprotein substances in the forage.

E. Management During Tapeworm Treatment

Because removal of mites may be just as important as removal of the tapeworms, removal of the herd from the affected pasture should be helpful. Regardless of the drugs used, all food should be withheld from the animals for at least fifteen hours before treatment. The treated animals should be confined in a small stall or lot. Twenty-four hours after treatment, all feces and tapeworms should be collected and burned, and the confinement area should be thoroughly cleaned and sprayed with a good phenolic disinfectant. In the author's experience, the environment of housed goats often contains extremely large numbers of mites in the bedding, stalls and floors. Immediately following treatment, thorough cleaning and disinfection of the premises may be well worth the effort.

F. Management to Control Lungworms

For large lungworm (**Dictyocaulus sp.**) problem situations, little can be accomplished unless every effort is made to prevent goats from eating fecal-contaminated feed or drinking fecal-contaminated water. (See **Forage Feeding Equipment** and **Sanitary Watering Equipment**.) For **Mulleria sp.** lungworms, goats should be removed from wet pastures and kept in dry lots. Drainage of the pastures and spraying with copper sulfate solution (11 lbs./130 gallons water/5 acres) to kill snails may be helpful. Do not put animals back onto the pasture until at least several inches of rain have fallen after application of copper sulfate solution to the pasture area. In the author's experience, removal of the animals from the pastures and dry lot feeding has been the only practical solution to this problem.

G. Medication

Baby kids usually do not need or benefit from worm medication during the time they are receiving milk or milk replacer. However, if allowed to remain with their dams, they may pick up sizeable worm burdens in a few weeks in spring and early summer. It is usually a good idea under humid eastern United States conditions to worm kids the first time after they have been weaned about three weeks.

The best time to use worm medicine is the time when it is strategically best to hit the worm population hardest. For example, in Pennsylvania when temperature and rainfall are high in late June, goats should be wormed for Haemonchus (stomach) worms and moved immediately to a new pasture paddock. The best worm medicine for that particular worm should also be used at that time. For the situation above, haloxon (Loxon, Copper and Nephews) would be the medicine of choice because it is highly efficacious against stomach worms and less than the usual dose will be sufficient, thus saving some money. Dairy goat herd owners should expect their veterinarians to work out for them a worm control program using the safest and most economical drugs available at the best strategic times to get the job done.

Following administration of worm medication, goats should be moved immediately to new pasture. If they are being kept in a dry lot, a thorough clean-up of manure and wasted feed should be done. In hot summer months, it may be necessary to treat goats several times at three-week intervals to accomplish much, if the chances for reinfection are great. For example: when the herd is kept on permanent pastures and there is excessive depth of forage furnishing larval worms good protection from the sun, one dose of medicine has very little total effect. The author has encountered herds under the above condition where regular treatment at monthly intervals had little effect on the worm burden of the herd.

A very good time to worm goats is at the end of the pasture season when burdens of adult worms may be high and the number of larvae entering or beginning their stay (histiotrophic phase) in the digestive tract lining may be very great. Mebendazole and Thibendazole in dosages three to five times the usual dosage may effectively wipe out many of the buried larvae. Levamisole is also effective, but goats will not tolerate more than the recommended dose.

Another strategic time to worm goats is about two weeks following kidding. This is especially true for does kidding the first time and for those kidding in spring or early summer. A 96 hour withdrawal period is usually specified for milking animals, but the milk loss may be well worth the benefits of worming at the proper time in herds which have persistent worm problems.

H.   Drugs Available For Treatment

Phenothiazine — This drug is only mentioned because it is now relatively cheap. It is effective against blood-sucking worms, but it is too toxic to use for severely infected animals and it may cause photosensitivity, especially in white-skinned animals. It has been widely recommended for worm control as phenothiazine-salt using one part phenothiazine to nine parts of trace mineralized salt. Sheep and cattle, and especially goats, disdain phenothiazine and will eat the mixture only when they desperately crave salt. Therefore, its use in this manner is not recommended. The author has seen heat exhaustion from lack of salt in cattle, sheep and goats in hot summer weather where the animals were expected to take salt mixed with phenothiazine to meet their needs.

Thiabendazole (Thibenzole - Merck) — This drug is highly effective against most of the blood-sucking worms of goats. It is virtually non-toxic so that it can be safely administered to does in late pregnancy and to weak severely parasitized animals. Thiabendazole-resistant Haemonchus worms have been reported in sheep, but there is no reported evidence that this has been found true for goats. Thiabendazole is virtually non-toxic. The author has seen no evidence of toxicity when three or four times the necessary dose was administered. The drug is supplied in several forms: wettable drench powder, a cattle-wormer pelleted form, bolets and a wormer paste form. The wormer paste form is ideal for treating goats. Unlike the pelleted form, the dose can be controlled, and one can be certain that each animal gets at least the necessary amount. Using a medicator, which is similar to a common caulking gun, the desired amount of the sticky paste can be put into the animal's mouth with no difficulty and the animals are unable to expectorate it. Be sure that animals to be treated have no forage available just before treatment. A very small amount of forage in their mouths will enable them to spit out the wormer paste. Thiabendazole,

Mebendazole (Telmin) and several other new similar compounds in the wormer-paste form are the current drugs of choice for removing blood-sucking worms from goats.

Mebendazole (Telmin - Pitman Moore Co.) — In addition to its use against blood-sucking worms, Mebendazole has been recommended against **Mulleria capillaria** worms at the rate of 25 mgms. per kgm. In the author's experience, it has been only moderately satisfactory for the purpose. Mebendazole, however, has a wide spectrum of activity against blood-sucking worms; it has a wide margin of safety and in two to three times the normal dose, it is effective against larvae buried within the digestive tract walls. Goats are able to tolerate 50 mgms. per kgm Mebendazole. In this dosage, the drug is effective against liver flukes and sequestered larvae of blood-sucking worms.

Albendazole (Smith Kline) — This new drug which has wide spectrum activity with relative safety demands attention by veterinarians for use in goats. There is evidence that birth defects are likely to occur when the drug is used during the first month of pregnancy.

Cambendazole (Camvet) — This drug is similar to Mebendazole. Either Mebendazole or Cambendazole in twice the label dosage would be the author's choice against whipworms.

Pyrantel (Strongid, Banminth) — This is another new anthelmintic which is not yet approved for goats but is widely used for horses and dogs. It is well tolerated, but it is extremely toxic to goats if they inhale its fumes. For this reason, the drug should only be administered by stomach intubation.

Haloxon (Loxon - Cooper and Nephews) — This organo phosphate drug is highly efficient against blood-sucking worms. The dose must be carefully regulated and the drug should not be used within two weeks of administration or external application of any other organo phosphate compounds. It is supplied as a wettable powder and administered as a drench. For Haemonchus worm treatment, a half-dose of haloxon is 100% effective and the cost per dose at that rate is far less than that for other compounds.

Levamisole (Tramisol - American Cyanamid) — This drug is highly effective against blood-sucking worms and is also recommended for Dictyocaulus lungworms. It is not effective for other lungworm species. Levamisole may be administered as a drench, in wormer pellets, in bolets, or by subcutaneous injection. Label specifications should be carefully followed. Slightly excess dosage in the author's hands has produced abortion in the last six weeks of pregnancy. Twenty-five percent excess dose in the author's hands produced collapse for several hours in half-grown kids. However, where Dictyocaulus lungworm infection is diagnosed, all of the young animals over two months of age should be treated. Breeding older ones should be delayed until they have been treated at least twice. Administration of more than one dose at three-week intervals has appeared to be necessary to achieve satisfactory results.

Drugs for Treating Tapeworms

Copper sulfate and nictotine sulfate — This old combination of drugs is not very effective and quite dangerous to use. Two ounces of nicotine sulfate solution (Black Leaf 40) and one ounce of copper sulfate are mixed in one gallon of water. The usual dose is one-half ounce for young kids and one ounce for yearlings administered with a drench syringe.

Phenothiazine with lead arsenate — The combination of drugs has low efficiency and rather high toxicity.

Niclosamide (Yomesan - Chem Agro) — This administered at the rate of 150 to 200 mg/kgm is the only relatively safe effective drug currently available. It is expensive but worth using on dairy goat kids. **Albendazole**, according to recent research reports, may be effective against roundworms, tapeworm, lungworms and liver flukes. At this writing it has not been approved for any domestic animal use.

I.   Liver Fluke Disease

Several species of liver flukes are capable of producing liver disease in goats. The disease in goats is not as common as it is in sheep in areas where liver fluke infection is an important problem in sheep. Liver damage caused by flukes influences growth, feed efficiency, and productivity. Because the flukes require intermediate hosts to complete their life cycle, consideration for control of these is important. Two species of Fasciola flukes (**F. hepatica, F. magna**) require intermediate development in snails (**Lymnae sp.**). The lancet fluke (**Dicrocoelium dendriticum**) requires both snails (**Cionella lubrica**) and ants (**Formica fusca**), for intermediate development. The young flukes cause tissue damage when they reach the intestine and migrate from it to the liver. Damage to the bile ducts causes blood leakage and inflammation of the bile ducts. Following treatment, damage is repaired but there is no increased resistance to the parasites.

Treatment — Eleven pounds of copper sulfate per 130 gallons of water per five acres should be used to spray all snail-infected wet pasture areas. The spray should be repeated in 21 days to destroy snails which were immature at the time of the first application. Goats should be treated twice at 21-day intervals before they are returned to copper sulfate treated areas. At least one to two inches of rainfall should be allowed to wash off treated areas before goats are returned to them, otherwise, copper sulfate residues may cause copper poisoning.

The treatment for liver flukes is rather dangerous, especially for weak animals or those under severe stress. Carbon tetrachloride is given intramuscularly at the rate of 1 ml. for adult flukes or 4 ml. for immature flukes. Hexachlorophene given orally or subcutaneously at dose rates of 15 to 26 mg. and 40 mg/kg of body weight for acute liver fluke disease and chronic liver fluke disease respectively, is safer than carbon tetrachloride but is not quite as effective. The new drug Albendazole shows promise as a safe effective treatment for fluke infection.

J. Cysticercosis (Bladderworm Disease, Gid)

This is a chronic parasitism of young goats caused by the cystic stage of **Taenia hydatigena,** a common tapeworm of dogs and coyotes in certain western areas of the United States. The pea-sized bladderlike cysts are found in the liver, the peritoneal cavity and occasionally the brain on post mortem, usually at slaughter. Young goats acquire the infection during summer and fall grazing when the microscopic oncospheres (embryonal tape worms) are liberated from tapeworm segments passed in the feces by dogs or coyotes. These contaminate food and water ingested by the goats. When they occur in large numbers, they cause poor growth and vague unthriftiness of kids. Control and prevention of serious cysticercosis demands regular tapeworm treatment of dogs, prompt disposal by burning or burial of sheep and goat carcasses, and coyote control where these animals are numerous. Prompt collection and removal of dog feces is an important sanitary precaution.

The best currently available tapeworm treatment for dogs is Nicosamide (Yomesan), at a dose rate of 50 mg/kg of body weight at three-month intervals where cysticercosis in kids is found. There is no treatment available for elimination of the bladderworm stage (cysticercosis) in goats or other animals.

K.   Nose Bots (Head Grubs, Oestrus Ovis Infection)

This common parasite of sheep only affects goats where goats are exposed to sheep which harbor it. This author has seen goats showing mild symptoms which were kept with badly infested sheep.

The bot fly, **Oestrus ovis,** is grayish-brown and about 12 mm. in length. The female deposits larvae in and around the nostrils without alighting. The flies are active in late spring and early summer. They cause huddling together, foot-stamping and snorting in sheep as the flies strike them to deposit larvae. Dairy goats are much more terrified of the flies than are sheep. They go into a dark shelter and refuse to emerge when bot flies are active.

The tiny larvae migrate through the nasal passages into the sinuses where they require as long as ten months to mature. Their activity in the nasal passages causes inflammation and damage to the epithelial lining, opens the way for other infections, causes copious discharge of mucous and pus, and great discomfort.

When the larvae reach maturity, they migrate toward the nostril where they are discharged and fall on the ground. There they remain dormant (pupate) from three to nine weeks, depending upon the weather. Cold wet weather delays their emergence as adults. As soon as they emerge, they mate and the females begin to deposit larvae shortly afterward.

Treatment — When dairy goats show evidence of nose bot infection, heavily infested sheep flocks within the immediate vicinity should be suspected. Little can be accomplished by treating goats without treating all the sheep within at least a quarter-mile radius. Rulene (Dow Chemical Co.) is highly effective for removal of nose bot larvae when administered orally. The same dosage and label recommendations for sheep would apply for goats. Levamisole (Tramisole - American Cyanamid) in the same dosage used for removal of blood-sucking worms is reported to be effective for removal of larval nose bot. The best time to treat the animals would be within six weeks after nose bot flies have been active and before the animals show severe symptoms.

L.   Herd Parasite Control — A Challenge To Veterinarians

Many highly efficient and relatively safe vermicidal compounds are available to dairy goat owners from many sources, including the veterinarian. Indiscriminate use of any of these drugs may be illegal, harmful to the animals, expensive, and non-productive.

Veterinarians have excellent training in both diagnosis and epidemiology of internal parasites. They can be of great value to dairy goat herd owners in setting up a management medication program for the elimination of internal parasite herd problems which can be effective and economically sound.

Any effort to enlarge dairy goat herds and intensify production on a relatively small acreage of land demands a good regularly monitored internal parasite program. When a veterinarian furnishes diagnosis, surveillance, and treatment recommendations, the cost is minimal and the rewards to the herd owner are great.

Additional Information and Reference — Williams, Jeffrey, V.B. Sc., M.R.C.V.S., PhD. Internal Parasitism in Goats, Proceedings of Sheep and Goat Practice Seminar 1976, Colorado State University.

CHAPTER X

EXTERNAL PARASITES AND THEIR CONTROL

A. Lice Infestation — Pediculosis 162
B. Goat Scabies 163
C. Demodectic Mange — Demodicosis 163

A.   Lice Infestation (Pediculosis)

Two common species of lice occur in goats in the United States: the red louse, **Damalinia caprae**, a very small louse which burrows into the hair follicles and causes intense itching, and the blue louse, **Linognathus stenopsis**, which is larger. It can easily be seen by the naked eye. It sucks blood and is commonly found on the sides of the neck, the underline, and behind and above the udder. Two other small species have also been reported.

A few common misconceptions about lice deserve discussion here. Lice are obligatory parasites. They must live constantly on their hosts to survive. Buildings and other facilities do not, therefore, become infested with lice and do not require lice treatment sprays. Lice are also host-specific. No other animals, with the possible exception of sheep, harbor lice which also live on goats. At least one louse, **Linognathus stenopsis**, the blue louse, can be found on both sheep and goats in the same flock.

Control and Eradication — Good safe pesticides available today make the presence of lice in a herd of goats intolerable. Lice cause loss of blood, extreme annoyance, irritability, and severe loss of milk production. The best time to treat a herd for lice is in the first cool weather of fall when the parasites revive from summer hibernation in crevices and skin folds on the body surface. Coumaphos (Co-ral manufactured by ChemAgro in the United States) has been approved for lactating dairy cows. It is safe and efficient for lice treatment of dairy goats. The secret in effective lice treatment is thorough coverage of the entire body surface. For large herds of goats, the only practical approach is the use of a dipping vat. Where a permanent or portable sheep-dipping vat is available, this is the ideal method for treatment. Select a cool calm day and use cold pesticide solution for best results. This prevents chilling and aids penetration of the pesticide suspension. Use 25% wettable Co-ral powder at the rate of 1 lb./100 gallons of water. In a small herd, the Co-ral suspension can be applied using a knapsack sprayer with good pressure to drive the spray material down into the skin surface. The spray material can also be effectively applied using a hand scrubbing brush and scrubbing the material over the entire surface of the body. Do not neglect the eyelids, corners of the mouth, ears, and under the legs and dewclaws. Treatment should be repeated in ten days to two weeks. If treatment has been thorough, lice can be totally eradicated from a goat herd, and they will not appear again until the animals have been exposed to infested sheep or goats.

The author has never attended a dairy goat show or sale where there was no obvious evidence of lice infestation in at least a small percentage of the animals. It is reasonable to expect all animals returning from shows to be infested with goat lice.

B.   Goat Scabies

Goat scabies is caused by infestation of the skin by **Chorioptes caprae**, the goat scabies mite. The disease is very rare in dairy goats, but it does occur in semi-feral animals and in Angora goats. The Chorioptes mites cause severe itching symptoms and loss of hair on the legs and belly within three months to twenty-one months after the scab mites have been transferred by contact between infested and susceptible goats. The appearance of scabby masses follows loss of hair. Diagnosis is simple; the mites are easily seen under the microscope or hand lens. The goat scab mite is relatively fragile and will not survive for more than a month, at most, off the host animal. Coumaphos (Co-ral) at the rate of 1½ lbs. of 25% wettable powder per 100 gallons of water used as a dip, twice, at two-week intervals is effective for elimination of this parasite. Goat scab is not infectious to other animals and man.

C.   Demodectic Mange — Demodicosis

Any skin condition of goats characterized by the appearance of skin nodules ranging from pinhead to larger than pea size should be suspect as demodectic mange. This disease is caused by a microscopic cigar-shaped mite which can easily be demonstrated from the waxy white contents which can be scraped from or squeezed out of a nodule. Little is known about its transmission from animal to animal. It is suspected that infection begins at a very early age. Demodectic mange is responsible for damage to hides, and it is an unsightly disease which ought to eliminate animals from the show ring. The nodules are most commonly found on the neck and on the rib area. A few of them might justify excision and treatment with tincture of iodine. Medication (Coumaphos, Famphur) effective for other forms of mange has been tried with doubtful success. Individual goats, like individual dogs may be affected with demodectic mange as a result of inherent faulty immune response.

CHAPTER XI

REPRODUCTION

A.   Physiology 166
    1.   Genital Tract in Pregnancy 166
B.   Artificial Insemination 166
C.   Improving Herd Fertility 168
    1.   Factors Which Affect Heats
       and Fertility in the Doe 168
        a.   Environmental 168
        b.   Nutritional. 168
        c.   Social 168
        d.   Hermaphrodism 169
        e.   Congenital Reproductive Hypoplasia 169
    2.   Pregnancy Diagnosis 170
    3.   Preparing Bucks for Breeding 171
    4.   Using Bucks to Best Advantage in Large Herds . . . 171
    5.   Heat Synchronization 171
D.   Problems of Reproduction 173
    1.   Abnormal Cycles 173
        a.   Weak or Silent Heats 173
        b.   Cystic Ovaries. 173
        c.   Heat During Pregnancy 173
        d.   Abnormally Long Periods Between Heats. 174
    2.   False Pregnancy 174
    3.   Metritis 174
    4.   Infertility Hazard in Polled Goats 175
    5.   Problems in Bucks. 176
        a.   Cryptorchidism (Undescended
           Testis, Retained Testis) 176
        b.   Varicocele 176
    6.   Causes of Abortion 176
        a.   Vibrionic Abortion. 176
        b.   Chlamydial Abortion. 176
        c.   Q Fever. 177

A. Physiology

1. The Genital Tract in Pregnancy

The reproductive organs of does at all stages of pregnancy very closely resemble, except for size, the anatomy and function of the reproductive tracts of cows. There is, of course, a higher incidence of multiple fetuses and they are distributed equally in both uterine horns. Migration of ova from the side where they were produced to the opposite uterine horn apparently occurs regularly in the goat. This is not the usual case in the bovine. The placental attachment is quite similar to that of the cow with the average number of cotyledons, about 99, and the placenta extending into most of the nongravid horn area where there was one. There is a marked difference between maternal cotyledons of the cow and the goat. In the cow they are dome-shaped, in the goat they are cup-shaped. Slightly more than 55% of pregnancies observed in a large study (328) in India were single pregnancies; this would seem to be a higher proportion than seen in american goats. In the Indian study, 40% were twin pregnancies, 5% were triplet, and 0.3% quadruplet pregnancies.[1]

B. Artificial Insemination

Because at least one new book about artificial insemination of goats is soon to be published by an expert on the subject, this author does not intend to provide an exhaustive treatment of dairy goat artificial insemination in this book.

Artificial insemination of dairy goats offers a tremendous opportunity for improvement of both type and production, provided, of course, that superior sires are used. The same criteria used for selection and evaluation of bulls for the dairy cow industry should be used for selection of bucks. Dairy cattle insemination floundered for years in the foolish use of "big name," "show bulls," "sons of hot cow families," etc. Significant progress was achieved only after the industry developed scientific genetically sound methods for selection of sires. In the current situation in the dairy goat industry, sire selection is about 25 years behind that universally used for selection of bulls. The only sound basis for sire selection is good milk production records. The AI sires worth using can hardly be found in herds where there are no good milk production recording systems. Because numbers of offspring are so important for finding superior sires, it seems logical that the most likely place to find them would be in the large herds where bucks would have not less than 25 daughters on test. Some sires used artificially may be identified as superior or worthless if they are used in a number of production-tested good producing herds. One of the most serious problems in the United States dairy goat industry is the presence of and the use of too many bucks. In the author's experience, it is extremely rare to find as many as ten does bred to a single sire. This is true even in many of the larger herds. There is simply no possibility for making real progress unless the production records of a large number of daughters can be compared with production records of their dams and their herdmates in a number of herds. In the American dairy cow insemination industry, it is possible for dairymen to select from a large number of available sires which have been proven superior on the basis of their daughters' comparative production records. In addition, detailed evaluation of type is published for the bulls. The dairy goat industry must set its sights toward the same goals. Without those goals, AI will remain a convenience service without any real improvement of the animals.

Artificial Insemination Techniques — The dairy goat industry's approach to the use of AI is reminiscent of the early days of AI in dairy cattle. Thirty years ago there was no shortage of experts who offered a host of ways to "properly inseminate cows." They used special specula; some used complicated techniques where canulas were "threaded" through the cervix, and semen was deposited in as many as five strategic places. The time of insemination recommended varied as widely as the techniques. In retrospect, it is difficult to see how cattle AI survived all the mistakes and faulty procedures of its early days. Good AI research solved many of the early problems. Most of that research can be applied to AI in dairy goats.

This author, for one, sees an increasing number of things in AI which portend no good for the future of the dairy goat industry. "Do it yourself" insemination, improper collection, evaluation, storage, and handling of semen, offer only frustration and lack of real progress for the dairy goat industry. The possibility of deliberate or accidental false identity of sires is frightening. Some dairy goat herd owners are rushing to buy semen from "big name" sires with nothing but name and show winnings for criteria.

Artificial insemination of dairy goats may be a tragic experience for those who are willing to go along with less than the best method for sire evaluation. For the first fifteen years of the use of AI in dairy cattle, there was little real progress. Using the selection tools available now, dairy cattle breeders have achieved tremendous results.

This author cannot be enthusiastic about what he sees in dairy goat AI. There is a desperate need for application of available research, new research, and sire selection based on proven criteria. Most of the dairy goat AI problems have had their day in dairy cattle AI. There is no need to learn by repeating mistakes.

C. Improving Herd Fertility

1. Factors Which Affect Heats and Fertility of Dairy Does

a. Environmental — Temperature — In the Swiss breeds especially, onset of regular heats is often postponed until the weather becomes cooler in fall. Fertility in males is usually very low when the temperature exceeds 85°F.

Light — Keeping does in total darkness for seventeen-hour periods each day induces early onset of heats and normal fertility after the beginning of June. If any attempt is made to induce early heat in does, the buck to be used to breed them should also be subjected to the seventeen-hour darkness periods. Results with reduced light are poor when attempts are made to do it during the spring months.

Time of Year — In our temperate North American climate, the normal breeding season for Swiss breeds of goats extends from the end of September until the end of January. Nubians usually come into heat a few weeks earlier but they normally only rarely come into heat after the beginning of January.

b. Nutritional — Regardless of the physical condition of does at the time of breeding, those gaining weight during the period of several weeks before breeding and at least three weeks following breeding show more easily detectable heat and produce more ova. This "flushing" process has been used for many years in management of all multipara (multiple birth) species to increase the number of offspring.

c. Social — The presence of a vigorous active buck, or at least the odor of such an animal, has a direct effect on the onset of heats in does. Where there is no buck on the premises, taking an old coat or burlap bag to a place where it will be in contact with a sexually active buck for a few days, and placing it where the does can smell it will result in heat signs in most of them within one week. This is a reasonably good way to synchronize heats in a small herd to be bred artificially. An active buck brought within sight and hearing of does will usually bring them into heat during the fall months. Where does have a choice, they will usually refuse the attentions of a deodorized buck, preferring one which is more odorous. Where it is desirable to use a deodorized buck where an intact one is also present, it may be worthwhile to remove the odorous buck from sight or sound when does begin to come into heat.

Although it is most undesirable to allow intimate association of milking does with a mature vigorous, odorous buck, his presence is the best stimulus for beginning of sexual activity in female goats. In nature, much of the breeding activity of bucks is concerned with fighting each other and segregating collected harems from other bucks. In domestication, with usual circumstances under which herds are kept, it is much better to hand-breed does at the onset of heat, and again just before they go out of heat, than it is to let them stay with the buck during the entire heat period.

d. Hermaphrodism — This is the most important cause of infertility in dairy goats. Konde in the Japanese Journal of Genetics (1952-53) published a survey of hermaphrodism in the goat and classified the intersexual types into five different groups. In this author's experience, hermaphrodism and genital hypoplasia are directly related to the polled or hornless characteristic, and both are more likely to result when both parents are polled. The semi-female hermaphrodites usually have a normal sized vulva and a much enlarged clitoris clearly evident when they are a month old. The vagina of these animals may be very short or atretic. Use of a lubricated glass rod the size of an ordinary lead pencil can be helpful to determine whether or not the vagina of a suspect kid is normal. This author has never been able to pass such an instrument more than about one inch past the vulva of a female type hermaphrodite kid. Most hermaphrodites can easily be determined at birth because external genitalia are clearly abnormal. Those which are most nearly female are the most difficult to detect. Konde found twice as many hermaphrodites in Saanens than in the other breeds.

e. Congenital Hypoplasia of the Reproductive Tract — This condition is also related to hornlessness, but in females, at least, the author has seen it in animals with one horned parent. In the very young doe kid, it is difficult to detect congenital hypoplasia, but the usual very small vulva becomes evident when kids reach seven - eight months, the normal age where they should come into heat. Most females with congenital hypoplasia show little or no evidence of heats or heat cycling. On necropsy, essential parts of the reproductive tract may be extremely small or absent.

In the male, congenital testicular hypoplasia is not at all rare in herds where many of the animals are polled, and polled sires have been in use. By the time buck kids reach four to five months of age, the smaller, softer than normal size and consistency of the testicles can easily be determined by comparison with normal buck kids of the same age. This author has observed young bucks with testicular hypoplasia to exhibit libido and normal buck behavior, but the typical hypoplastic buck has neither the usual male appearance nor behavior.

2. Pregnancy Diagnosis

A palpation technique developed by C.V. Hulet, USDA, for pregnancy diagnosis in sheep is equally useful for diagnosis of pregnancy in goats. It is virtually error-free if does bred from 70 to 110 days are examined. Hulet examined 200 ewes per hour using this method. It is not necessary nor is it desirable to handle dairy goats that rapidly. It is possible to examine 60 bred does per hour with great accuracy and with minimal likelihood of injury.

Best results are obtained when all feed is withheld overnight. The animal is placed on her back in a laparotomy cradle or ordinary low table about 24 inches off the floor. One person on either side of the animal holds the fore and hind leg together on each side to relax the abdominal muscles. A rounded plastic rod 50 x 1.5 cm. is lubricated with mineral oil and passed into the rectum forward beyond the edge of the pubis in front of the udder. A piece of 3/8 inch coroseal or plastic tube rounded on one end and stiffened by insertion of a metal rod into it works very well. The rod is moved toward the abdominal wall and the gravid uterus can easily be palpated through the abdominal wall using the other hand. The empty uterus lies under the udder and it remains small so that it cannot be palpated. There is little reason to use this method after does are bred 120 days, but it can be done if fetal movements are not observed otherwise. This method for pregnancy diagnosis was more rapid and more accurate than two different electronic devices tested.

Why diagnose Pregnancy? — It is most important that bred milking does be diagnosed pregnant by 80 days. If they are not pregnant, they can be moved closer to the buck where they will often return to heat. If rebreeding is no longer desirable at that time, the doe can be kept in the milking string and milked for an additional five or six months.

Open milking does which are not bred often milk profitably for at least a year. The author has seen individual open does milk as much as four pounds daily for four years without kidding. It is a great disappointment and it is expensive to dry off a milking doe thought to be pregnant, only to learn two months later that she was not.

3. Preparing Bucks for the Breeding Season

A serious management fault in many dairy goat herds is neglect of the buck before breeding season begins. Often the entire breeding season is gone before the herd owner realizes that something is wrong with the buck's fertility. Routine worming of the buck at least twice, at three-week intervals, is a good precaution before the breeding season begins.

The feet of the buck should be trimmed and long hair from the belly, the penis sheath, and areas around the scrotum should be clipped. The buck should be fed at least two pounds daily of the same concentrate fed to the milking herd throughout the breeding season. It is normal for bucks to lose weight during the breeding season. Many vigorous adult bucks will lose weight almost to the point of emaciation during periods of sexual activity. It should be of no serious concern to the herd owner as long as the animal will take some food and water and he remains active and vigorous. The author has had repeated anguished inquiries from novice herd owners about the loss of condition of bucks during breeding season. The fertility of a buck which gains weight during the breeding season should be of more concern than that of one which is normally losing weight.

4. Using Bucks to Best Advantage in Large Herds

Artificial insemination is the logical approach to efficient use of herd sires. Where artificial insemination is not practiced, does should be hand bred to the buck. A good practice is to allow the buck to serve the doe as soon as she will accept service. Remove him and allow him to serve her again twelve hours later. If the buck is allowed to run with the herd, certain females in heat may be ignored because of preference for others. If more than one buck is present, does in heat may not receive service because the bucks are continually fighting. Two bucks with a herd of females to be bred are often about as effective as no buck at all.

5. Heat Synchronization

Much research has been conducted on heat synchronization in

sheep, and enough of it has been done with goats to show that all of it is useful for goats. These are some good reasons for consideration of heat synchronization:

The long hours of close observation through the kidding season can be shortened when does kid within a few days. For part-time herdsmen, it is much simpler to breed most of the does within a few days, especially if they are to be bred artificially. Also, having larger groups of kids born within a few days of each other simplifies their management.

The use of intravaginal sponges (Synchromate — Searle Upjohn) appears to be the simplest of the synchronization methods. The sponges which contain 20 mg. flugesterone acetate are placed and allowed to remain for sixteen to twenty days. At removal of the sponges, 500 IU of pregnant mare serum and 500 IU human chorionic gonadotrophin are administered. The administration greatly increases the number which show heat and ovulate. Best breeding results are obtained where the entire group of synchronized animals are allowed to go un-bred until the onset of the next heat period. This eliminates the need for the biologic injections, and conception rates are equal to those where does received the pregnant mare serum and Hcg injections.

Signs of Heat — One of the best early signs of approaching heat in a milking doe is a sudden increase of milk output about eight hours before symptoms are seen. Anxiety, repeated bleating, tail wagging and frequent urination with swelling and reddening of the vulva are good signs. If a buck is present, or even if some object which has been near a buck is present, the doe will show great interest in it. Other does usually mount the doe in heat if she is not too high on the "peck order" in the herd. The period between heat cycles in goats varies between individuals from 17 to 23 days. However, the same length period between heats is the rule in individual animals. The length of the heat period varies greatly, influenced by the same factors which affect heats. (See **Factors Which Affect Heats.**) Weak, nearly silent heats may last for only a few hours. Strong heats under the best environmental, social, and nutritional conditions may last two or three days. Ovulation usually occurs in the last few hours of standing heat until eight hours beyond it. When breeding does artificially, best conception rates are obtained during this period.

Detection of Heat Using a Speculum — At the onset of heat, the cervix becomes hyperemic (reddened) and there is marked engorgement of the vaginal wall. Swelling of the cervix produces many apparently normal variations of its shape. Secretions in the cervical orifice at the onset of heat are clear and watery, rapidly thickening and becoming grayish white in color. This accumulates on the vaginal floor and at the proper time for breeding, cheesy material is present and the cervix is extended farthest into the vaginal cavity.

Following heat, engorgement of the cervix and vaginal walls subsides and the normal pale pink color returns to the vaginal walls while the cervix assumes its normal pearly white color. During pregnancy, a plug of thick viscid brownish mucous forms in the cervical opening (os).

D.   Problems of Reproduction

1. Abnormal Cycles

a. Weak or Silent Heats — Anemia is the commonest cause of weak heat signs in milking does. For this reason alone, worming a herd of female goats two weeks before breeding them may be very important in herds where blood-sucking worms are a problem. Anemic does often show longer periods between heats than do normal does.

b. Cystic Ovaries — Cystic degeneration of ovarian follicles produces continuous heat or abnormally short intervals between heat periods. The causes of cystic ovaries are not clearly known and they may be complex. Estrogen in white clover, birdsfoot trefoil, subterranean clover, and to a much less extent, alfalfa varieties, influence ovarian activity with resulting reduced fertility. Certain molds in feeds produce estrogens which shorten periods between heats, intensify and prolong heat and cause continuous enlargement of the vulva in does.

Early treatment of cystic ovaries is usually successful when 500 units chorionic gonadotropin is administered intravenously. When, as a result of several weeks of cystic ovary activity, does show relaxed pelvic ligaments and develop buck-like activity, treatment is usually unsuccessful.

c. Heat During Pregnancy — It is not at all uncommon for does to show some signs of heat during pregnancy. These heats are not really normal heats. According to Germann (1963 Schw. Arch. Tiescheilk 105), they do not ovulate and they show none of the characteristic signs of heat when examined intravaginally using a speculum. An ordinary large pyrex glass modified test tube such as that commonly used for artificial insemination of does is adequate for vaginal examination. A small headlamp worn by the examiner facilitates inspection.

d. **Abnormally Long Periods Between Heats** — When embryonic death occurs before the eleventh day following ovulation, resorption is rapid and the time interval between heat periods is not affected. However, when embryonic death occurs after the fifteenth day following ovulation, the time interval may be greatly extended because the corpus luteum of pregnancy is already established and a considerably larger amount of embryonic material must be resorbed. When periods between heats exceed 25 to 30 days, embryonal death from uterine infection is a possibility.

2. False Pregnancy

Bred does occasionally go full term without returning to heat when in false pregnancy. Most of the usual signs of pregnancy occur (regression of milk flow, abdominal enlargement, both drying off and often "springing" of the udder). At parturition (kidding time), a large volume of clear fluid is passed and the doe usually cries incessantly, searching for her kid. If the animal's value or production justifies keeping her, normal pregnancy usually follows. Some does with false pregnancy come into normal milk production; however, the majority of them do not.

3. Metritis

Inflammation of the endometrium (lining of the uterus) and the maternal placenta (cotyledons) frequently follows difficulty with kidding and with retained placenta (see **Retained Placenta**). Metritis may be an acute infection accompanied by high fever (T. 105-107°F.), severe depression, and indifference to the kids. Dark red discharge is often observed in the cervix and vagina. This may occur within 24 hours after kidding.

Intravenous broad spectrum antibiotic therapy (250 mgm. tetracycline, oxytetracycline, or chlortetracycline three times daily for four days, or very large doses of penicillin-streptomycin combinations containing at least 1,000,000 IU penicillin intramuscularly for four days) has been effective in the author's hands. Intravenous administration of 5% dextrose and normal saline or Lactated Ringers' solution for supportive therapy are desirable.

Chronic metritis is characterized by mild fever, less depression, and abnormal discharge from the vulva. If the animal is otherwise healthy, the chronic metritis may abate spontaneously. If the cervix is open sufficiently to pass a catheter easily, uterine lavage with sterile warm saline and hydrogen peroxide (4:1) may help in removing the excessive uterine discharge.

In the eastern and central United States and presumably other areas where selenium deficiency occurs, more than an occasional case of metritis in a herd should make one suspect selenium-Vitamin E deficiency as the most likely basic cause. This author has observed the presence of white muscle disease in the uterine smooth muscle tissue and in other muscles of the abdominal wall and loin in goats which had died from both acute and chronic metritis. Work at Ohio State University and others has shown that selenium deficiency ought to be suspect where metritis, uterine atony, and chronic uterine discharge occur regularly in post-parturient cattle. In the author's experience, primarily with dairy cattle herds in Pennsylvania and Virginia, selenium deficiency is one of the most important causes of metritis and subsequent infertility.

Prevention — (See **Selenium-Vitamin E Deficiency.**)

4. Infertility Hazards in Polled Goats

With cattle, horns can be eliminated from a herd using polled sires without any of the problems which accompany repeated use of polled bucks in dairy goat herds. The polled characteristic in goats carries with it a tendency toward hermaphrodism in females and testicular hypoplasia in bucks. When polled bucks are used to breed polled does, as many as 20% hermaphroditic females may be born. In the usual herd situation, polled females should always be bred to horned (or disbudded) bucks. Disbudded or horned females may be bred to polled bucks. Another characteristic in males closely associated with polled parentage on both sides of the pedigree is **testicular hypoplasia,** congenitally small soft testicles which do not produce spermatozoa. Such animals are infertile. Any young polled bucks to be used as herd sires should be carefully examined for testicular hypoplasia and the size and consistency of their testicles compared with other horned buck kids the same age.

The process of dehorning or disbudding baby kids is so simple, safe, and sure nowadays that it is usually better to use only horned or disbudded sires for the average herd. Those who practice line breeding may have to use polled bucks on polled does, but they should recognize the danger of hermaphrodism and testicular hypoplasia that is present when breeding polled animals.

5. Problems in Bucks

a. Cryptorchidism (Undescended Testis, Retained Testis) — This is a developmental abnormality which occurs in all breeds of dairy goats. Usually the affected testicle may be retained at any location in its normal path of descent. If the testis later descends partially, no semen is produced by it, but androgens are. Semen quality is naturally impaired. There is a definite possibility of inherited tendency to unilateral cryptorchidism. Monorchid buck kids should be slaughtered at an early age. Bilateral cryptorchidism is extremely rare in buck goats. When it does occur, no semen is produced.

b. Varicocele — This is a local disturbance of the circulation in the internal spermatic vein. It is recognized as a sacular dilation in the spermatic cord above the testicle. It may be bilateral or unilateral. Excessive fluid surrounds the cord. Semen quality is usually not seriously affected and the animal is not seriously hampered in movement unless the varicocele reaches large size. This constitutes a major health hazard to the animal as it matures. Finding of a varicocele upon examination of a prospective herd sire should eliminate him from consideration. The exact cause of the problem is not known. Fortunately, it is even more rare in goats than it is in sheep.

6. Causes of Abortion

a. Vibrionic Abortion — This common cause of abortion in cattle and sheep has only been reported twice in the United States in dairy goats. The disease is primarily spread by carrier animals and forage contaminated by aborted fetuses, discharges and infected placentae. In cattle, the disease is primarily spread to susceptible females via natural service by an infected bull. Streptomycin has been added to bull semen used in AI for more than twenty years to eliminate vibriosis.[2]

b. Chlamydial Abortion — This disease in sheep is known as Enzootic Abortion of Ewes (EAE). Similar outbreaks of abortion in goats have been reported from Cyprus and Bulgaria. An outbreak of this disease was reported in California in a large herd of goats. In this outbreak, about 12% of the kids were aborted, born alive and weak, or were stillborn. Vaccines have been used in Cyprus where the disease is endemic. One of the best aspects of this form of abortion is that animals in all of the reported outbreaks conceived and kidded normally following the abortion experience.[3]

Q Fever — Q Fever is caused by a rickettsial organism, **Coxiella burnetii,** formerly known as **Rickettsia burnetii.** It is maintained in wild rodent populations from which it moves into domestic animals and to man. In man, Q Fever exhibits symptoms similar to influenza. There is increasing evidence that **C. burnetii** can cause abortion. Serological evidence of Q Fever is not at all rare in the United States. Dairy cattle herds in most of the dairy states and goats and sheep in California have shown serum titres.

Infected animals excrete the organism in all body secretions and it has been possible to isolate the Q Fever agent from the air of infected premises. Diagnosis of Q Fever can be made by most state health departments or state veterinary diagnostic laboratories by submission of blood sera from animals which abort.[4]

References:

1   *K.P. Nair, Indian Veterinary Journal 50 (1) 42-50, 1973*

2   *Dobbs, E.M. and McIntyre, R.W., California Veterinarian 1951, Vol. 4, pg. 19.*

3   *1976 Williams, Christine, Proceedings — Sheep and Goat Practice Symposium, Colorado State University.*

4   *1976 Williams, Christine, Proceedings of Sheep and Goat Practice Symposium, Colorado State University, pages 50-52.*

CHAPTER XII

ANESTHESIA
AND SURGERY

A.   Anesthesia For Dairy Goats. 180

B.   Surgical Procedures. 183
        1.   Dehorning Adults 183
        2.   Disbudding Kids — Descenting, Wattle Removal . . 183
        3.   Castration of Buck Kids 186
        4.   Foot Trimming. 186
        5.   Caesarian Section 187

A. Anesthesia For Dairy Goats

Goats are very similar to sheep in their response to the various anesthetic agents and very little research work has been done specifically with the goat. A few recent reports have appeared, however, and will be discussed later in this section.

Goats do not tolerate pain connected with even minor surgical procedures well and will lapse into shock quickly if sufficient analgesia is not provided. Local analgesia and anesthesia have a definite place in goat practice, but care should be taken to completely anesthetize the surgical area. With the advent of the newer tranquilizing agents that produce a more profound state of sedation and analgesia, and the cyclohexamines which produce the dissociated state, local analgesia is not practiced as widely as was once the case.

As with any ruminant animal, care should be taken to avoid ruminal tympany, regurgitation and aspiration of rumen contents. If the procedure is an elective one, fasting and withholding water for 12-24 hours, depending upon the age of the animal involved, should be routine practice. In the case of a non-elective procedure, endotracheal and rumen tubes should be placed when appropriate to avoid bloat and aspiration of rumen contents into the lung fields.

For general anesthesia and analgesia, the use of atropine preoperatively in ruminants is controversial.[1] The author prefers to use atropine at a dosage rate of 2 mg/100 lbs. for procedures lasting more than 45 minutes. This will reduce the salivary flow. In short procedures such as dehorning, etc., the use of atropine preoperatively is probably of little value. In abdominal procedures, the use of atropine is useful in reducing the effects of the vagal reflex. When the abdomen is first opened and the viscera manipulated, the pulse rate and peripheral blood pressure should be monitored carefully to observe the bradycardia and hypotension that are characteristic of this reflex. Peripheral blood pressure can be monitored successfully for this procedure, either on the lingual artery or the digital artery in a forelimb. If this response is noted, then additional atropine should be administered intravenously until the abdominal viscera can be manipulated without illiciting the vagal response. In the author's experience, an additional 1 mg/100 lbs. is usually sufficient to accomplish this.

In field situations, the tranquilizers and cyclohexamines are very useful restraint, and analgesic drugs for minor procedures require minimal monitoring of the patient during the anesthetic procedure.

General anesthesia with barbiturates and inhalation anesthetics can be used successfully in goats, but are more safely and efficiently administered in a hospital setting.

Recommended Anesthetics for Dairy Goats

Ketamine hydrochloride (Ketaset, Bristol or Ketalar, Parke, Davis — 100 mg/ml) — is not FDA approved for food animals. However, its use in dairy goats has been reported. The drug is usually administered intramuscularly. It may be administered intravenously but the more rapid effect may be preceded by a short period of excitement. The solution used is irritant and it may produce transient local muscle pain during induction. Full anesthetic effect lasts only 15 to 30 minutes, but injection of further small doses can be used to prolong anesthesia. A great advantage for its use is the fact that there is minimal excitement as the drug takes effect. Used alone, ketamine does not produce sufficient muscle relaxation to be useful for abdominal procedures. It can be used safely and effectively for most surgical procedures.

Dosage — Administer intramuscularly 0.75 ml to 1.5 ml for baby kids, 1.5 ml to 3.0 ml for those between 8 weeks of age and yearlings. For mature does, use 2.5 ml to 5.0 ml. Large mature bucks may require 8.0 ml for general anesthesia. It is best to administer a light dose and add to it after five to eight minutes if necessary. Spaulding[2] recently reported use of 200-700 mg (2-7 ml), depending upon the size of the goat, for dehorning. This dose will produce restraint and analgesic for 15 to 30 minutes.

Rompun (Xylazine - ChemAgro Div. Bayer) — This drug is highly effective and safe as a tranquilizer and restraint drug for all ruminant animals. As the dose rate is increased, its effects are more profound and the duration of restraint and analgesia is prolonged. It is highly effective as a general anesthetic, but it is quite dangerous if used haphazardly. Induction and recovery are rapid and without excitement. The author has seen kids recover from deep anesthesia within a few minutes without any side effects or after effects. The small animal dilution is recommended because the dose is so small. As with ketamine, this drug should always be used first in the minimal amount. Deep anesthesia may continue for as long as one to six hours, depending upon the dose. There are no available drugs available to counteract the effects of Rompun, and goats are quite variable in their tolerance of it; therefore, the smallest necessary dose should always be administered first.

Dosage — For disbudding and/or castrating kids up to one month of age, administer 0.2 ml to 0.4 ml of *small animal* Rompun (4-6 mg). For young goats up to yearling size, 0.5 ml to 1.0 ml is usually sufficient. Adult does may require from 1.0 to 3.0 ml (20 to 60 mg) and mature bucks may require as much as 3.0 to 4.0 ml of *small animal* Rompun (60 to 80 mg) for deep anesthesia.

Ketamine-Xylazine combination — For long procedures involving exploration of the abdomen such as Caesarian section, this combination may be very useful. The combination produces sufficient muscle relaxation without severely depressing the fetus. The simultaneous use of this combination has been recently reported in the goat[5]. Xylazine was used at the rate of 0.22 mg/kg (0.1 mg/lb.) five to ten minutes prior to the injection of Ketamine at the rate of 11 mg/kg (5 mg/lb.). The animals were chemically restrained in three to six minutes and approximately 40 - 45 minutes of analgesia were realized from the initial dose. Supplemental dosages were given to maintain the animal for periods of up to three hours. With this procedure, the laryngeal reflexes were depressed sufficiently to permit tracheal intubation to prevent aspiration of rumen fluids.

Barbiturates — Goats are highly variable in their response to pentobarbital and for most field procedures its use should be discarded in favor of the safer drugs now available. The ultra-short-acting barbiturates, thiopental and thiamyal, may be administered to goats very safely and will produce good surgical anesthesia and analgesia for periods of 10 - 20 minutes. The initial dose rate is usually of the order of 20 mg/5 lbs. (1 cc of 2% solution), but this should only be used as a guide. Care should be taken to administer the smallest amount of the drug necessary to produce the desired effect. Acidotic patients will require considerably less of this anesthetic than normal ones. Supplemental doses may be given to increase the period of anesthesia, but this may lead to a more prolonged recovery period with mild excitement.

Inhalation Agents — Halothane and methoxyflurane may be used as inhalation agents quite successfully. Kids and animals under 50 lbs. can easily be induced on a mask with 4% halothane, intubated and maintained on 1 - 2% halothane at a flow rate of 1 liter of O_2/min. Older animals are first induced with a barbiturate and then maintained on the inhalation agent. The author prefers the use of halothane over methoxyflurane in goats due to the shorter induction and recovery times. If methoxyflurane is used, care should be taken to keep the animals lightly anesthetized after induction. This will keep recovery time within acceptable limits.[4]

B.   Surgical Procedures

1. Dehorning Adults

Horned animals have no place in the modern dairy goat herd. The daily assertion of "peck order" continually raises the possibility of injuries. The more timid younger does in the herd never milk up to their potential if most of their time is spent watching and avoiding the dominant members of the herd. Fear and intensity of watchfulness increase as the proportion of horned animals increases. Horned goats also can inflict injuries on human caretakers. However, such injuries are usually accidental. It is very unusual that a horned doe willfully tries to injure one who handles her. Bucks, however, are a different story. They can and will, without provocation, use their horns. The sharp edge of a triangular horn can inflict severe wounds.

The dehorning of adult goats is a difficult procedure with plenty of hazards. Removal of large triangular horns necessitates opening a large area of the frontal sinuses. Smaller rounded horns are relatively easy to remove. General anesthesia is necessary to prevent severe pain and shock and to provide necessary restraint. Wire embryotomy saws or bone saws are most commonly used. The skin area surrounding the horn should be shaved. At least a quarter inch of skin should completely surround the base of the horn when it is removed. Arteries around the horn base should be ligated or pulled if necessary. Sulfonamide powder should be applied to the wounds and an adhesive bandage should be used to cover the wounds for at least the first postoperative week before it is removed. Special care to keep dust and chaff out of the wounds should be taken. Dehorning of adult goats, especially bucks, is a major operation. Unless it is performed correctly so that horns will not grow back little will be gained. Improperly dehorned mature goats develop ugly misshapen masses of horn tissue that are usually worse weapons than the original horns.

2.   Disbudding Kids

Disbudding or dehorning baby kids is easily accomplished using an electric disbudding iron made especially for the purpose, or a modified electric calf dehorner which does a good job, too. The most important requirement for a good electric dehorner is that it gets hot enough to show a cherry red color. The use of those electric dehorners which do not become cherry red is inhumane, because it requires too much time to penetrate the skin at the base of the horn bud and the excessive length of heat application may damage bone and brain tissue beneath. If an electric kid dehorner is used, be sure that it is hot enough. Some types on the market do not reach cherry red color.

The Sunbeam electric dehorner used for dehorning young calves burns much more tissue than is necessary for dehorning kids. Healing is a long tedious process and permanent ugly scars may follow its use. If the soldering tip manufactured for use with the Sunbeam electric calf dehorner is cut off and the end drilled out, an excellent dehorner for kids results. This does minimal damage and one can easily flip out the burned-out horn bud with it.

Many people routinely dehorn kids without use of anesthesia, using clever boxes to hold them, or by getting someone to hold the kid with the hind quarters under one arm and the head flexed downward by the hands. The experienced operator with a good cherry red hot iron and good help can perform the job satisfactorily and very quickly. However, anesthetics are now available which make the job more humane and accurate. From 0.25 ml. to 0.4 ml. of small-animal Xylazine (Rompun-ChemAgro) using a tuberculin syringe for accurate dosage and intramuscular administration is excellent for the purpose. Use the smaller dose for kids under two weeks of age up to the larger dose for kids five to six weeks old. Within five minutes, kids go under deep anesthesia which lasts about ten minutes. After that, they rise with no after effects nor do they show any awareness that anything has happened to them. The dehorner, when it is hot enough, is applied over the horn bud for about half a second, burning through the skin. The isolated horn bud and skin can be lifted out using the dehorner itself or a pen knife. It is important that the burned area be at least a quarter inch from the base of the horn bud. Often scurs develop when the dehorner is used on a triangular-shaped horn bud. Be sure that the burned area completely isolates the developing horn and entirely penetrates the skin. One of the best arguments for the use of anesthesia is the likelihood that the job will be done correctly.

Removing Odor Tissue — Most of the odor of bucks is produced by sebaceous cell masses which in the young kid are located medially and posteriorly (toward the mid-line and behind the horn buds). In order to know how much tissue must be destroyed it is necessary to remove the odor glands. It is a good idea to shave the area with a fine clipper blade or razor before dehorning the first few buck kids. After you are able to identify and locate the small yellow masses (about the size of small match heads), then further shaving of kids is unnecessary.

Because a few doe kids also have a much smaller amount of the sebaceous gland tissue, it may be a good precaution, especially in some Toggenburg and Alpine breeds, to burn a small additional elliptical area toward the inside and behind the area disbudded. With baby buck kids, the sebaceous gland area is usually not more than three-eighths of an inch wide at its greatest width. Simply removing the additional tissue will remove practically all of the buck odor and prevent goaty flavor of the milk of females which have any of the sebaceous gland tissue. The appearance of scurs (abnormal horny growths) following use of an electric dehorner results when the skin surrounding the horn button has not been totally destroyed. Off-center placement and insufficient dehorner heat are the usual reasons for development of scurs. These usually become unsightly weapons as bad or worse than horns. With good anesthesia, the operator is able to do a much better job.

Rubber-Band Dehorning — The use of elastrator bands at the base of horns is often attempted for their removal. When they are used on horns which have emerged, they will do the job if they are applied correctly. Anesthesia is required for the necessary restraint. A cut should be made below the base of the horn at the anterior-medial corner (the sharp angle of the horn) to prevent the band from slipping. Tincture of iodine should be thoroughly scrubbed into the area and the elastrator bands should be soaked in iodine for at least ten minutes prior to application as an aid in preventing tetanus. Administration of tetanus antitoxin at the same time is worthwhile. Rubber-band dehorning is a poor alternative for hot-iron disbudding.

Caustic Paste Dehorning — Caustic paste containing potassium hydroxide or potassium hydroxide sticks are frequently used for dehorning calves and some people also use either form for dehorning kids. Control is not good and kids may rub their heads and develop permanent unsightly damage to their heads and ears as a result of the caustic material.

Removing Extra Teats — At the same time doe kids are dehorned, extra teats can be easily removed. If there is any question at all as to which teat is the extra one, removal should be postponed. A small curved serrated-edge scissors should be used and the cut line should be made in the same direction as the long axis of the body to minimize scars.

Wattle Removal — Whether or not wattles should be removed is a matter of the owner's preference. They are rarely subject to injury, but some prefer them off to improve the "dairy character" of the head and neck. Wattles are easily removed when kids are dehorned, using a curved serrated sears or a small Burdizzo emasculator.

3. Castration of Buck Kids

If it is desirable to keep buck kids until they are three to five months old for use as meat, they should be castrated. Castrated bucks are much easier to handle; they develop little or no buck odor; and they can be kept with doe kids. They fatten very well and produce excellent carcasses at three to five months. Milk-fed bucks to be slaughtered at four to eight weeks need not be castrated.

The best way to castrate buck kids is with a sharp knife. The lower third of the scrotal sac should be cut off and the testicles squeezed out through the opening. The spermatic cords are usually scraped through with the knife, or a canine emasculator is used.

Elastrator bands may also be used for baby kids, but care must be taken to prevent tetanus. Dipping the bands in tincture of iodine and thorough disinfection of the area where the band is applied are necessary precautions. Be especially careful when applying the band to see that the band is between both testicles and the body wall.

4. Foot Trimming

Depending upon the amount of exercise goats get and the terrain on which they move, more or less foot trimming must be part of the management program for every dairy goat herd. Those animals which have daily exercise in rocky or sandy surfaces may require minimal trimming. Those kept in a sodded dry lot may require foot attention at intervals of as low as six weeks. Burdizzo foot-trimming shears, garden pruning shears, or a sharp knife may be used.

The important thing to remember about foot trimming is that the ground contact edge of the wall of the hoof should be exactly parallel with the coronary band (the top edge) of the foot. Weight should be borne on the entire horny hoof wall and not on the sole or heel. The tough rubber-like heels of goats grow fairly rapidly. In the natural rocky habitat of goats, this helps to give the animals good footing. However, under dry lot conditions, the heels become excessively long if not trimmed off regularly. They cause spreading of the toes and curled-under outside walls of the hooves. The novice at foot trimming should first study the feet of top animals in the larger dairy goat shows to determine what a normal foot should look like. Unless one understands how to trim the feet and how much to trim off the feet, especially the heels, effort may be wasted and much damage done.

5. Caesarian Section

The ventral midline approach using Ketamine-Xylazine combination is most widely used. Prognosis is good when fetuses are alive and active. Where fetal death and decomposition have begun prognosis is, at best, guarded. C-sections offer the best approach to dystolia in many cases.

References:
1. Bryant, S.H.: *General Anesthesia in the Goat. Fed Proc 28:1553, 1969.*
2. Spaulding, C.E.: *Procedure for Dehorning the Dairy Goat. VM/SAC 72:228, 1977.*
3. Kuman, A., et.al.: *Clinical Studies of Ketamine HC1 and Xylazine HC1 in Domestic Goats. VM/SAC 71:1707, 1977.*
4. Soma, L.R.: *Textbook of Veterinary Anesthesia. Williams and Wilkins. Baltimore, Maryland, 1971.*

CHAPTER XIII

POISONOUS PLANTS

A.   Factors Involved in Plant Poisoning 190
      1.   Starvation 190
      2.   Accidental Plant Poisoning 191
      3.   Amount of Plants Eaten 191
      4.   Desire for Browse 191
      5.   Fertilization Practices and Weather 191
B.   Locoweeds 192
C.   The Nightshades 192
D.   Nitrate-Accumulating Plants 192
E.   Ornamental Plants 193
F.   The Prunus Family 193
G.   Plants Which Contain Oxalic Acid 193
H.   Plants Which Cause Photosensitivity 194

Poisonous plants are, perhaps, more important to those who manage dairy goats than for any other class of livestock, including brush or range goats. The dairy goat in America is an animal kept mainly in confinement. Any opportunity the dairy goat finds to eat green browse of any sort is usually seized upon.

The goat kept on range soon learns to avoid the toxic plants. In Virgina, the author has seen scrub goats used solely to clean up areas to be developed for cattle pasture. After they ate all of the honeysuckle and poison ivy, they systematically attacked everything edible. The really poisonous plants like hellebore sp., blood root, nightshade, etc., were carefully avoided, even after the goats were forced to resort to eating tree bark and other rough sources of food.

Because so many plants that are not poisonous to goats affect the flavor of their milk, it is not very practical to attempt to pasture a milking herd unless the animals are put into an improved pasture with no access to wild or ornamental plants. Goats make economical use of this pasture only when it is strip grazed with electric fence. This grazing method has serious disadvantages because the forage is used at all stages of development. Therefore, it seems to be more practical to confine the milking herd in a clean dry lot and feed them green forage or hay cut at the optimum stage of growth so it will provide the most palatable material with the highest protein and energy and the least amount of fiber. If the goat farm has extensive area of permanent pasture land or brushy range land, this should be reserved for young stock or dry stock. As long as animals have plenty of forage when using these areas, the danger of plant poisoning is relatively small. Browse of all kinds is extremely useful for restoration of rumen function in high-producing does and for good rumen development in growing kids.

A. Factors Involved in Plant Poisoning

The factors that contribute to the ingestion of poisonous plants are a more serious consideration than the mere presence of potentially poisonous plants. They are:

1. Starvation

Too often, animals are placed in woodland "pastures," or unimproved pastures which offer very little safe nutritious food. They refrain from eating poisonous plants until they are forced by hunger to do so. In the author's experience, starvation is the most important reason why all types of domestic animals eat poisonous plants. Unless there is a large amount of land available in a "woodland pasture lot," putting goats into it offers almost certain hazard of plant poisoning unless supplementary forage is offered.

2. Accidental Plant Poisoning

Poisonous plants may be fed with other safe material unknowingly. This may occur when forage is green-chopped and dangerous poisonous plants are accidently included with the safe material. In Pennsylvania, deadly nightshade has been field-chopped with alfalfa or corn for green feeding with disastrous results. The same material fed with alfalfa without chopping would doubtless have been sorted out and rejected by the animals.

3. The Amount of Plants Eaten

Poisonous plants are often well tolerated and eaten by goats if they have adequate safe material to eat at the same time. The author has seen goats completely remove bracken fern, dog bane, mountain laurel, wild cherry and other plants from wild areas containing an adequate amount of safe material (birch, wild grapes, aspen, maple, honeysuckle, woodbine, etc.). The animals serve a useful purpose with little danger to themselves in doing this. However, if they have access to poisonous material when they manage to break out of the best of pastures or from dry lot feeding, the result can be disastrous. Certain plants cause photosensitivity when white-skinned animals eat enough of them in bright sunny weather.

4. Desire for Browse

Dairy goats on the best of rations crave woody plant material. It is important when feeding goats in a barn or dry lot that they be prevented from any access to woody plant material or weeds unless they are given safe material harvested for them by the owner. As every goat owner knows, goats fed the best of feed will struggle to reach anything outside the fence and eat it, whether or not it is poisonous.

5. Fertilization Practices and the Weather

Many plants which are safe sources of forage are made poisonous when faulty fertilization practices and abnormal weather affect normal plant metabolism. In cold wet weather of early spring and fall, small grain and grass pastures become deficient in magnesium and may have toxic levels of nitrates. In periods of drought, sorghum and sorghum-sudan hybrids may contain excessive amounts of cyanide even if feeding is delayed until the plants reach the height generally recommended to be safe. Certain plants (pigweed, smartweed, lambsquarter, elderberry — to mention a few) become accumulators of toxic levels of nitrates under droughty conditions.

B. Locoweeds

These important addictive poisonous plants of western United States are members of the Astragalus family. The poisonous principle elaborated by the plant is similar in its effects to that found in various lathyrus sp. (vetchlings and peas). Lack of muscular control, tremors, and endless wandering, rigidity of the limbs and pushing against objects are usual symptoms terminating in death. In addition to the lathyrogen symptoms, locoweeds have addictive properties which apparently cause animals to hunt for them once they have begun to eat them.

C. The Nightshades

These plants contain solanine compounds in the leaves and their green berries. Because they are very bitter, goats will usually not browse nightshade species. The green berries of many nightshades (including potatoes) are extremely poisonous. The ripe berries of some (including deadly or black nightshade) are often used to make delicious jellies and preserves.

D. Nitrate-Accumulating Plants

Many plants under normal conditions can be safely eaten by goats. Some of them (red root pigweed, thistles, lambs' quarter) are palatable and useful feeds. However, when these plants are affected by drought, they may accumulate toxic quantities of nitrates (up to four or five percent). Then when eaten by the animals, the excessive nitrates are reduced to nitrites. These combine with hemoglobin of red blood cells to limit the oxygen-carrying capacity of the blood. Nitrate poisoning commonly causes abortion and extreme shortness of breath (dyspnea) from exercise. Severe nitrate poisoning can produce rapid death from suffocation. Mild cases may show digestive upset with colicky symptoms and severe drop in milk production. The common elderberry (Sambucus Canadensis) is a notorious nitrate accumulator in dry weather. Does due to freshen in fall months may abort if they have access to elderberry plants in hot dry late summer weather.

E. Ornamental Plants

Almost without exception, dairy goat owners may assume that most ornamental shrubs, hedges, garden flowers, and perennial flowers, with the exception of roses, are to be considered unsafe.

The one single fact that the author wishes to stress most about plant poisoning for dairy goats is that given adequate forage of all kinds, goats are less likely to suffer poisoning than are any other domestic animal. They are extremely adaptable to utilizing all kinds of forage and roughage. Only when they are allowed to eat toxic plants through faulty management on the herdsman's part do problems develop.

F. The Prunus Family

The leaves of all members of the Prunus family (wild cherries, cherries, plums, peaches, apricots) contain a glucoside. As long as the leaves are fresh, they are harmless. However, when the leaves wither, hydrogen cyanide and a sugar are released. For a short time, until the leaves dry and the HCN is dissipated, the leaves are extremely poisonous and a handful can kill a goat. During the period when the leaves are poisonous, they appear to be more palatable, perhaps, as a result of the presence of the sugar.

Hydrogen cyanide combines with hemoglobin, the oxygen-carrying component of red blood cells, and the animals literally die of acute suffocation.

Methylene blue solutions are used by veterinarians for the treatment of cyanide poisoning. But, it is rarely possible to administer the drug early enough to effect recovery.

G. Plants Which Contain Oxalic Acid

Rhubarb leaves contain large quantities of oxalic acid and hungry goats might eat enough rhubarb leaves to die of acute oxalate poisoning. Oxalates tie up blood calcium and produce milk fever-like symptoms first, but this is followed by severe kidney damage with death occurring within 36 hours after the first signs of abdominal pain and convulsions.

All ruminants are much less susceptible to oxalate poisoning than are other animals. A source of urinary oxalate calculi in buck goats might very likely be repeated access to a few rhubarb leaves or repeated feeding of beet leaves, swiss chard, or mustard leaves. These contain oxalic acid which causes precipitation of oxalates in the kidney tubules and formation of masses of crystals in the bladder or urethra where they sometimes prevent urination (urinary calculi, urolithiasis).

H. Plants Which Cause Photosensitivity

The important plants involved in this group are buckwheat, alsike clover, rape, St. John's Wort, and to a lesser extent, ladino and white clover. With the exception of St. John's Wort, all of the plants are quite palatable and nutritious. White-skinned animals eating enough of these plants (those that produce lush growth in ideal weather are the worst) in bright sunny weather develop anything from sunburn to severe sloughing off of the white-skinned areas.

For example, a herd of Saanen goats eating aftermath buckwheat after harvest of the grain in late September in northeastern United States might experience severe "sunburning." A group of darker colored goats could safely eat the forage at the same time with no problem.

There are three basic requirements for development of photosensitivity when goats eat these plants: the animals must have white skin, the animals must eat a minimum quantity of the plants, and they must be exposed to bright sunlight for at least one-half day at the same time.

CHAPTER XIV

CHEMICAL POISONING

A.   Ammonium Sulfamate (Ammate) 196
B.   Arsenic 196
C.   Borax...196
D.   Dinitro Compounds 196
E.   Fluoride 197
F.   Lead..197
G.   Pentachlorophenol 198
H.   Salt..198
I.   Sodium Chlorate..................................199
J.   Trizine Compounds 199

A. Ammonium Sulfamate (Ammate)

This widely used herbicide is often suspected of poisoning. While research trials have indicated little danger of toxicity from correct use of this herbicide, some field reports persist that it is toxic to deer and cattle.

B. Arsenic

Arsenic is still widely used as a weed- and brush-killing spray along highway and railroad rights of way. It no longer is widely used as a pesticide in agriculture. Organic arsenical compounds (arsonilic acid, carbasone, roxarsone, and nitrasone) are widely used in poultry and swine production in medicated feed. Accidental incorporation of any of these in goat feed could be a source of poisoning for goats.

Symptoms — Severe watery diarrhea with blood and repeated straining are seen. Dehydration, weakness, severe depression, weak pulse, and abdominal pain follow. The onset is usually rapid and the course most often requires only a few hours but chronic arsenical poisoning may require weeks to manifest itself.

Common findings with chronic arsenic poisoning are dry exfoliative dermatitis and cracking of the skin.

Diagnosis — Excess of 3 ppm (wet weight) of arsenic in liver and kidneys 24 hours after animals have been exposed to arsenic is diagnostic of arsenic poisoning.

C. Borax

This compound is widely used as a soil sterilant and for fly control in compost and manure piles. Cases of poisoning would only likely occur from accidental incorporation of borax into feed, and dairy goats of all domestic farm animals, would be least likely to eat it. Symptoms include diarrhea, dehydration and convulsions preceding coma and death. There is no known antidote.

D. Dinitro Compounds

Dinitrophenol and Dinitrocresol are both highly toxic when animals have immediate access to sprayed foliage. Later on, residues on foliage are not toxic to livestock. Characteristic yellow discoloration of the skin and hair around the mouth and nose, and high fever are common symptoms. Dyspnea, tachycardia, and convulsions precede rapid death and rapid onset of rigor mortis.

Treatment — This is rarely successful in goats. Chlorpromazine to reduce the fever, parenteral injection of Vitamin A and large amounts of intravenous five percent dextrose are indicated.

E. Fluoride

Fluoride poisoning most often occurs from gases and dusts emanating from chemical plants, aluminum production, certain enameling operations, and phosphate processing plants. Air pollution may affect forage for several miles from such plants.

Goats are more tolerant of fluoride than are cattle. Where fluoride poisoning is suspect, cattle in the same area should be showing more severe symptoms than the goats.

Symptoms — Dry stiff hide, acute lameness usually in one or two legs, abnormal hoof growth, and diarrhea are usual symptoms. Excessive wearing and staining of permanent teeth formed during exposure to fluorides is the most dramatic evidence of exposure to fluorides.

Diagnosis — Normal bone contains up to 1000 ppm fluorine. Fluorine levels in bones of poisoned animals may reach ten times that amount. Fluorine content of normal urine is 5 ppm; excess fluorine intakes may produce values exceeding 10 ppm.

F. Lead

Goats are relatively resistant to lead poisoning. The author has seen several instances where cows suffered from acute lead poisoning which did not affect goats under the same circumstances.

Sources of lead — Automobile battery salvage operations are common sources of lead poisoning both by water and air pollution. Lead-containing paints may be important where goats chew on wood covered by such paints. Lead acetate (sugar of lead) is a lead compound very palatable to cattle, sheep, and goats. Lead arsenate sprays, rarely used today, and lead arsenate-phenothiazine combinations are possible though improbable sources. Lead is slowly soluble from the digestive tract.

Symptoms — Nervous disturbances predominate. Blindness,

circling, grinding of teeth, exaggerated leg movement when walking, and pressing the head against firm objects are common symptoms.

Treatment — Extensive injury to the liver, kidneys, and brain often makes treatment of little value. Administration of 20% calcium disodium versenate solution intravenously or subcutaneously at the rate of 2 mg/lb. body weight daily is the treatment of choice for lead poisoning.

Diagnosis — Lead values in unclotted blood exceeding 0.2 ppm and in kidney and liver tissue exceeding 4 ppm are good diagnostic indicators of lead poisoning.

G.   Pentachlorophenol

This commonly used wood preservative can be directly absorbed through the skin and via the lungs. Goats should not be allowed access to, or be housed in, pentachlorophenol-treated lumber until the lumber has thoroughly dried and there is no longer evidence of the typical pentachlorophenol odor. Gates and feed troughs or any other wooden structures likely to be chewed by goats should not be treated with pentachlorophenol.

Symptoms — Nervous symptoms, rapid pulse, and convulsions followed by death are characteristic. Neither effective treatment nor antidote is known.

H.   Salt

Goats appear to be more resistant to salt poisoning than swine, cattle and sheep in that order. The only likely situation where salt poisoning might appear would be where salt is suddenly supplied to salt-hungry animals followed by lack of water or failure to drink water. In goats, sudden depressed intake of water during cold winter weather might be a likely source. Salt poisoning rarely occurs when animals have adequate drinkable water.

Symptoms — Weakness, depression, ataxia and blindness with rapid weak pulse and nervousness. The course is usually rapid. Salt poisoning may be difficult to differentiate from clostridial entero-toxemia.

I. Sodium Chlorate

This old, but rather common, herbicide is very unlikely to produce poisoning in goats. The minimal lethal dose must exceed about 1300 mg/lb. It would likely only cause poisoning where it was accidentally added to feed instead of salt.

J. Trizine Compounds

(Atrazine, promazine, simazine, prometone, pyrometryne) and Plant Hormone Herbicides (2,4D and 2,4,5T) — All of these compounds and especially the plant hormone herbicides (2,4D and 2,4,5T) are widely used today. When used under label recommendations and leaves have died, there have been no authenticated poisonings. However, the action of these herbicides on nitrate-accumulating and cyanide-producing plants may increase these toxic elements in the plants.

For example, sprayed wild cherry leaves may be toxic during the immediate period when they are wilting. Similarly, elderberry and other nitrate-accumulators may be more than usually toxic when treated with these herbicides during dry or unusually cool weather.

CHAPTER XV

ROUTINE HERD HEALTH PROGRAM FOR DAIRY GOAT HERDS IN MID-ATLANTIC STATES OF THE U.S.

A.	Seasonal Health Considerations	202
B.	Health Recommendations for Classes of Animals	203
	1. Dry Does	203
	2. Kidding Does	203
	3. Baby Kids	204
	4. Weaned Kids	204
	5. Milking Herd	204
	6. Bucks	205

T here are certain herd health recommendations best considered
on a seasonal basis. These are listed first. Where certain herd
disease problems are present, routine procedures for their control
and/or elimination can be added to the routine herd health program
below. It is not necessary that all of the procedures be performed by a
veterinarian. However, a herd health program is meaningless unless it
is accompanied by the constant professional surveillance and super-
vision of a veterinarian.

A.   Seasonal Health Considerations

Fall and Early Winter
Clean the barn thoroughly before the onset of bad weather. Clean
and disinfect kidding pens and housing for baby kids. Keep these clean,
dry and free of bedding until needed.

Parasites — It is generally prudent to administer doses of a broad
spectrum worm medicine to all animals in the herd before the winter
confinement season. All animals in the herd should be given two
thorough cold water sprayings at Coumaphos (Co-Ral-ChemAgro)
1 - 1½ lbs. 25% wettable powder per 100 gallons water at two-week
intervals during calm weather, at least several weeks before the onset
of cold weather. It must be emphasized that **thorough spraying** be done.
Actually, dipping is much preferable to spraying and it should be done
where it is practicable. Check and trim feet where necessary.

Winter
Check Housing to be sure that there is no moisture condensation
anywhere inside. Be sure bedding remains dry and there are no drafts
which will unnecessarily chill animals. Check watering facilities for
cleanliness and proper function. Goats will drink much more water if it
is at least 15° above freezing and milk production will benefit greatly
from it. Check feet and trim if necessary. Remove horns and scurs from
animals which are using them.

Spring
Check fencing and gates in lots and pastures. Two weed chopper
electric fence wires placed on the inside of woven wire or other
permanent fencing will prevent fence damage and goat injury. Remove
all sources of injury from lots and pastures. Check and trim feet if
necessary.

Summer

Provide dry shade and cool fresh water for all animals. Only loose salt will enable animals to consume adequate amounts during hot weather. Use only trace mineral salt. Check bucks for physical condition and vigor. Feed them additional grain (dairy feed) to be sure they are gaining in condition before the onset of the breeding season. Physically examine all bucks for genital abnormalities or injuries. Check the herd for internal parasite burden during the height of the summer and treat, if necessary. Check and trim feet, if necessary.

B.   Health Recommendations for Classes of Animals

1. Dry does

All does bred 70 - 110 days should be examined for pregnancy before drying them off. Examine udders carefully after does are dried off. Those which have had clinical evidence of mastitis, or older animals which have large pendulous udders, may benefit from administration of one quarter dose of a dry cow mammary infusion in each udder half. There may be justification for routine treatment of all glands when they are dried off where mastitis is a herd problem. Strict cleanliness and antiseptic teat end preparation is necessary for safe dry treatment. Dip teats for at least three days after drying them off. Examine udders carefully during the dry period. Strip them out and treat them again if they show any abnormal signs.

Feeding — Be sure dry does are gaining in condition for the last month before kidding. Control calcium intake for the last month before kidding. Restrict alfalfa feeding and feed a grain mix containing no added calcium supplementation if any alfalfa forage has been fed.

Selenium-alphatocopherol Injection — Administer a dose of selenium-alphatocopherol 60 days before kidding. Repeating the dose may be indicated again 15 days before kidding.

Biologics — Administer a booster dose of **C. perfringens CD** toxoid bacterin and a booster dose of tetanus toxoid not less than 21 days before kidding. Blackleg bacterin or other clostridial bacterin may be administered where indicated at this time.

2. Kidding Does

Make sure they have adequate exercise right up to kidding. Confine in maternity pens when kidding is imminent. Be sure both the doe and the maternity pens are clean at kidding time. Wash udder and soiled hindparts of the doe at the end of kidding. Assist doe to clean and dry kids. Dip navel cords of kids in tincture of iodine immediately. Remove kids and hand feed at least 2 - 3 ounces of colostrum as soon as possible. Remove placenta and discharges as they are expelled by the doe. Retained placentas should be removed after 24 hours. Examine does which show anxiety with straining after kidding.

3. Baby Kids

Keep a small supply of antibiotic bactericidal scours medicine available for use if a kid develops diarrhea. Examine all kids carefully for navel infection. In some herds, it may be advisable to re-treat all navels the second time with tincture of iodine. Check all kids for congenital abnormalities (atresia ani, genital hypoplasia, hermaphrodism, cleft palate, etc.). Disbud kids at three days to three weeks of age. Castrate surplus bucks, remove wattles and extra teats at the same time.

Coccidiosis — In some herd situations it may be advisable to administer two or three daily doses of sulfamethazine to kids at three weeks of age. In most herds, a course of coccidiostat (preferably amprolium) should be administered two to three weeks following weaning.

Biologics — Administer the first dose of **C. perfringens CD** toxoid bacterin and the first dose of tetanus toxoid at three to four weeks of age and repeat both in two weeks. All animals in the herd including bucks should be receiving booster doses of **C. perfringens** toxoid bacterin at least annually.

4. Weaned Kids

Check for internal parasites one month after weaning. Administer contagious ecythma vaccine at least two weeks after weaning and not less than three weeks before the first show. Segregate buck kids from doe kids at three months of age or earlier. Recheck polled kids for genital abnormalities. Trim feet before turning kids out.

5. Milking Herd

Feed animals grain, individually, according to their needs.

Prebreeding Recommendations — Be sure does are gaining in weight for at least two to three weeks before breeding. Record all heats noticed, length of heat, intervals between heats and all breeding dates. Breed doe kids at seven to ten months of age — as soon as they are large enough to breed. Check all animals for parasites or routinely worm the herd one month before breeding.

Mastitis — Avoid milking injury. Develop a good milking routine. Wash and dry udders before milking. Use a strip plate. Dip teats routinely in a **non-irritant** teat dip after milking. Check milk with the CMT every two weeks or when there is any reason to suspect mastitis (swelling, fever, tenderness, abnormal milk).

6. Bucks

Administer to bucks all biologic injections and all parasite treatments at the same time these are given to the other animals in the herd. Provide abundant exercise. Keep feet trimmed. Administer selenium and alphatocopherol at the same time dry does receive it and again several weeks before the beginning of the breeding season. Be sure that bucks are in good flesh at the beginning of the breeding season. Examine all bucks for genital abnormalities or genital injuries before the beginning of the breeding season.

CHAPTER XVI

DAIRY GOAT RESOURCES

by Dr. Duane Miksch
Extension Veterinarian
University of Kentucky

ASSOCIATIONS

American Association of Sheep and Goat Practitioners, Don E. Bailey, DVM, Sec.-Treas., 248 NW Garden Valley Road, Roseburg, OR 97470.

American Dairy Goat Association, Box 865, Spindale, NC 28160. PH: (704) 631-3801.

American Goat Society, 1606 Colorado St., Manhattan, KS 66502. PH: (913) 537-7751.

BOOKS

Belanger, Jerry, *Raising Milk Goats the Modern Way.* Garden Way Publishing Co., Charlotte, VT 05445. $3.95.

Devendra, C. and M. Burns. *Goat Production in the Tropics.* 1970. Commonwealth Agricultural Bureau, Farnham Royal, Bucks, England. Approx. $12.00.

Eberhardt, Jo. *Good Beginnings with Dairy Goats.* 1973. Dairy Goat Journal, Box 1908, Scottsdale, AZ 85252. $6.00 (plus 50¢ postage).

French, M. *Observations on the Dairy Goat, FAO.* 1970. Unipub, Inc., 650 1st Avenue, Box 433, Murray Hill Station, New York, NY 10016. $5.50.

Hungerford, T.G. *Diseases of Livestock.* 1971. Lawrence Verry, Inc., 16 Holmes St., Mystic, CT 06355. $40.00.

Jeffrey, H.E. *Goats.* 1975. Diamond Farm Book Publishers, Dept. DG, Box 266, Alexandria Bay, NY 13607. $3.95.

Leach, Corl A. *Aids to Goatkeeping.* 8th Edition, 1975. Dairy Goat Journal, Box 1908, Scottsdale, AZ 85252. $10.00 (plus 50¢ postage).

Leach, C.E. *The Goat Owner's Scrapbook.* 1961. Dairy Goat Journal, Box 1908, Scottsdale, AZ 85252. $7.50 (plus 50¢ postage).

Lindahl, Ivan L., Nutrition and Feeding of Goats in *Digestive Physiology and Nutrition of Ruminants, Vol 3 — Practical Nutrition,* D.C. Church, Senior Author and Editor. OSU Bookstores, Inc., Box 489, Corvallis, OR 97330. $12.90.

MacKenzie, Davis. *Goat Husbandry.* 5th Edition, 1975. Diamond Farm Book Publishers, Dept. DG, Box 266, Alexandria Bay, NY 13607. $17.75.

Owen, Nancy Lee. *The Illustrated Standard of the Goat.* Dairy Goat Journal, Box 1908, Scottsdale, AZ 85252. $10.00 (plus 50¢ postage).

Shields, Joan and Harry. *The Modern Dairy Goat.* 1972. Dairy Goat Journal, Box 1908, Scottsdale, AZ 85252. $5.00 (plus 50¢ postage).

Walsh, Helen. *Starting Right with Milk Goats.* 1972. Garden Way Publishing Co., Charlotte, VT 05445. $3.00.

BREED CLUBS

Alpines International Club, Lelia Ramey, Sec.-Treas., 7155-D Redwood Retreat Rd., Gilroy, CA 95020.

American LaMancha Club, Mary R. Vickery, Sec.-Treas., 148 HWY 9, Sedro Woolley, WA 98284.

National Nubian Club, Jean Van Voorhees, Sec.-Treas., RD 1, Box 416, Glen Gardner, NJ 08826.

National Saanen Club, Della Frazier, Sec.-Treas., 9132 Hastings Blvd., Riverside, CA 92509.

National Toggenburg Club, Ellen Shew, Box 131, South Bristol, ME 04568.

BULLETINS

American Dairy Goat Association, Box 865, Spindale, NC 28160. *Dairy Goats Breeding/Feeding/Management,* Leaflet No. 439 (1966). $1.25.

California Goat Dairyman's Assn., Box 934, Turlock, CA 95380. *Miracle Goat Milk — Recipes For All The Family.*

Canada Department of Agriculture — Information Division, Ottawa, K1A OC7. *The Dairy Goat in Canada,* Publication 1441(1976).

Minnesota Dairy Goat Assn., Box 377, Silver Lake, MN 55381. *Caprine Cookery.* $1.75.

New Mexico State University — Agricultural Publications, Las Cruces, NM 88001. *Keeping a Goat for Home Milk Production,* Guide

400D-701 (1972). *Breeds of Dairy Goats*, Guide 400D-702 (1975). *Housing and Equipment for Dairy Goats*, Guide 400D-703 (1972). New York State College of Agriculture-Agricultural Publications, Cornell University, Ithaca, NY 14853. *The Dairy Goat*, Extension Bulletin 1160.

Oregon State University-Agricultural Publications, Corvallis, OR 97331. *Dairy Goats for Farm Milk Supply*, Extension Circular 866 (1976). *Dairy Goat Housing and Care*, Extension Circular 867 (1975).

Rutgers University-Agricultural Publications, Box 231, New Brunswick, NJ 08903. *Dairy Goat Management*, Extension Bulletin 334 (1972).

Texas A&M University-Agricultural Publications, College Station, TX 77843. *Dairy Goats Care and Management*, MP-1178 (1975).

U.S. Government Printing Office, Washington, DC 20401. *A Dairy Goat For Home Milk Production*, Leaflet No. 538 (1973).

University of California-Agricultural Publications, Davis, CA 95616. *Dairy Goat Day, Proceedings, March 31, 1975.* $.50.

University of Florida-Agricultural Publications, Gainesville, FL 32611. *Dairy Goat Production Guide*, Dy 73-13 (1973).

4H PROJECTS

University of Arkansas, Box 391, Little Rock, AR 72203. *Dairy Goat Project Book*, N-102. *Dairy Goats*, N-202.

University of California, Davis, CA 95616. *Your Dairy Goat*, AXT-243.

University of Florida, Gainesville, FL 32611. *4H Dairy Goat Record Book*, 4H264. *Fitting and Showing 4H Dairy Goats*, DY 75-38 (1975).

University of Minnesota, St. Paul, MN 55108. *Dairy. . .Kids & Goats*, 4H B-12 (1975). *Caring For Dairy Goats*, Extension Folder 319 (1975).

North Carolina State University, Raleigh, NC 27607. *Dairy Goat Youth Project Record Book*.

Ohio State University, 2120 Fyffe Road, Columbus, OH 43210. *Dairy Goat Production Project Record Book and Guide*, 4H Circular 132 (1974). *The Dairy Kid*, 4H Circular 131 (1974).

Oregon State University, Corvallis, OR 97331. *4H Dairy Goat Project*, 4H 1120 (1975).

Pennsylvania State University, University Park, PA 16802. *Dairy Goat Project* (1976).

Virginia Polytechnic Institute, Blacksburg, VA 24061. *4H Dairy Goat Record Book*, Record Book 96 (1975).

PAPERS

Baker, Norman F., *Control of Parasitic Gastroenteritis In Goats.* 1975. JAVMA 167:1069.

Barnard, Sidney E. and Donald L. Ace., *Manufacture of Goat Milk Dairy Products.* 1973.

Booth, Robert L., *Coccidiosis In Goats.* 1976.

Guss, Samuel B., *Dairy Goat Herd Health Problems.* 1975. JAVMA, 167:1076.

Guss, Samuel B., *Don't Let Them Get Your Goat.* 1974.

Guss, Samuel B., *Some Things Veterinary Practitioners Should Know About Dairy Goats.* VM/SAC, July 1974.

Hammond, R.C., *Caseous Lymphadenitis — A Common Goat Problem.* 1976.

Lindahl, Ivan L. *Goat's Milk — A Review of Its Properties.*

Williams, Christine S.F., *Anthelmintics For Dairy Goats.* 1975. Extending Animal Health/Michigan State University, Vol 75, No. 5.

CORRESPONDENCE COURSE

Pennsylvania State University, University Park, PA 16802. *Dairy Goats*, Course 105. $5.00.

PERIODICALS

Countryside and Small Stock Journal, Portland Road, Waterloo, WI 53594. $9.00 per year.

Dairy Goat Gazette, Box 1217, Vanderhoof, B.C., Canada VOJ 3A. $3.00 per year.

Dairy Goat Journal, Box 1908, Scottsdale, AZ 85252. $9.00 per year.

The Australian Goat World, G.P.O. Box 4317, Sydney, N.S.W., Australia 2001. $3.00 per year.

The Smallholder, Argenta, B.C., Canada VOG 1NO. $3.50.

RESOURCE PERSONS

Ace, Donald L., Extension Dairy Specialist, 213 Borland Laboratory, University Park, PA 16802. PH: (814) 865-5491.

Baker, John S., DVM, School of Veterinary Medicine, Purdue University, West Lafayette, IN 47907.

Booth, Robert L., DVM, Box 307, Middleburg, VA 22117.

Bowen, Joan S., DVM, 5036 East County Road 60, Wellington, CO 80549. PH: (303) 568-3613.

Caruolo, Edward V., PhD, 1147 Grinnells Animal Health Bldg., North Carolina State University, Raleigh, NC 27607. PH: (919) 737-3319.

Guss, Samuel B., VMD, 115 Animal Industry Bldg., University Park, PA 16802, (retired).

Hammond, R.C., VMD, Department of Veterinary Science, University of Maryland, College Park, MD 20740. PH: (301) 454-4631.

Kruse, Sue, 4H Program Specialist, 448 Agriculture Hall, Oklahoma State University, Stillwater, OK 74074. PH: (405) 372-6211 Ext. 7018.

Lindahl, Ivan L., Nutrition Institute Agricultural Research Center, Beltsville, MD 20705.

Long, Norman D., Extension Specialist — 4H and Youth, Cooperative Extension Service, Purdue University, West Lafayette, IN 47907.

Miksch, Duane, DVM, Extension Veterinarian, West Kentucky Substation, Box 469, Princeton, KY 42445. PH: (502) 365-5597.

Smith, Mary C. Cole, DVM, College of Veterinary Medicine, Cornell University, Ithaca, NY 14853. PH: (607) 256-2175.

Williams, Christine S.F., MRCVS, Center For Laboratory Animal Resources, Michigan State University, East Lansing, MI 48824.

Young, Grady H., DVM, Box 958, Thomasville, GA 31792.

SUPPLY SOURCES

American Supply House, Box 1114, Columbia, MO 65201. PH: (314) 449-6264.

Hoegger Supply Company, Box 490099, College Park, GA 30349. PH: (404) 996-9240.

NASCO, 901 Janesville Ave., Fort Atkinson, WI 53538. PH: (414) 563-2446.

INDEX

A

Abortion 102, 176-177
    Brucellosis. 102
    Chlamydiosis. 176
    Enzootic. 176
    Listeriosis 115
    Q Fever 177
    Vibriosis. 176
Abscesses 92-97
    Causes 92, 96, 97
    Occurrence of C. ovis. 94
    Other Types 96
    Symptoms 95
    Control 92-97
    Treatment. 94, 96
Abomasal Ulceration. 83
Acetonemia (see Ketosis) 83-84
American Goats 2
    Herd Size. 7
    Popularity 7
    Production Leaders. 6
    Purebred Breeds 2, 3
    Registrations 1969 — 1976 4-5
    Shows 1970 — 1976 7
    Spotlight Sales Prices. 8
Ammonium Sulfamate (Ammate) Poisoning 196
Anaplasmosis. 97-98
Anesthesia 180-183
    Atropine In 180
    Barbiturate. 182
    Inhalation Agents 182
    Ketamine Hydrochloride 181
    Xylazine. 181
Anthrax. 98-99
Appetite — Effects of Exercise 52
Arsenic Poisoning 196
Arthritis
    Non-suppurative 99
    Suppurative 100
    Navel Ill. 140
    Nutritional 88
Autogenous Bacterins (see Abscesses) 92-97

B

Birth Chilling (see Hypoglycemia) 139
Black Leg 116
Black Scours 102, 141
Bladderworm Disease (see Cysticzrcosis). 159
Bloat 82
Blood Chemistry 16
Bluetongue 101-102
Borax Poisoning 196
Brucellosis 102
Buildings (see Housing)

C

Caesarian Section 182, 187
Calcium Milk Fever 86
    Normal Blood Values. 16
    Nutritional Arthritis. 88
Captan — Ringworm Treatment 106
Castration 186
Cerebrocortical Necrosis 89
Chemical Poisoning 196-199
Chlamydiosis
    Abortion 176
    Arthritis 100
Chlortetracycline
    Abscess Treatment 96
    Anaplasmosis Treatment 98
Chorioptic Mange 163
Circling Disease 114
Coccidiosis 102-104
    Relation to Toxoplasmosis 129
Colibacillosis 138-139
Congenital Reproductive Hypoplasia 176
Contagious Ecthyma 104-106
Cryptorchidism. 176
Cyanide Poisoning 193
Cystic Ovaries 173
Cysticercosis 157

D

Demodicosis (Demodectic Mange) 163
Dermatomycosis 106
Diarrhea Medication 140

Differential Cell Counts 16
Dinitro Poisoning 196

E

Economics — Goat Milk Production 10-12
Elastrators — For Castration 186

F

False Pregnancy 174
Fascioliasis (see Liver Fluke Disease) 156-157
    Snail Control 152, 157
    Medication 157
Fecal Samples 149
Feeding 46-60
    Additives 59
    Colostrum 46
    Sour Colostrum 48
    For High Milk Production 53-55
    Forages 55-57
    Grains to Complement Forage 52
    Herd Sires 50
    Kids Grain and Forage 49
    Milk Replacers to Kids 48
    Minerals 59
    Preferences For Grain Mixtures 50
    Requirements 60
Fencing 32-35
    Dry Lots 34
    Electric Fence 35
    Herd Sires 32
    Training 35
Fertility
    Factors Affecting Does 168
    Factors Affecting Bucks 50
Fertilization
    Practices and Poisoning 191
    Practices Affecting Palatability of Forage 57, 58
Fluoride Poisoning 196
Foot Abscesses 109-110
Foot Rot 109-110
    Eradication Program 109
Forage 56, 57, 58
    Optimum Time to Cut 56
    Factors Influencing Palatability 58
    Feeding Fresh Forage 57

216

Founder (see Laminitis)..85-86
French Alpines 2, 3
Fringed Tapeworms 148

G

Gestation Time 16
Goiter 72

H

Haematology...16
Head Grubs — Oestrus Ovis 158
Heat
    Abnormal..173-174
    Cycle Length...16
    Determination Using Speculum 172
    Discharges...172
    During Pregnancy 173
    Silent Heats 173
    Synchronization...171
Herd Health Program 201-205
Hermaphrodism
    Relation to Polled 169
    Relation to Genital Hypoplasia............................110
Housing...30-41
    Air Requirements 21
    Baby Kids 30
    Free Stall..27
    Herd Sire..32
    Light Requirements 21
    Loose Housing 27
    Temperature Requirements 21
Hypocalcemia (see Milk Fever)................................86
Hypoglycemia (see Birth Chilling) 139
Hypotemic Electrolyte Solution 140

I

Indigestion..82, 83
    Acute 82
    Chronic..83
    Bloat...82
    Choice...83
Infectious Bovine Rhinotracheitis (IBR) 110

Infectious Keratoconjunctivitis (Pink Eye) 111
    Cause, Prevention, Symptoms 111
    Vitamin A Treatment 112
    Antibiotic Treatment 112
Internal Parasites **144-159**
    Blood Sucking Worms 144
    Control of Life Cycles 144
    Diagnosis 148
    Drugs for Treatment 154-156
    Facilities and Management Effects 149
    Lungworms 148
    Management for Lungworm Control 152
    Management During Tapeworm Treatment 152
    Medication 153
    Symptoms of Excessive Worm Burden 149
    Tapeworms 147-148

J

Johnes' Disease **112-113**

K

Ketamine Hydrochloride **181**
Ketosis **83-85**

L

LaMancha Goats **3**
Laminitis **85-86**
Lead Poisoning **197-198**
Leukoencephalomyelitis (Progressive Paralysis) **113-114**
Lice Infestation **162**
Lipolytic Rancidity **66**
Listeriosis **114-115**
Liver Fluke Disease **156-157**
Locoweed Poisoning **192**
Lungworms
    Species 148-149
    Control 152
    Treatment 155

M

Malignant Edema **116**

Magnesium
Normal Blood Levels.................................... 16
Hypomagnesemia Blood Levels 73
Effect of Potash Fertilization on 73
Malta Fever (see Brucellosis)............................. 102
Management
Baby Kids... 44-48
Dry and Freshening Doe.............................. 36-37
Drying Off Udders.................................... 36
Freshening Does' Udder 119
Herd Sires.. 50
Kidding Doe....................................... 42-43
Lungworm Control................................. 151-152
Preparing Bucks for Breeding 171
Preparing Herds for Breeding 168
During Tapeworm Treatment........................... 152
Methylene Blue for Cyanide Poisoning 193
Milk Fever (see Hypocalcemia) 86-88
Milking
Hand... 121
Injury.. 120
Let Down.. 120
Machine... 121
Machine Performance................................ 123
Machine Tester 123
Pulsation Rate 122
Systems... 29
Vacuum Lines...................................... 122
Milk Quality 64-67
Factors Influencing 64-65
Holding Temperatures............................... 67
Off Flavors...................................... 65-66
Rancidity.. 66
Somatic Cells 67
Monezia Expansa Tapeworm................................ 147
Muelleria Capillaris 148

N

Natural Environment 14
Navel Ill.... 140-141
Nutritional Arthritis...................................... 88
Neoplasias 131-137
Classification.................................... 131-132
Incidence 135
Papillomata....................................... 133

Lympho Sarcoma..133
Nervous System Tumors...............................134
References..135
Nightshade Poisoning..192
Nitrate Poisoning..192
Nose Bots..158
Nubian Goats..2
Nutrition (see Feeding)
Nutritional Deficiency Diseases 69-79
Calcium Deficiency 70
Cobalt...70
Copper Deficiency 71
Energy Deficiency 71-72
Iodine Deficiency.....................................72
Iron Deficiency.......................................73
Magnesium Deficiency 73
Phosphorus Deficiency...............................74
Protein Deficiency....................................75
Salt Deficiency 75
Selenium Deficiency................................75-77
Sulfur Deficiency 77
Vitamin A Deficiency...............................77-78
Vitamin B Complex Deficiency 78
Vitamin C Deficiency 78
Vitamin D Deficiency 78
Vitamin E Deficiency...............................75-78
Zinc Deficiency.......................................79

O

Oestrus Ovis Infection 158
Omphalitis 140-141
Orf 104-106
Ornamental Plant Poisoning 193
Osteopetrosis 88
Over Eating Disease 106-109
Oxalic Acid Poisoning 133
Oxytetracycline
Abscess Control......................................96

P

Parasites Control
External..162-164
Internal...144-159
Paratuberculosis (Johnes' Disease) 112-113
Pentachlorophenol Poisoning 198

Pastures 32-34, 51, 151-152
Pediculosis 162-163
Photosensitivity From Plants 194
Photosensitivity From Phenothiazine.......................... 154
Physiological Data 16
Pink Eye.. 111
Plant Poisoning... 190-194
Pneumonia..................................... 21, 28, 127-128
Poisoning
    Chemical.. 196-199
    Plant 190-194
Polled Goats... 175
Pox... 128-129
Pregnancy
    Diagnosis... 170
    Duration.. 16
    Disease 83-85
Progressive Paralysis 113-114
Pseudopregnancy... 174

Q

Q Fever.. 177

R

Resources
    Books... 207-208
    Breed Clubs.. 208
    Bulletins.. 208-209
    Correspondence Course 210
    4H Projects 209
    Papers... 209-210
    Periodicals.. 210
    Persons.. 210-211
    Supply Sources... 211

R

Rickets 78
Ringworm 106
Rompun 181

S

Saanen Goats... 3
    Papillomatosis In 133

Salmonellosis... 141
Salt Poisoning... 198
Scabies 163
Snail Control... 152, 157
Sodium Chlorate Poisoning 199
Somatic Cell Counts in Milk................................ 67
Sore Mouth.. 104-106
Stressors Which Lower Resistance 21, 117, 141-142
Supernumerary Teats...................................... 185

T

Tapeworms 147
  Treatment 152, 155-156
Teat Dipping.. 126
Teat Ends... 40
Teat Injury 120
Thyanosoma Actinoides 148
Toggenburg Goats 2
Toxic Indigestion 106-109
Toxoplasmosis.. 129
Traumatic Testiculitis................................ 129-130
Trizine Compound Poisoning............................... 199
Tumors 131-137

U

Udder
  Abscesses... 96-97
  Drying Off 36-38
  Impetigo... 97
  Management at Freshening 41-42
  Normal Dry Secretion.................................. 37
U.S. Dairy Goat Industry 1-10

V

Vibrionic Abortion....................................... 176
Vitamin Deficiency..................................... 77-79

W

Warts 133
Water
  Facilities 28
  Feed Value 51, 61

Worms (see Internal Parasites Control)
Worm Free Herds 150
Worm Medication For Dry Does. 42

X

Xylazine
      Analgesic.. 181
      Anesthetic... 181

Z

Zinc Deficiency 79